8168659

Marketing in Perspective

Previous titles by the same author
International marketing – a strategic approach to world markets

Marketing in Perspective

SIMON MAJARO

London
George Allen & Unwin
Boston   Sydney

George Allen & Unwin (Publishers) Ltd,
40 Museum Street, London WC1A 1LU, UK

George Allen & Unwin (Publishers) Ltd,
Park Lane, Hemel Hempstead, Herts HP2 4TE, UK

Allen & Unwin Inc.,
9 Winchester Terrace, Winchester, Mass 01890, USA

George Allen & Unwin Australia Pty Ltd,
8 Napier Street, North Sydney, NSW 2060, Australia

First published in 1982

Copyright © 1982 Simon Majaro

British Library Cataloguing in Publication Data

Majaro, Simon
   Marketing in perspective.
1. Marketing
I. Title
658.8 HF5415
ISBN 0-04-658234-7
ISBN 0-04-658235-5 Pbk

Set in 10 on 11 point Times by Gilbert Composing Services
and printed in Great Britain
by Billing and Sons Ltd, Guildford, London and Worcester

To Pamela

Preface

The 1970s was a trying decade for most marketers. Nonetheless, the more creative and effective members of the marketing fraternity have managed to cope with the shocks of a turbulent era. They succeeded in steering their respective enterprises between the economic, commercial, political and social hazards of our modern world.

The challenges of the 1980s may yet prove greater than those of the 1970s. If this happens the marketing concept may assume a different role in the life of most firms. It is doubtful whether basic principles will change but the areas of emphasis and attention will probably be different. I personally believe that among the preoccupations of the next decade will be three major areas: 'productivity', 'creativity' and 'integration'.

We have already witnessed a great interest in productivity at macroeconomic and manufacturing levels. I am convinced that 'productivity' will represent an important issue both at the macro-marketing level and also in relation to the various ingredients of the marketing mix. Marketing in its most quantitative form is concerned with the allocation of resources. It is therefore right that each expenditure area should yield a commensurate level of results. This will certainly present the marketer of the 1980s with an intellectual and methodological challenge.

'Creativity' is a notion to which marketers have been accustomed to pay considerable lip-service. In practical terms many firms have failed to develop an environment in which creativity can spawn. There is little doubt that whenever one encounters a successful marketing case study one detects an imaginative and creative strategy underlying it. 'Creativity' is a vital component in an effective marketing effort and management must apply itself to the task of ensuring that this element is developed throughout the organisation.

The third area which I predict will receive fresh attention is the question of 'integration'. Marketing activities can be said to be effective only when they are fully integrated with corporate strategies and also with the activities of all other functions. There is no such thing as an effective marketing function *per se*. If all the components of a modern enterprise are properly integrated, one is likely to achieve a high level of productivity.

This book covers a wide range of topics. Some appear to be of a disparate nature. However, the three ingredients – 'productivity', 'creativity' and 'integration' – are the *leitmotif* throughout. I have attempted to re-visit well established marketing concepts and principles from the vantage point of today's world. A few of the chapters represent ideas that I have been preaching to my many students for a number of years, but I have now re-orientated them to the needs of a more challenging environment. This is not a textbook on marketing. It is a collection of essays on vital topics which affect most managers at one stage or another of their careers. It aims to close gaps that I have encountered in the marketing literature.

For some readers this book will offer an opportunity to re-think principles with which they are familiar within a fresh perspective. For others specific chapters will present practical ideas for dealing with operational problems. For instance, Chapter 4, dealing with 'successful acquisition – a marketing approach', offers a step-by-step checklist for pursuing an acquisition strategy.

I hope that educationalists will find this book a useful aid for effective training programmes. In writing this book I drew considerable material, information and inspiration from the various clients I have served as a consultant and the many managers I have taught as a trainer. Their number is too great to be thanked individually. Nonetheless, through these pages I wish to thank them all collectively.

London, October 1981   SIMON MAJARO

Foreword by Michael Rines

A couple of years ago Simon Majaro and I were planning a one-day seminar, tailor-made for the U K subsidiary of a major American company. Simon outlined to me his ideas for the programme and said he would start as soon as dinner was over with a two hour introduction on some of the more basic aspects of our subject.

The idea that ten very senior executives would submit to a two hour lecture, in the inevitably mellow state that follows a veritable banquet, without either protest or snores, was quite preposterous. I protested and told Simon that trouble was sure to follow.

However, when after a sumptuous meal with plentiful wine Simon stood up and started into his marathon session, he showed me how wrong I was. Dinner finished at around ten o'clock, I suppose, and it was not until some time after one in the morning that Simon was allowed to stop by a still attentive audience.

How did he do it? He manifestly does know what he is talking about and is a genuine enthusiast, but there are lots of management authorities who have those qualities. He has the advantage of not being academic in his approach. What he has to teach is essentially practical, and he never produces an idea without being able to back it up with anecdotal evidence, very often from his personal experience, and quite often a copy of an advertisement or some promotional artefact from his bulging case to illustrate his story. And there are not too many who can do all that. But I think what really picks Simon Majaro out from the rest, and what kept those ten executives riveted for more than three hours, are two other qualities. The first is his ability to illuminate the ideas of others and make them relevant and practicable where before they may have seemed purely a matter for theorists. The second is his undoubted capacity for original thinking. And all this is put over in such a way that his audience goes away feeling that they have learned something they can go away and *use*.

Simon's writing is no different from his speaking. Over the eleven years in which I have occupied an editorial seat on *Marketing* magazine, I believe we have published only about a dozen articles that have made a genuine contribution to the advance of marketing thought and which have at the same time been so written that the practising marketer could take the ideas away and apply them. Simon was the author of about half of them, and that is why this book is such a welcome addition to the literature of our profession. And what is particularly valuable is the fact that the book re-examines a number of long established marketing ideas that have been in danger of becoming ossified in their 1960s' and 1970s' forms at a time when the different circumstances of the 1980s demand their revision.

Perhaps the best example of this is the chapter on market share (Chapter 8), in which Simon demonstrates how dangerous it can be to base any kind of marketing analysis on the unthinking application of a concept that has come to be accepted almost without question. In the first place, there are plenty of different ways of measuring market size. It can be done, for instance, in terms of value, volume, customers or orders, and the answer may be quite different, depending on which measure is chosen. Again, taking any of these measures, there is a danger that the total size of the market may be incorrectly assessed, perhaps because the market has been defined too narrowly, in terms of the company's own product or brand rather than in terms of the needs it satisfies. An electric razor manufacturer, whom Simon takes to illustrate his point, might well define his market in terms of electric shaver users when he ought to be thinking in terms of all shavers – women included.

But Simon's contribution here is not just negative. Having pointed out the dangers he goes on to show how, by deliberately measuring share of a market in a number of different ways, the concept can be turned into a very powerful analytical tool which can highlight with great clarity the company's marketing weaknesses and opportunities.

The chapter on sales aids (Chapter 9) is another that takes a tired and apparently pedestrian subject and injects new meaning and life into it. Until I read Simon's ideas on it I had, I suppose, like most people, regarded it as a matter of minor importance and considerable tedium. But when Simon Majaro takes us back to first principles and defines a sales aid as something that 'seeks to help the salesman to clinch a deal by overcoming well defined obstacles to a sale' the subject takes on a new importance and interest. The development of a new sales aid then becomes an analytical process in which the obstacles to selling are first identified, objectives set, and sales aids designed and then tested. The examples adduced, as always, prove the practicality of the theory.

These two chapters, the one taken from the strategic end of the marketing task and the other from the front-line tactical end, are just two examples from the illuminating content of this excellent book. Other chapters deal with much of what goes on between these two extremes, and all of them have in common a careful relationship with the whole of the marketing activity and the corporate plan. I particularly welcome the chapters on marketing for the three service industries, transport, banking and insurance, because the marketing of services is still not well understood and, by comparison with the marketing of tangible products, has been too much neglected. I believe that Simon Majaro's new book is an important contribution to the marketing literature and that it will provide refreshment and inspiration for the established marketing executive; and for the student or the marketer on the way up it will bring to life and clarify what is so often pedestrian and platitudinous in other books.

London, October 1981   Michael Rines
                                                        Editor, *Marketing*

Contents

PART I

The Marketing Concept – A Strategic Perspective for the 1980s

1
The Many Faces of Marketing

During a seminar conducted by my company a group of senior personnel were asked: 'What is the role of marketing in your organisation?' Surprisingly, we received as many answers as participants. Most answers were sensible, but it was difficult to believe that the various participants were talking about the same function. Admittedly the question was vague, but the answers that emerged on anonymous cards were even vaguer. When posing the question we did not expect either a definition or a conceptual articulation of the marketing creed. We simply hoped to hear a practical description from senior managers of what 'marketing' meant to them and their respective firms. It must be emphasised that none of the participants worked within the marketing field.

My immediate reaction to this surprising confusion was that the marketing managers of the firms represented in my sample had failed in the fundamental task of 'brainwashing' their peers in the philosophy of marketing. As every competent marketing executive knows, the first task in developing an effective marketing function is an educational one. Marketing cannot thrive in an organisation which is unable or unwilling to appreciate the immense value that the function can impart to its overall success. Moreover, marketing has an enormous number of interface areas with other functions, and, if the non-marketing personnel do not fully understand these interfaces, it is difficult to see how marketing can attain its legitimate position in the firm.

But perhaps the position is not quite as simple as it seems. Perhaps marketing by its very nature defies a single cohesive and all-embracing definition. The Institute of Marketing defines marketing as 'the management process responsible for identifying, anticipating and satisfying customer requirements profitably'. This is probably the most satisfactory of the many dozens of definitions which one encounters in the literature. Nonetheless, in practical terms it does not always help management in the process of ascribing specific tasks to the marketing function and its many sub-activities.

For example, the planning of effective sales aids is certainly part of the marketing process. Yet the definition given above hardly covers this very important aspect of marketing. The same comment applies to such areas as corporate identity, social responsibility, strategies relating to the world at large rather than to the consuming public, and the cost effectiveness of logistics services. Many other examples of activities which fall within the marketing orbit but do not emerge clearly from an academic definition can be listed. In reality marketing is too complex a process to be capable of a definition adequate for all situations.

This book is addressed to the following people: (a) managers who find themselves operating in a new business environment; (b) marketing personnel who as a result of promotion find that their responsibilities have changed; (c) managers who attempt to introduce a marketing function into their organisation for the first time.

In other words the various messages incorporated in this book could apply to most managers at one stage or another in their careers.

The main propositions put forward here are as follows:

Proposition 2   Marketing has many faces. It presents a different face in different business environments. This is perfectly normal and it is wrong to attempt to ascribe a universal role to this function in respect of every conceivable environment.

Proposition 2   The true role of marketing in an organisation depends on a myriad of influences: the managerial vantage point from which it is perceived; the firm's structure; the industry and its products; the geographical dimension and the time scale involved.

Proposition 3   Before determining the precise role of marketing in a given enterprise top management must identify, with some clarity, the strategic and tactical impact that each of these dimensions can have on the firm's destiny. The synthesis of all these elements should form a balanced platform from which a sound marketing philosophy can be developed. Every firm must undertake this task in relation to its own needs.

Proposition 4   Once the task has been completed the role ascribed to the marketing function must be communicated throughout the firm. A full appreciation of what marketing means is as important as understanding the firm's organisation chart. It is intolerable that people of some seniority do not understand the role of marketing in their own firms.

Managers often lose sight of the very important fact that marketing has many perspectives. These perspectives vary not only from enterprise to enterprise but also inside the same firm. In practical terms marketing conveys different connotations to the president of General Motors than to the sales director of one of General Motors' operating units in Germany. To the former, the emphasis in marketing lies on a sound public relations activity, a good corporate image, the effective handling of institutional and sociopolitical lobbies and an informative public communication strategy. To the latter effective marketing probably means the planning and control of a sales organisation, the allocation of sales objectives, the recruitment, training and motivation of sales personnel and the requisition of sales aids. Both men work for the same firm and both seek to achieve a complementary set of objectives which in the end will help to attain the firm's overall objectives. Nevertheless, if asked what the role of marketing is in General Motors, they would probably express different answers. Both answers would be right, but would present different, though compatible, faces.

Similarly, a firm that is decentralised into a large number of diverse activities, e.g. ICI, Unilever and Beecham, will no doubt admit that marketing has as many different faces in their respective organisations as there are product groupings. The face of marketing is inevitably different in a pharmaceutical division from that in industrial chemicals. Trying to impose a standard package throughout the organisation is like forcing all nations to speak a single language.

The major elements

It is appropriate to attempt to specify the major dimensions that influence the kind of face that marketing and its allied sub-activities are likely to present at the points of implementation. One must endeavour to identify the main elements that contribute to a change in perspective as to what marketing can do for a firm. Some of these elements are external to the firm: the majority are internal and hierarchical. Table 1.1 lists the major elements.

Table 1.1 The many faces of marketing: the influencing dimensions.

Influencing dimensions		Common variables	
management levels	strategic*	management	operations
the structure	macropyramid (centralised)*	umbrella (decentralised)	conglomerate
geography	national	multinational	international
time scale	short term	medium term	long term
product/market	industrial raw materials fabricating materials and parts installations accessory equipment operating supplies	consumer convenience shopping goods speciality	services

*The terminology used here is adapted from the author's book *International marketing – a strategic approach to world markets* (London: George Allen & Unwin).

The table presents a large number of permutations and the main hypothesis is that each permutation deserves a thorough exploration as to what marketing tasks should be performed by those within that specific orbit. Thus, for a member of the strategic level of a multinational firm manufacturing diesel engines (industrial goods) in a decentralised type of organisation and seeking to plan the long term future of the corporation, 'marketing' will entail one set of tasks. To the manager who markets toothpaste in a national environment and in a firm which is centralised and plans the future on a very short term basis the marketing tasks will be totally different.

All this is of course logical, but nonetheless very few companies bother to go through the process of analysing the implications of their specific anatomy in relation to the external environment. They tend to adopt a textbook approach to marketing, presenting a stereotyped face towards the world at large, as well as inside the firm, and feel that they have thus embarked on an effective marketing route.

It would not be practical to prescribe rigid rules as to the kinds of perspectives that a firm is likely to identify in relation to the marketing activities and tasks in every given set of circumstances. Each firm must undertake the process in some depth and generate an inventory of influencing factors that need to be brought into account in determining the most suitable face for the firm as a whole and for its major strategic and tactical vectors.

It is an intellectual process, but the pay-off can be of long term value. The risk that such an important function as marketing will be shrouded with a mystique will be obliterated once and for all. The main aim of the whole exercise is to define the role of marketing in a given firm and to ascribe clear tasks to individual departments and/or people in such a way that they can all blend into a cohesive and effective whole. The many faces must be translated into a single-minded army.

The major areas of emphasis

In attempting to mould an appropriate marketing philosophy for a specific firm the various influencing dimensions listed earlier must be analysed with some care. Against each dimension it is necessary to specify the possible areas of managerial emphasis which need to be undertaken in the given circumstances of the organisation. In practice it entails a conceptual simulation of the types of activities which would result from the nature of each one of the environmental and/or organisational dimensions identified.

The various tables which follow illustrate the kinds of information that one would expect to list as a result of this exercise. The items shown are purely illustrative and it must be recognised that every firm will identify a different list of activities in respect of each dimension. The more time and thought devoted to this task the clearer it becomes to the firm's strategists what shape and face marketing needs to assume.

The important thing to remember about the level dimension (Table 1.2) is that the marketing tasks change with the levels of management. A man who finds himself performing the job of a marketing director after having held for many years the position of marketing manager must shed his well established perception of the role of marketing. Otherwise he runs the risk of having been promoted in name but not in real terms. The new face of his marketing tasks must be real and not illusory.

Table 1.2 Management levels and their impact on the firm's marketing.

Levels of management	The face of marketing / the emphasis
strategic	need to define 'what business we are in'
	identifying the firm's 'stakeholders' and defining their respective expectations – striking a balance among these expectations
	defining the firm's objectives and determining criteria of corporate success (e.g. market share, segmentation, product innovation, etc.)
	evaluating future marketing opportunities
	developing a climate for creativity
	planning a corporate image strategy
	social responsibility policy
	organising for marketing effectiveness (including succession planning)
management	detailed marketing planning
	allocation of resources to the various elements of the marketing mix
	ascribing standards of performance to each of the above
	control of marketing activities
	planning and authorising marketing intelligence activities
	controlled experimentation
operations	selling
	advertising and/or sales promotion activities
	brand management
	service
	physical distribution
	training sales personnel

Again, as Table 1.3 shows, it is important to recognise that the centre of gravity of the marketing tasks will rest in different parts of the organisation, depending on the firm's structure. Ignoring such a fundamental truth can only lead to unnecessary problems.

Table 1.3   Company structure and its impact on marketing.

The structure	*The face of marketing/the emphasis*
macropyramid (centralised) structure)	centralised marketing planning strong standardisation of policies in relation to product design, branding, distribution strategies, etc. high standards of performance laid down from the centre
umbrella (decentralised) structure)	co-ordinating a high level of product differentiation sensitivity to local market needs (especially in relation to international operations) communication difficulties among decentralised units need to be resolved low synergy among operating units – a problem to be overcome by all functions, and marketing in particular problem of integration
conglomerate	considerable marketing freedom allowed among individual units most marketing tasks performed in a decentralised fashion main criterion of success is financial residual marketing responsibility at the centre for corporate identity; public communication (e.g. annual reports) and appraisal of new projects contact with governmental institutional bodies (especially where the conglomerate is multinational)

Table 1.4   Geography and its impact on the firm's marketing. For the purpose of this table 'national' means a company operating in a single domestic market; 'internatonal' means a firm marketing its products in a number of markets.(See the present author's earlier book entitled *International marketing – a strategic approach to world markets*. London: George Allen & Unwin).

Geography	*The face of marketing/the emphasis*
national	in-depth coverage of the market need for detailed knowledge of the market high market share objective high level of research and testing to reduce risk effective selling heavy promotional effort
international	ability to select the best country opportunities need to respond quickly to changing market conditions need for comparative research capability sensitivity to marketing ecologies must be developed need for good communication and co-ordination activities on a global scale understanding of the workings of international agencies

Table 1.4 is self-explanatory. It seeks to highlight how marketing gains many demanding tasks when it moves from national to international strategies. The significant aspect that should emerge from Table 1.5 is the recognition that as the time scale moves towards the more distant future the marketing face becomes blurred, inasmuch as the borderline between this function and the others, notably R & D and production, becomes less distinct.

Table 1.6 deals with one of the biggest pitfalls, namely the nature of the product and its relationship with the market it seeks to serve. In this area many a whizz-kid has broken his neck. Trying to impose a consumer marketing face in an industrial goods environment is like getting a paediatrician to perform the job of a vet.

It is clear from the tables that marketing is not a homogeneous philosophy that can be retrieved from a textbook and applied to every situation. It is complex, it is subtle, and it needs to be moulded into a suitable and clearly defined creed. My major aim in this chapter has been to provoke the more alert marketer into a greater effort at identifying the main parameters of a balanced marketing function within a set of commercial and environmental dimensions. The ultimate aim is to provide marketing with a meaningful face, not just a pretty face.

Finally I wish to emphasise the need to present the output of all these investigations in a document, a manifesto, a little 'red' or 'blue' book, or

Table 1.5 Time scale and its impact on the firm's marketing

The time dimension	The faces of marketing/the emphasis
short term	operational effectiveness in each element of the marketing mix ability to react quickly to deviations from objectives speedy and accurate control procedures emphasis on results knowledge of quantitative techniques for measuring results training emphasising cost effectiveness
medium term	familiarity with planning methods knowledge of quantitative techniques, especially those that help in forecasting (e.g. regression correlation, least squares methods) high level of fact-finding and analytical skills competence at evaluating alternative strategies
long term	need to forecast the long term future knowledge of techniques such as Delphi, scenario writing, technological forecasting strong interface with R & D function high level of creativity and innovation

a 'White Paper', in which the marketing creed and its concomitant activities are defined. Such a document must of course go to all marketing personnel, but ideally it should also be communicated to personnel carrying out other functions. After all, they are also involved in making marketing aspirations come true. Over the years I have come across a few of these marketing 'tablets from Mount Sinai'. I have little doubt that the companies that have gone through the laborious process of giving birth to them know what marketing means – and such knowledge should not be the prerogative of the few.

Table 1.6   The product and its impact on the firm's marketing

Product type	The face of marketing/the emphasis
consumer goods	need to research and identify generalities in a horizontal market
	ability to handle large promotional budgets and measure effectiveness
	alertness to market standing, market share and consumer satisfaction
	motivating skills and good sales force management
	understanding human behaviour
industrial goods (varies considerably among the types of products listed in Table 1.1)	good knowledge of customers and buying patterns and specific levels (buyers, deciders, influencers, users and 'gatekeepers')
	effective selling
	need to develop creative sales aids
	negotiating skills
	emphasis on individual service
service industry	more or less the same as industrial goods

2
Marketing Integration

The *Shorter Oxford dictionary* defines the word 'integration' as 'the making up of a whole by adding together or combining the separate parts or elements'. The principles underlying the modern marketing concept always suggest that 'integration' is one of the most vital elements of a successful marketing effort. There is hardly a textbook on marketing which does not emphasise the need to 'integrate' marketing strategies with other parts of the organisation. In fact 'integrated marketing' has become almost synonymous with effective marketing. Nonetheless, if one asks experienced and competent marketers as to what precisely they understand by the expression, they would probably shrug their shoulders in disdain as if to say that the whole concept is no more than one additional jargon expression coined by tiresome academics. They would feel that it has little practical value. Unfortunately such cynics would be very wrong!

Let us explore the meaning and scope of integration in a well managed marketing function and consider the practical implications for the firm as a whole. 'Integration' is one of the major challenges for managers in the 1980s, and the full import of the content of this chapter should be grasped not only by marketing personnel but also by managers with other functional affiliations. Marketing has to be integrated with many activities and in many directions. The ability to achieve such an integrative process is probably one of the most important forces that provides an enterprise with the dynamic momentum which enables it to steer the firm's plans and operational activities from policy determination to the final consumption which is the ultimate objective of every firm. This is not a new concept. Yet many firms both in manufacturing and in service industries find it difficult to achieve. Poor integration is normally a source of great operational weakness, whereas a firm that is able to integrate the many conflicting pressures within the organisation into a cohesive and results-orientated whole is very likely to succeed.

As a generalisation it may be useful to put forward the proposition that modern management is less effective at the integration game than the old-fashioned managers of fifty years ago! This is a harsh statement to swallow. However, a brief moment of reflection should highlight the reasons for such a phenomenon and perhaps some useful lessons could be derived therefrom.

Modern technology and managerial methods have developed at an exponential rate during the last few decades. Whilst these developments are most welcome, they have had a serious side-effect on the overall performance of individual managers. The level of specialisation in each function has become so great that barriers have sprung up between individuals involved in different disciplines and having different functions. It is virtually impossible for one manager, however brilliant he may be, to muster the inventory of complex knowledge that is available in the multidisciplinary armoury of a modern organisation. Communication barriers develop not through malice or desire for self-aggrandisement but simply as a result of the very natural fear of the mysterious and the unknown. Thus the production person tends to isolate himself from the machinations of the marketing department simply in order not to expose himself to ridicule. The finance manager looks askance at the costly and often inexplicable goings on in the R & D department. Everybody snipes at the personnel department – especially when they start resorting to fancy methodologies for grading people and evaluating their job contents. Specialisation has created a so-called confidence gap among the various organs of the enterprise, and this in turn has become the cause of many hidden and overt conflicts.

I recently came across a sad story where what appeared to me as a progressive and useful technique was allowed to die as a result of fear and ignorance among those managers who were supposed to be the main beneficiaries of the outcome thereof. The method in question was a computer modelling technique developed as an aid to new product design and/or improvement of existing ones. Basically it was a simulation model into which major ergonomic, structural and cost-effective factors were incorporated. The computer-aided design system was capable of generating many configurations and monitoring their relative performance in simulated conditions. The only people who understood what the process was all about were two clever engineers in the design office. The others, including the marketing personnel, were convinced that the whole idea was a major confidence trick on the part of the consultants who had sold the 'package'. It so happened that the technology was capable of increasing engineering productivity and reducing the lead time between design ideas and feasibility studies. The mystique associated with the modelling technique derogated from its final usefulness. It was not capable of being integrated into the design and marketing management of the firm. Who was at fault? One can blame the management of the firm for showing such a limited level of enlightenment. At the same time one can blame the two smart engineers who were unable to communicate to their peers the intricacies of a useful technique in a simple language that ordinary mortals are capable of decoding. The method was abandoned. The firm was the ultimate loser. Somewhere along the line a major failure of integration had taken place. The behavioural reasons were obvious, but the management failed to respond to the challenge in a creative and decisive manner.

Every manager will probably be able to recount other instances where valuable techniques or concepts failed or were abandoned for the simple reason that interfunctional constraints had made their integration into the firm's environment impractical.

Our industrial ancestors had in this area fewer problems. Managing a business was a less complex process. The demarcation between functions was blurred. Present-day techniques and sophistication did not exist, with the result that the manager of that era was able to acquire a thorough knowledge of every nook and every cranny of the firm and its facilities. With such a comprehensive understanding of the enterprise he was in full charge of all the variables and was able to integrate them into a cohesive and well structured whole.

Oddly enough one can still encounter such an all-embracing capability to manage among the smaller firms. The problem of integration does not afflict them quite as much as it affects the larger and often multinational firms. Unfortunately the larger the firm the greater is the problem of integration.

I hope that at least some non-marketing personnel will read this book. In such an event I must explain that I am not trying to prove that marketing is an elitist function which initiates and dictates the firm's overall policy and direction. I know that this impression may be gained by what will be said later. However, I must remind readers, irrespective of their function, that the firm's main role is to undertake the production of goods or services which are needed or desired by the customer and in the process of so doing to meet the firm's objectives. This is not only the most popular definition of marketing but is also the most cogent mission for most firms. Any manager who is prepared to accept this fundamental truth must recognise that marketing is the locomotive that pulls all the carriages of the organisation towards a destination. A manager who refuses to accept this simple axiom is defying the basic law of industrial gravity. Viewed in this light marketing has a co-ordinating and integrating role which ensures that all other functions perform their respective tasks in a homogeneous direction. This part of the marketing task is often neglected or simply not understood, especially by non-marketing personnel. This is why I hope that the various thoughts expressed here will not be read by marketing people only. If we are going to achieve integration, everybody must take part in the process.

The Meaning and Scope of Integration

What does one mean by integration? Integration with what? Integration will be viewed here from the vantage point of a marketing director, although the subject can be viewed from the perspective of each functional head in turn.

A firm can be compared to an orchestra consisting of many

instruments. The chief executive is the conductor and his task is to ensure that every instrument plays its part at the right time and with the appropriate contribution. The score is the firm's corporate plan. A player who does not know his portion of the score is likely to be in trouble when his contribution is required. The head of the marketing function, by virtue of his co-ordinating role, is the leader of the orchestra – the first violin. The competence of the first violin is essential if the orchestra is going to perform well. This does not mean that one can tolerate mediocrity among the rest of the orchestra. Nonetheless, the quality of the leadership of the first violin is invariably of paramount importance. So is the role of the head of the marketing function.

To the marketing director the word 'integration' should convey three distinct, albeit interrelated, tasks – the integration of (a) all the sub-activities of the marketing department; (b) the various ingredients of the 'marketing mix'; (c) marketing planning and the overall planning process of the firm. An effective head of the marketing function must try to achieve all three integrative tasks. All three are important, and inadequacy in any of these is likely to lead the organisation to major problems.

Each one of the headings listed above contains a range of important implications, the understanding of which will help the 'leader' of the team to harmonise the activities of his 'instruments' with the overall theme of the ensemble.

Integration of the sub-activities of the marketing department

Marketing, like any other function, consists of a large number of sub-activities that fall into four interrelated categories: the gathering of 'input'; the setting of 'objectives'; 'operations' and 'control'.

The interrelationship between these sub-activities is illustrated in a simple model shown in Figure 2.1. The role of each one of these activities is explored briefly below.

'INPUT'

These are the information-gathering activities which every sound planning process calls for. The marketing people require information about markets, customers, environments, competition, consumer motivation, price elasticity, institutions, etc. Market research, marketing research and motivation research are some of the tools that the marketer can use in order to obtain the information which he requires.

Obviously every function needs information, and it is up to the head of each department to prepare a list of his information needs. In the ideal world he would define with precision the information he needs and the

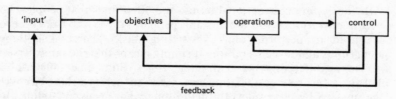

Figure 2.1 The sub-activities of the managerial process – a simple model.

cost–benefit ratio of obtaining it. Subject to the dynamism of the market-place the marketer will stick to the inventory of his 'input' requirements – he will not ask for more, neither will he ask for less.

'OBJECTIVES'

Once the 'input' gathered has been distilled and understood it is possible to define the department's objectives. Having collected all the relevant information about the external environment and the consumer, as well as the appropriate data about the firm's competitors, it is possible to prescribe 'what we aim to achieve'. It is a logical corollary to a thoroughly researched and well analysed 'input'. The marketing objectives will be defined in such terms as profit, growth, return on investment, market share, image, level of penetration, etc.

It is evident that an endeavour must be made to integrate the information-gathering activities with the nature of the firm's business and the probable objectives likely to be set. Too much or irrelevant information is a waste of resources and indicates an inadequate integrative skill.

At this point – and at the risk of pre-empting what will be covered later – it is important to emphasise the fact that during the objectives-setting stage an additional area of integration must be considered: the marketing objectives must be compatible with (a) the corporate objectives and (b) the objectives of each of the other functions. If either of these two integrative tasks is not carried out effectively, the plans contain the seed of potential trouble.

'OPERATIONS'

These are all the activities that the firm must undertake on a routine day-to-day basis in pursuance of the firm's objectives or the marketing objectives. These are the tasks which one can describe as the 'doing' activities. Selling, advertising and running an after sales service department are all 'doing' tasks. Well performed 'operational' tasks help the firm to achieve its objectives. If the 'doing' is unrelated to the objectives laid down, something has gone wrong with the integrative process. This may sound like a truism, yet it must be stated.

Obviously, in organisational terms, one often finds that people who perform operational tasks are the same people as those who from time to time need to perform 'objectives-setting' tasks. There is nothing incongruous about such a notion. It simply means that the same person undertakes different tasks at different times. Sometimes one has to 'plan' and the rest of the time one seeks to achieve the objectives encompassed by these plans through doing what needs to be done. In small firms the same person may have to undertake all the tasks described in our model. There is nothing wrong with it. However, in practical terms it is important to be able to categorise one's activities within the managerial framework described. It is a useful tool for planning one's time allocation and also for ascribing productivity levels to specific tasks. Thus a manager can say, 'Last year it took me four days to prepare our plans and budgets; this year I managed to do it in three days. I am getting better at it!' Or, 'It costs us £120 to gain an order for a tractor; last year it only cost us £85 to gain the same order. The trend is disturbing and an analysis of the reasons must be undertaken'. The fact that the same person may be carrying out both tasks does not derogate from the validity of the model. In the age of productivity which we seem to be heading for, a logical division of tasks should help to monitor the quality of sub-activities.

'CONTROL'

No managerial process is complete without control procedures. These are the methods for evaluating the quality and quantity of the results achieved. We need to control the whole managerial process in order to ensure that what we have done conforms to what we set out to achieve. Control procedures normally seek to perform three important and interrelated evaluation and measurement activities:

(a) To evaluate the quality of the firm's operational tasks: 'Have we performed our "doing" jobs effectively?'
(b) To gauge the level of attainment of the pre-set objectives.
(c) To provide new and up-to-date 'input' for the next planning cycle. The aim is to collate the lessons learnt from successes and/or failures into valuable and well proven data for future planning. By doing this one is in fact closing the loop and a continuous process of planning is developed. In time the quality of the 'input' should improve, partly through improved skills and partly through the experience that the control procedures impart to the planners.

This summarises the first major integrative task of the marketing supremo. Four important and interrelated tasks have been described.

They are all interdependent and if any one of them is out of step with the others the whole ceases to be a cohesive and integrated assemblage. Thus if the 'Input' gathered is unrelated to the planning process, the objectives set may be based on wrong premises and assumptions. In turn the 'operational' activities are likely to be conducted without clear objectives and direction. Inevitably there will be little point in measuring results.

It may be useful at this stage to translate what has been said into a practical structuring of a marketing organisation. Under each of the four headings ('input', 'objectives', 'operations' and 'control') one could list the kinds of sub-activities that one would expect to see in a typical marketing department. This is illustrated in Figure 2.2. The diagram is self-explanatory and could form the basis of internal deliberations pertaining to the development of suitable organisation patterns for specific marketing environments.

One point must be emphasised: under the heading 'objectives' an

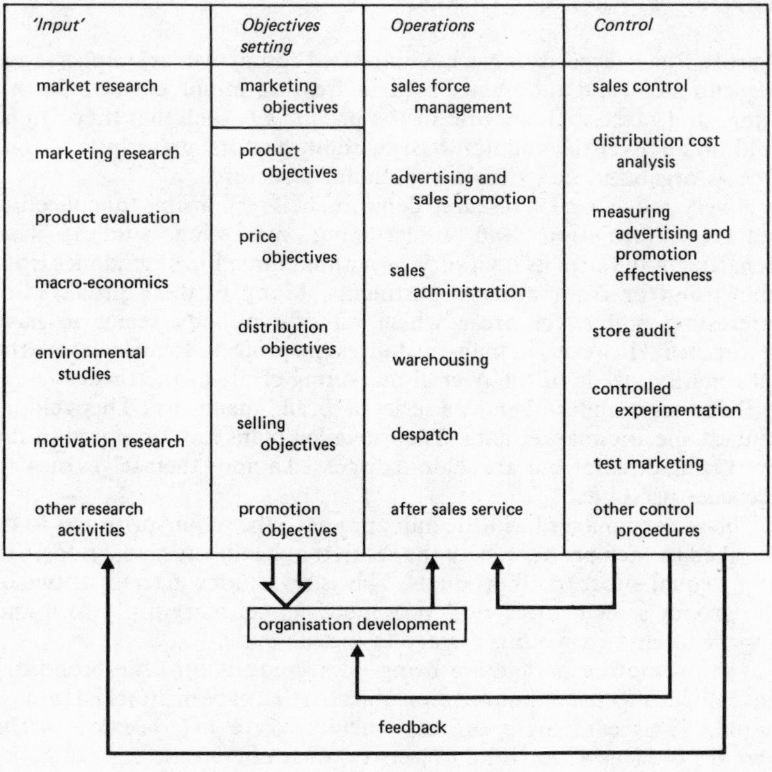

'Input'	Objectives setting	Operations	Control
market research	marketing objectives	sales force management	sales control
marketing research	product objectives	advertising and sales promotion	distribution cost analysis
product evaluation	price objectives	sales administration	measuring advertising and promotion effectiveness
macro-economics	distribution objectives	warehousing	store audit
environmental studies	selling objectives	despatch	controlled experimentation
motivation research	promotion objectives	after sales service	test marketing
other research activities			other control procedures

organisation development

feedback

Figure 2.2 The sub-activities of the marketing function.

arrow points to 'organisation development'. The implication here is that one should not meddle with organisational structuring and development until one has defined the firm's objectives! As long as one does not know what one is trying to achieve it seems futile to explore the kind of organisation that one needs to develop.

In summary, integration is achieved at this level when the marketing sub-activities are so dovetailed as to perform their respective tasks in ways which support each other – and also the marketing effort as a whole – with the underlying aim of attaining the firm's overall goals. On paper this seems a simple enough job; in practice it calls for a determined and well thought out allocation of tasks and resources. A well integrated team representing the four sub-groupings described can impart to the organisation a most potent stimulus towards success.

A simple case history will help to illustrate some of the messages contained in what was said so far.

AURORA PHARMACEUTICALS

Aurora Pharmaceuticals is a medium sized company marketing a range of semi-medicinal ointments used in treating minor cuts, sunburns, stings and rashes. The nature of the products is such that they can be sold on an 'over the counter' basis without doctors' prescriptions. The firm is organized in a simple 'functional' structure.

A very active market research department is responsible for collecting market information and undertaking marketing studies. This department initiates its own surveys without direction or guidance from above and/or from other departments. Many of these projects are interesting and cover areas which hitherto nobody seems to have researched. However, in many instances the projects do not relate to the information needs of the overall marketing effort of the firm.

Planning is undertaken by a series of 'brand managers'. They seldom request specific market data. Their detailed plans are submitted to the marketing director but are seldom discussed among themselves or with the sales personnel.

The sales manager has little guidance as to the selling priorities to be ascribed to each product, with the result that he directs his sales force to apply equal effort to all products. This is regrettable in so far as two of the products seem to carry a very much higher margin of profit and appear to enjoy a 'younger' stage in the life cycle.

The promotion people are being given budgets for each brand but have no idea what communication objectives have been attached to each brand. Their campaigns are extremely creative but, because of the absence of clear advertising objectives, their effectiveness is not being measured.

Potentially the team is capable of performing well. They know their instruments. They even know the score. Yet the lack of integration means that they are opening at a sub-optimal level.

The cure is simple. It needs clear direction from above with a well defined allocation of tasks supported by job descriptions. Moreover, improved and frequent communication between personnel involved in the various sub-activities, in the form of briefing sessions, short meetings and bulletins, can enhance the integration process – without which the marketing department cannot function effectively, if at all.

Integration of the Various Ingredients of the 'Marketing Mix'

The marketing mix, as every marketer would know, is the assemblage of ingredients aimed at achieving customer satisfaction. At the same time it is so designed as to achieve the firm's own objectives. In considering whether an ingredient should be included in the 'mix' or not, the final test is whether it is capable of offering the customer and/or consumer satisfaction. There is absolutely no point in spending resources on an ingredient which neither offers the customer satisfaction nor is capable of making the marketing process more productive from the firm's point of view.

The marketing mix has been described in different ways by different writers. For the purposes of our discussion we can take the fairly traditional approach to the concept, as shown in Figure 2.3. The diagram shows five segments in the inner circle – product, price, promotion, selling and distribution. These are known as the controllable ingredients of the 'mix'. These are the five elements that the

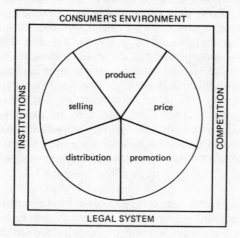

Figure 2.3 The marketing mix – the controllable and uncontrollable elements.

marketer can mould and change until he manages to attain maximum customer satisfaction. The square box outside the circle lists four elements: the consumer's environment, competition, institutions and legal system. These are the external (also known as the uncontrollable) ingredients of the mix. Each one of these ingredients affects each one of the internal (controllable) ones. All the four external ingredients must be fully congruent with each one of the controllable ones. The slightest incompatibility will affect the ultimate effectiveness of the marketing effort. In the case of the uncontrollable elements of the mix one needs to acquire full knowledge and understanding of their intensity and impact on the internal ingredients. In the case of the controllable elements the marketer can evolve strategies and policies in relation to each one of them. He can allocate resources in whichever way he thinks appropriate and can modify them as and when required. However, he must always remember that the aim is to provide customer and/or consumer satisfaction. It is remarkable how often the most experienced marketers forget this very fundamental truism.

The ingredients of the mix described above are of validity in most situations. Nonetheless, there are environments in which the mix ingredients must be adapted to the specific needs of the marketplace. Thus firms marketing cosmetics have been known to add 'packaging' to the mix. Some firms in the domestic appliance business add 'after sales service' to their mix. Mail order firms would normally obliterate 'selling' in so far as their whole strategy is based on the elimination of any selling effort. Promotion expenditure in the form of catalogues and advertising is increased at the expense of selling costs. Some textbooks talk of the marketing mix in terms of the 'four Ps' – product, price, promotion and 'place'. Others talk about seven Ps and one A – product, packaging, price, personal selling, promotion, publicity, physical distribution and advertising. It is almost a pity that one cannot find a synonym for the word 'advertising' starting with a 'P'. We could then talk about eight 'Ps'. This is a wonderful subject for endless debates. Students love arguing for hours as to which of the various approaches is correct. In fact they are probably all correct; each one in its own marketplace environment. It is always helpful to remember that the decision as to whether an ingredient should be incorporated in the mix is not a capricious one. It is a decision based on very sound and logical reasoning. The following considerations should help the marketer to take a decision as to whether a specific ingredient deserves a separate existence in the mix:

(a) *The level of expenditure spent on a given ingredient*   Normally an insignificant ingredient can be attached to one of the others. Basically it is a question of resources allocated to each ingredient which matters. Thus a firm that spends an insignificant amount of money on publicity would be fully justified to add that small budget to the total promotional budget or to the advertising budget. Similarly, a firm that spends very little on packaging would not bother to give this ingredient a separate existence. It will attach it to the 'product' or to the 'promotional mix', whichever appears more appropriate in the circumstances.

In other words, every ingredient involving a significant expenditure would normally earn its separate identity. After all, every area of resource allocation must be measured!

(b) *The perceived level of elasticity and consumer responsiveness* Where the marketer knows that a change in the level of expenditure (up or down) of a given ingredient would affect results it must be treated as a separate tool of the mix. Price is invariably an important element of the mix, especially where the marketer is able to alter the supply–demand relationship through price changes. However, he can only do that where he knows that elasticity exists. In fact, by reducing the price in situations where such elasticity exists he allocates resources through reduced margins. He will probably have to reduce the allocation of resources to the other ingredients of the mix. In fact he needs to 'mix a new mix'.

On the other hand, a firm enjoying a monopoly, or where the price is fixed by government edict, is justified in relegating price to a less important role. In fact it may obliterate the price from the mix altogether. It virtually ceases to be 'controllable' ingredient within the jurisdiction of the marketer. The consumer may not like it but there is little that the marketer can do about it. The latter will have to identify other ways for achieving consumer satisfaction. Thus the gas companies in the UK cannot talk about price being an integral part of the marketing mix. The government has taken out of their hands the freedom to use the pricing tool. They should therefore identify some other ingredients which are within their jurisdiction and which are capable of providing consumer satisfaction. Thus they may have to design a cost-saving advisory centre or a 'twenty-four hour maintenance service'. These will be within their controllable resource allocation authority. Before choosing any such strategy and placing it as an honourable member of the 'mix' they must ensure through research that the consumer is likely to respond to such an offering. If he is going to shrug his shoulders and say, 'So what?', that ingredient should have no home in the marketing mix.

(c) *Allocation of responsibilities* This is always a useful acid test as to whether an ingredient should become a full member of the mix. Invariably a well defined and well structured marketing mix reflects a clear-cut allocation of responsibilities. Thus, where the firm requires the services of a specialist to help to develop or design new packaging, as is the case in cosmetics firms, it is perfectly proper to say that 'packaging' is an important and integral part of the mix and deserves a separate existence therein.

The whole question is not just an academic one. The decision as to which are the ingredients of the mix depends on a combined analysis of the most effective and results-orientated way of allocating funds and responsibilities coupled with a thorough understanding of what would provide the maximum responsiveness from the final arbiter, the customer.

Now comes the vital problem of integration. It is all very well choosing the right ingredients, but if they are not properly integrated the whole effort is futile. As stated earlier the mix represents a number of important ingredients which require money and effort aimed at satisfying the customer's needs. These ingredients must be designed to be in a state of total harmony with the marketplace as well as among themselves. Any single ingredient of the mix which is out of empathy with the rest can upset the whole assemblage.

The product, price, distribution and selling may be perfect in relation to a target consumer and yet the whole mix may prove ineffective due to a poor promotional effort which simply fails to communicate the right messages to the right audience. Each ingredient in turn can be an offending element in attaining the overall aim of the marketing effort. Invariably the problem stems from poor integration.

Once again a short case study would help to place what has been said in a practical context.

CASA HOMES LIMITED

Casa Homes Limited designs, builds and sells houses. They are classified as one of the medium-sized house builders offering for sale around 800–1000 units per annum.

A recent 'interfirm comparison' undertaken yielded disturbing data. The firm's performance in terms of profits, return on investment, growth and market share in the segment in which they have been operating was exceedingly poor when compared with the nearest competitors.

Moreover, the various ratios of marketing productivity indicated that the firm was spending too much on promotion and selling for each unit sold. A few competitors were able to achieve results at around 50% of the amount spent per unit sold by Casa Homes.

A firm of consultants was invited to carry out a 'marketing audit'. The following facts emerged:

(a) Whilst Casa's target group had been defined as the A, B socio-economic class, the product (namely the house itself) seemed to fail to match the needs of members of that group. The level of finish and the general surroundings were marginally below the expectations of members of the A, B class.

(b) The price seemed to match the expectations of the target group and was in line with competitive offerings.

(c) The advertising was all wrong inasmuch as a major portion of the advertising budget was spent in media with a limited A, B readership. Obviously the response rate was relatively low from members of the selected segment.

(d) The sales effort was carried out in a number of show houses, one in each estate. This, the consultants felt, was a suitable strategy, but they were extremely critical of the choice of sales personnel. They felt that the personality of these sales persons should better match the type of visitors that the company sought to attract.

The example speaks for itself. These are just a few of the details that emerged from the marketing audit. The diagnosis is fairly clear: the integrative process among the marketing mix ingredients and the marketplace itself was virtually non-existent.

Integration of Marketing Planning with the Overall Planning of the Firm

This is a very complex area and deserves a considerable amount of attention and thought; it is probably one of the most difficult integrative tasks in any organisation. This is partly due to the fact that very few organisations have the 'focal point' to initiate and demand a high level of integration. Integration seldom happens by itself – it needs pressure and persuasion from a key person at the top. Without such initiative from the strategic level of the firm the chance of having the various components of the corporate plan integrated into a cohesive whole are fairly slender. To a great extent the problem is attitudinal rather than methodological, and attitudes normally stem from the top of an organisation.

When talking about the need to integrate the various components of the planning process one must remember that this entails two integrative tasks: (a) the integration of the 'top down' and/or 'bottom up' plans; (b) the integration of the horizontal functional plans.

Figure 2.4 describes these two aspects of the planning process diagrammatically. Perfect integration is achieved when both the vertical and horizontal planning modules are dovetailed into a single and logical whole. All the carriages should be moving together towards a clearly defined destination. The management-by-objectives philosophy has sought to achieve the same aim. Unfortunately, in many instances through excessive bureaucracy, the approach failed to achieve the need to integrate the various members of the team.

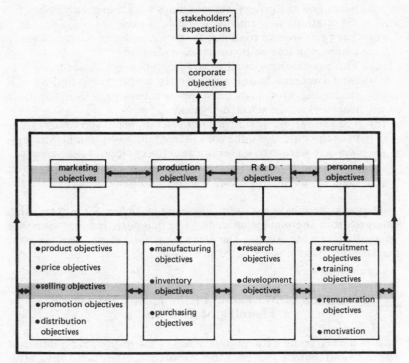

Figure 2.4 The hierarchy of objectives and their integration.

INTEGRATING THE VERTICAL PLANS

A firm exists to 'meet the expectations of its stakeholders'. These vary from firm to firm and from period to period. Stakeholders' groups consist of shareholders, managers, other employees, creditors, suppliers, bankers, the government, the community, channels of distribution and of course the consumers. The planning process starts and finishes with the stakeholders. The whole purpose of the process is to determine what the firm should be doing and what the firm is capable of doing in order to meet their expectations. Obviously one has to analyse these expectations on a regular basis and ascribe priorities thereto in accordance with the political, social and economic realities of a dynamic marketplace. The most important stakeholders of the 1980s are not necessarily those of the 1970s. This exercise needs to be undertaken by every company, large and small. They all have stakeholder groupings. Their number normally increases with the size of a firm and their demands become more complex, but the principle is the same.

The *corporate objectives* represent a manifesto as to what the firm must try to achieve if all the firm's stakeholders in their proper sequence of priority are to have their respective expectations met. Stakeholders' expectations are often contradictory and sometimes excessive – in defining the corporate objectives the firm's strategic level strives to assemble the best compromise between these demands. It is rare for a firm to be able to meet everybody's expectations all the time.

This highlights the subtlety of having to integrate company objectives with the ultimate and often more elusive purpose of the organisation.

Once the corporate objectives have been set it is possible to finalise the definition of the functional objectives. Thus marketing, production, personnel and R & D departments can define their goals. Each one of those must be fully congruent with the corporate objectives. Thus, for example, if the corporate objectives prescribe a market share objective (for reasons which were analysed and accepted, and – it is to be hoped – after verifying the feasibility of attaining such an objective), the marketing department must build such an objective into its own plans. It would be absurd for them to feel that what is stated in the corporate plans does not bind them in their own departmental plans. Nonetheless, such absurdities *do* occur. The same level of integration must take place between the corporate plans and plans of each of the other departments of the organisation.

Now the process can be taken further down the planning hierarchy, as described in Figure 2.4. The marketing objectives must be supported by sub-plans with their appropriate objectives for the product, price, selling, promotion and distribution. These must be integrated brick by brick with the marketing plan. A similar process must take place in the production, R & D and personnel areas. The best plans are those which are logically integrated. It is a mistake to think that large and detailed volumes representing plans for a myriad of departments are necessarily good plans. The plans can be brief and concise. The way in which they hang together is the test of sound planning.

INTEGRATING THE HORIZONTAL PLANS

So far we looked at the need to integrate marketing planning (and the other departmental plans) with the overall planning process of the enterprise. Equally important is the need to integrate the various plans horizontally. Marketing plans and strategies must be dovetailed with those of each of the other functions. Thus, for example, if one of the marketing objectives of a firm is to increase market penetration for a specific product through an increased selling effort, the plans would envisage the recruitment and training of additional salesmen. This must reflect itself in the plans of the personnel department and also in the 'recruitment' and 'training' sub-plans. It is so obvious that it is almost superfluous to mention it. Nevertheless, it is remarkable to observe how often such obvious ideas fail to materialise in our modern commercial world, which seems to prefer complex concepts to simple and well proven notions.

Among the case studies provided in the last part of this book the readers will find a case study on Opticol Products Limited, which can form a useful vehicle for discussing the problem of integrating marketing and R & D strategies. The case study illustrates the kinds of problem that occur when an organisation allows the R & D department to operate without a set of objectives that have been integrated with the aims of the marketing department.

In Conclusion

This chapter is presented as an intellectual challenge to serious disciples of the marketing creed. Marketing cannot live alone. It is an integral part of an increasingly complex structure which is seeking to attain maximum productivity in all directions. The great challenge is to know how to integrate a large number of cells into an organism which moves in unison towards a common goal. The secret seems to lie in the ability to integrate a large number of activities and in many directions. The person who can achieve this formidable task is sure to become the star performer of the 1980s.

3
How to Vector Markets

The 'marketing concept' is no longer a new concept. It has been in existence as a creed for over a quarter of a century. Yet, although it has become an increasingly important activity within many firms, one is often disappointed to observe what a superficial hold the marketing creed, as a way of life, has attained in many organisations. A 'way of life' means that marketing is a force that must pervade the entire firm and not only a single function which one calls 'marketing'. It must transcend functional areas and every decision-maker in the organisation, regardless of his or her level and functional affiliation, must be vigilant as regards the needs of the customer who is likely to be satisfied by the firm's offerings. Peter Drucker summarised this simple notion many years ago by saying, '*Until the customer has derived final utility, there is really no "product"; there are only "raw materials"*'. In other words the production people must be involved; the R & D department must be cognisant of the customer and his needs, and so must the personnel and finance functions. The paramount objective is to ensure that the customer derives final utility and satisfaction; without them there is no 'product'.

If this statement is true, one is entitled to ask a very fundamental question: 'What is the product?' This question represents a very subtle shibboleth. The reader may recall the biblical story of Gileadites who could identify their enemies by asking them to say 'shibboleth'. Whoever responded by saying 'sibboleth' was an enemy and was slain. The inability to pronounce the test word correctly betrayed the person's party, nationality, etc. Ask a person, 'What is your "product"?', and the answer will help you to judge the level of understanding and commitment that the interlocutor has towards the 'marketing concept'. It is a far better test than asking him whether he belongs to the Institute of Marketing or some other prestigious body to which marketers belong. This may sound a strange test, but its common sense will become clear.

The Various Faces of the 'Product'

A 'product' has many faces. What the manufacturing person sees can be very different from what the marketing person should be seeing. Take as an example a company manufacturing ball bearings and roller bearings in a vast assortment of sizes, alloys and configurations. The production manager will respond to the question, 'What is your Product?', by simply saying 'ball bearings and roller bearings'.

The marketing man should be punished if he gives the same reply. To him the product or products are 'anti-friction' devices. They are aids to the reduction of friction in a number of machines or instruments such as motor cars, machine tools, etc. The marketing man will know in detail the various sectors of the Standard Industrial Classification and will be able to enumerate the needs for 'anti-friction' devices of each of the sectors listed. Where there is no friction there is no need for the 'product' – to be more precise there is no 'product' in Peter Drucker's terms. This example is quite simple. Let us look at some more complicated cases.

A pharmaceuticals company manufactures a number of drugs. By the nature of the industry and its level of technology the drugs represent complex chemical compounds. The production people and the R & D people are very tempted to define the product in units of the 'wonder drug' that the firm produces. The enlightened marketing person will describe the 'product' in terms of the illness which the drug combats or the discomfort which it alleviates. The production-orientated man will boast about the units of the antibiotics which the firm manufactured and sold in a given period; the truly marketing-orientated person will talk about the number of pneumonia sufferers who were cured by 'our product'. When attempting to measure the firm's market share he will do so in relation to his perception of the 'market', namely the number of pneumonia cases that occur in the course of the year.

Normally the more intricate the product and the more sophisticated the technology the greater the chasm between the perceptions of the 'product' among the various functions of the enterprise. Obviously the R & D person who has been instrumental to the development of a highly innovative analgesic would prefer to talk about the complex chemical molecule of the product rather than the headache-alleviation nature of the product. Both definitions are correct; the former talks about the physical properties of the product; the latter talks about what the product does for the consumer. In marketing terms the latter utility is the one that really matters. Unless you have a headache you are not in the marketplace and the product has no relevance to you. If you do have a headache you become passionately interested in the product but not because it contains the x or y wonder ingredients but simply because it will alleviate your condition.

A manufacturer of diesel engines will tend to talk about the number of units, the size of the units and the number of cylinders that he has produced in the course of the year. 'What is your product?' will inevitably be answered with, 'diesel engines of 50 horsepower or 75 horsepower, etc., configuration.' The marketing man should say, 'We manufacture energy-producing units of a particular design as an auxiliary facility in process plants or ships or hospitals and at a cost per unit of electricity of x pence, etc.'. The marketing person must respond to the question as if he were the buyer of the product.

The message should be fairly clear. The marketer who has absorbed the marketing concept as a way of life will always seek to identify the product in terms of what it does for the customer and the cost–benefit relationship which it is capable of generating for the consuming environment, whether it is an industrial environment or a domestic one.

The 'Product' – A New Dimension

Much has been written about the product life cycle and as to what happens to the product sales and profitability during its course. The concept is a useful one, but one of its pitfalls is the fact that we often forget to identify the 'product' in terms which are really meaningful to the marketing process. The product may be progressing well towards 'growth' in the context of its technology or manufacturing processes yet it may have reached its 'saturation' point in terms of its market or segment penetration. The two levels of performance are not necessarily congruent. Let us take an example.

A manufacturer of running shoes supplies the fraternity of professional and quasi-professional athletes with a specially designed shoe that provides arch support when running or sprinting. The sales follow a classical pattern that indicates that a 'product life cycle' is in operation. As a result of the ravages of competition and the fact that the 'product' has reached the 'saturation' point in the cycle, pressure on margins is heavy and erosion of profitability is taking place. Nonetheless, rather unexpectedly the life cycle takes a twist upwards and sales are starting to boom again. The obvious implication is that the laws of gravity have been defied and that the theory of the 'product life cycle' should be relegated to academic manuscripts only.

What has really happened is that the 'marketing ecology' has changed. A new market has sprung up for the firm's product: the amateur joggers, people of all ages who have read about the health value of jogging and decided to join the throng of early morning enthusiasts. In truth what has happened is that a new market has developed and for all intents and purposes the product has acquired a new face and should be treated as a new 'product'. On this basis one would have a 'product' for the professional runner and one for the enthusiastic jogger. The physical product may be the same but the 'marketing product' will be different and each will deserve its separate analysis vis-à-vis the life cycle evaluation.

In the light of this it is instructive to re-examine the earlier example from the pharmaceuticals industry. Imagine that Stanton Chemicals manufactures an antibiotic product – Stantalyn – which is used effectively in the treatment of a wide range of infections. If one looks at the product as a technological package, one could trace its life cycle on the basis of its overall sales and profitability. On the other hand, one can rightly assume that each infection type represents a separate market, with the result that one can plot the life cycle performance in relation to each sickness or 'indication'. Thus, without getting too involved in the technicalities of a complex industry, one can have a product life cycle in respect of each identifiable 'indication': infections of the throat, ear, lungs, bile duct, etc. Each 'indication' will have its own 'product' (with or without different brand names) and each one of these products will have its own 'life cycle'.

The situation can be further embellished by saying that the drug used by children in relation to one kind of illness is a different 'product' from the one used by adults. Thus we finish by getting a three-dimensional matrix of product, market and segment *vectors*. It is quite possible that the 'product' will need to undergo a slight differentiation process, such as the production of a sweetened syrup for children to facilitate absorption or swallowing, but essentially the 'product' characteristics in technical terms are probably unchanged. Thus this illustration would suggest that we have many 'products', as shown in Figure 3.1, and not just one. If this is so we can now look at the new dimension of the product life cycle by plotting the cycle of each 'vector' in turn, as illustrated in Figure 3.2.

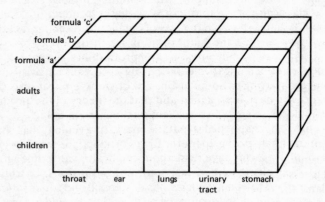

Figure 3.1   Product, market and segment vectors.

This concept opens a new perspective for the marketer inasmuch as the product life cycle gains a meaningful and more practical dimension. The product becomes the instrument of satisfaction for each market segment and it is the progression of the product in relation to each sub-market which is being monitored. The marketer who learns how to monitor the product in this way will also acquire the skill of applying the

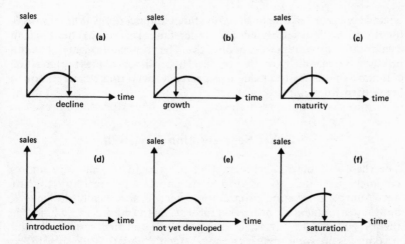

Figure 3.2 Vector life cycles. (a) Vector 1: formula 'A' against throat infection in adults. (b) Vector 2: formula 'A' against ear infection in adults. (c) Vector 3: formula 'A' against lung infection in adults. (d) Vector 4: formula 'C' against urinary tract infections in children. (e) Vector 5: formula 'C' against stomach infection in children. (f) Vector 6: etc.

most appropriate marketing tools for each stage of the 'vector' life cycle.

'Vector' in mathematics means a quantity having direction as well as magnitude, denoted by a line drawn from its original to its final position. To the marketer 'vector' means the market segment which is 'satisfied' by a specific product. The segment in question may be capable of 'satisfaction' by a number of products offered by the firm. Each 'product–segment' unit of activity is a vector. In other words, what is being suggested is that instead of talking about the progress of a product or a brand along the life cycle one should plot the behaviour of the vector life cycle, namely the 'utility rendered to a specific market segment'. Thus, if a diesel engine manufacturer has designed a small power-generating plant that can supply energy for a factory and also propel a vessel, he has two distinct 'vectors'. One is the supply of energy to a plant; the other is the supply of propulsion to ships. The physical and technical product may well be the same, but in marketing terms two separate vectors exist and their development will probably take totally separate patterns towards growth and success. Top management often expects identical performance from all its 'products'. In many instances this is neither possible nor justifiable. Different 'vectors' have to cope with totally different marketing environments, and to expect the same level of results from such environments just because the physical product is the same is of course illogical. The level of competition, the cost–benefit requirements and the distribution problems can tilt the balance in favour of one product–segment and make the other one look unattractive. Marketing people understand this much better than accountants or production people do. The last-mentioned feel that a machine is a machine and that the level of profit it provides to the selling company should be the same irrespective of who uses it and what it is being used for.

Market Segmentation Reviewed

The theory of market segmentation has taught us that very often a company is better off to devote its efforts and creativity towards developing a marketing programme which is specifically designed to appeal to a segment of the market rather than the market as a whole. The theory goes on to say that having studied the firm's strengths and weaknesses in some depth the marketer decides to seek to satisfy a selected part of the market rather than attempt to be all things to all men. However, when approaching the market with a segmentation policy it is necessary to recognise that it is essential to gain a significant portion of the sub-market whilst a small market share of the totality would have sufficed.

Segmentation policies often fail for the simple reason that, having decided to 'segment' the market and concentrate one's effort in that area, one has acquired too small a share of the segment in question. It is therefore vitally important that the person who decides to concentrate on a segment seeks to dominate or obtain a significant part of that segment. Normally one recommends to the would-be segmenter that he or she carries out thorough market measurement studies in order to establish beyond all reasonable doubt that the selected segment justifies the marketing firm's attention. After all, having opted for a part of the market instead of its totality one takes the risk of 'placing all one's eggs in one basket'; before taking such a decision one must be satisfied that the strategy selected is correct.

Market segmentation offers considerable scope for creativity. It is an area in which the innovative marketer can identify opportunities which competitors have missed or have decided to ignore. Thus when one looks at the more successful car manufacturers in the world, such as BMW, one soon recognises that the real reason for their success is based on the fact that they identified a very attractive (albeit small) unexploited market segment. However, in selecting one's target segment for marketing development one must ensure that three fundamental conditions are adhered to: (a) the segment must be measurable; (b) the segment must be sufficiently substantial to justify the effort to be invested therein; (c) the segment must be accessible in the sense that the institutional systems that facilitate the marketing process (e.g. channels of distribution, media availability) exist.

These three conditions are of course interrelated and perfectly logical. Yet it is sad to watch how often fairly experienced marketers fall into the trap of selecting segments which do not meet one or more of these conditions, and consequently fail in their aims. A further pitfall is the fact that many marketers seek to 'cheat old age' of a declining product by simply differentiating it vis-à-vis a specific segment which in turn happens to be on the decline as well.

In our modern and very competitive environment it is not enough to assume that a segmentation policy is *per se* a formula for ·success. One must refine the concept beyond what we have attempted to do in the past. Before indulging in product planning we must break down the market into consuming-orientated and cost–benefit-orientated sub-markets or 'vectors'. Obviously there is nothing to stop the marketer from standardising a product for a cluster of 'vectors', but it must be by design and not by accident. This is not dissimilar to the kind of problem that one encounters in international marketing, where the effective marketer seeks to identify the needs of each country but then attempts to standardise the product for as many countries as lend themselves to such standardisation.

For example, a large transport company has decided to specialise in the field of carrying very heavy cargoes (over 150 tonnes per cargo). This is in itself a segmentation policy in as much as the firm has opted out of the very competitive field of transporting ordinary cargoes. One hopes that before embarking on this strategy, which demands a very costly 'infrastructure', it has gone through the process of *measuring* the size of the market for 'heavy cargoes' and found it to be *'substantial'* in marketing terms. Furthermore, one hopes that the firm has established that the segment in question is *accessible*.

The strategy may prove to be reasonably successful, but if the firm wishes to pursue the logic of my argument a step further it must undertake a vector analysis. That would help it to ensure that the marketing effort is more directly geared towards the real 'marketing opportunities'. The 'product' will be totally congruent to the needs of each vector. How should they go about it? They should analyse step by step with suitable quantification details of who needs to carry very heavy cargoes. The Standard Industrial Classification offers a useful division of the industrial scene. Thus the marketer will analyse the 'needs of mining and/or quarrying', the 'needs of chemical industries', the 'needs of shipbuilding', etc.; each one of these is a vector and each one probably needs a different 'product'. Moreover, some of these many vectors will offer better marketing opportunities than others.

If one could plot all these opportunities on a 'dart-board' type of chart (see Fig. 3.3), the best will fit into the 'bull's eye' centre, the next on the adjacent circle, and so on. Once the implications of this philosophy are grasped by the creative marketer he or she will have acquired an excellent tool for planning. First, the product will be more directly designed to meet the best vector's needs. Secondly, the promotional mix could be geared towards the most attractive target audience. Thirdly, the sales force could be directed towards the 'bull's eye' buying environment. It is a totally different story from sending a sales force in search of people who need to transport very heavy cargoes!

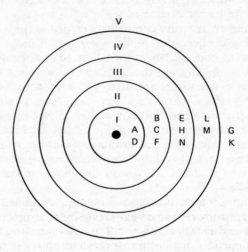

Figure 3.3 The relative attractiveness of 'sub-markets' for a 'heavy cargoes' transporter. (Note that the classification shown is purely for illustrative purposes; it does not purport to relate to the SIC classification.) I, Extremely attractive sector (A, energy and water supply industries; D, brewing and malting); II, attractive sector (B, cement, lime and plaster; C, shipbuilding; F, railway and aerospace); III, fairly attractive sector (E, construction; H, pharmaceuticals; N, textile machinery); IV, poor sector (L, pulp, paper and board; M, rubber, plastics); V, must be avoided (G, food and drink; K, animal feedstuffs).

Organisational Implications

It is worth exploring the organisational implications of what has been suggested. Many companies have so-called product managers or brand managers. Quite a few of these firms must reflect upon the real roles of these managers and their appropriateness to a truly marketing-orientated business. In many situations these managers are the hidden manifestation of a bias towards the 'product' as seen by production people rather than the one seen by marketing people. What, for instance, is the marketing relevance of a flooring product manager in a firm that manufactures and supplies flooring for domestic, industrial and institutional markets? Surely what such a company needs is a domestic flooring *market* manager, industrial flooring *market* manager and institutional flooring *market* manager. I emphasise the word 'market' because the 'product' as such does not exist until such time as the market–segment–vector in question exists. It is the needs of the 'market' which the manager has to satisfy and not the needs of the 'product'. In seeking to meet the needs of the 'market' the marketer has to develop a total marketing mix and not only a 'product'. By calling him or her a 'product manager' we simply fog the issue and derogate from the importance of the job.

It is not suggested that the role of product manager has disappeared. In many firms such managers are most appropriate and their role is an important one. At the same time it is recommended that before opting for a structure that encompasses the product management concept, top management must explore the alternatives and consider the relative merit of each in relation to the marketing aims of the firm. In fact in certain circumstances one can envisage solutions which embrace both product management and market management in a matrix* combination.

The whole essence of the matrix approach to organisation development is based on the theory that two vital, albeit slightly overlapping, structures can co-exist. One of the structures is traditional, hierarchical and results-orientated. The other structure is co-ordinative, integrative and in many instances seeks to impart a truly marketing-orientated dimension to a system which by its very nature is less capable of being dynamically so. Referring back to the earlier example of Stanton Chemicals, one can envisage a matrix-type organisation like the one shown in Figure 3.4.

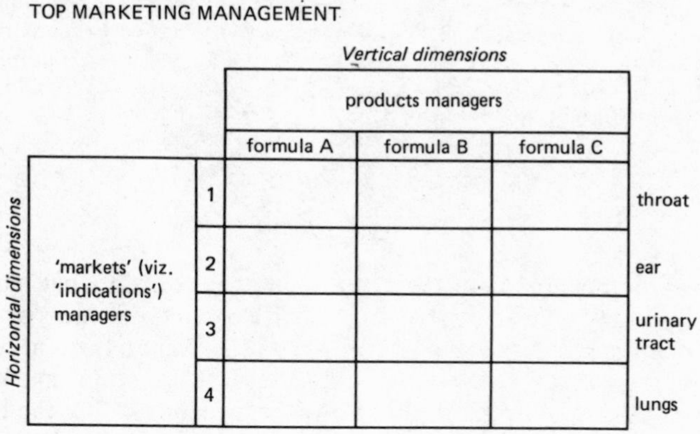

TOP MARKETING MANAGEMENT

		Vertical dimensions			
		products managers			
		formula A	formula B	formula C	
Horizontal dimensions	'markets' (viz. 'indications') managers	1			throat
		2			ear
		3			urinary tract
		4			lungs

Figure 3.4 Matrix organisation for Stanton Chemicals.

*See Chapter 11 in S. Majaro, *International marketing – a strategic approach to world markets* (London: George Allen & Unwin).

A structure like the one shown in Figure 3.4 may well prove to be an admirable solution for combining the more traditional way of managing the 'product' with the much more progressive, albeit more complex, way of becoming a faithful adherent of the marketing creed. To the latter the ideas propounded here should provide fertile food for thought.

Finally a simple checklist for the more enlightened reader:

(a) Do not attempt to structure your organisation until you have established clearly what your 'products' are.

(b) Before defining what your 'products' are, attempt to identify the size and accessibility of the various market vectors that your company is best equipped to satisfy. The 20% of the vectors that offer 80% of the results for your firm will direct you towards the most sensible and effective structure.

(c) Maintain enough flexibility in your structure to enable you to cope with the dynamism of the marketplace. The matrix approach to organisational structuring can offer such a flexibility in many situations.

(d) Never forget that the most successful marketing takes place when the company knows exactly whom they are trying to satisfy!

4
Successful Acquisitions –
A Marketing Approach

Soldiers during a battle recognise that the probability of them getting killed, injured or maimed has increased when compared with citizens at home. Yet they prefer not to think about this unpalatable truth. They go to battle with a conviction that they are the ones who will return unscathed. The shells, the shrapnel, the bullets are all there, but somehow many soldiers feel that providence has bestowed upon them a touch of immortality and divine protection from these flying objects.

Similarly the gambler is often able to isolate himself from the realities of the laws of probability and conjure to himself a 'make-believe' world in which the rewards for small stakes are far superior to those prescribed by the rules of the game. He is convinced that his own chances are superior to those that apply to ordinary mortals.

Despite the most persuasive evidence that has accumulated over the last two decades about the high risk of failures of mergers and/or acquisitions, many managers seem to be able to ignore this risk quotient. They persevere with an acquisition strategy, hoping that their own track record will be a better one than the norm. Managers are supposed to be rational people; they are expected to evaluate their actions in a systematic and unemotional fashion. Nonetheless, the failure rate and the cost of failures is so high that one starts wondering whether some managers suffer from some degree of amnesia when plunging into the merger–acquisition arena. Pirelli and Dunlop merged in a jumbo deal. The outcome was so catastrophic that many years will pass before the extent of the disappointing marriage can be quantified. More recently Chubb found that its acquisition of Gross Cash Registers Limited proved to be an unqualified disaster.

The number of sad and costly stories in the field of mergers and acquisitions that can be recounted is legion. Nonetheless, the corporate predator is undeterred; he continues to stalk his prey with the conviction that his own hunting exploit will count among the more successful ones. He pursues his victim with the feeling that his own endeavour will yield success in terms of enhanced profits, growth and market share dominance. Providence will look after the corporate righteous with the same care as it looks after the fighting soldier and the gambler. Or will it? The saying that God looks after those who look after themselves is certainly a most appropriate message in this area.

In an interesting study carried out a few years ago by J. Kitching ('Why do mergers miscarry?' *Harvard Business Review*, 1967) and later in a similar study undertaken in Europe ('Acquisitions in Europe', summarised in *Business International* in 1973 and also in *Management Today* in November 1974 under the title 'Why acquisitions are abortive') the level of failure rate was quantified. Kitching's research suggested that around a third of all acquisitions were unqualified failures. At the same time Kitching's findings suggested that when acquiring firms *'bought' a market share* the relative outcome was more satisfactory where the 'market share' thus bought was high. The higher the market share bought the lower the incidence of failure. Kitching's findings are summarised in Table 4.1.

Table 4.1 Success and failure relative to market share purchased during an acquisition strategy.

Market share bought	<1%	1–5%	5–10%	10–25%	25–50%	>50%
Incidence of success	43%	42%	58%	61%	70%	73%
'Not worth repeating'	22%	23%	24%	20%	12%	24%
'Incidence of outright failure'	35%	35%	18%	19%	18%	3%
	100%	100%	100%	100%	100%	100%

In another study, *Disappointing marriage: a study of the gains from merger* by G. Meeks (Cambridge: Cambridge University Press, 1977), the efficiency gains from mergers carried out in the UK were evaluated and summarised. The study concentrated on mergers, although the author used the term in a broad context to include acquisitions. The study suggests that in the majority of post-merger years the typical amalgamation experienced a decline in profitability when compared with the pre-merger level. The study appears to support the logical hypothesis that on the whole an acquirer who is relatively strong and successful before a merger is less likely to be unsuccessful after a merger. It is very sad that one needs to talk in such terms when the underlying rationale for an acquisition is to be more successful and not just less unsuccessful!

It almost sounds as though pursuing an acquisition policy is like playing Russian roulette? It may not be a fatal game in terms of human life, but the evidence also seems to suggest that the probability of failure, on average, is greater than the 'one in six' hit rate of Russian roulette. Is it not possible to undertake an acquisition strategy with a higher level of success? Is it not possible to mitigate the risk? The purpose of this chapter is to review the rationale for acquisitions and explore the kind of 'homework' and systematic procedures that the corporate strategist should pursue. Acquisitions are not new phenomena. There are many case studies, successful and unsuccessful, which the planner can analyse. The emphasis in this chapter will be on the importance of approaching acquisitions studies with a marketing orientation. The aim here is to alert the reader to the thought that one of the main reasons for failure in achieving successful acquisitions is the fact that inadequate attention is paid to the marketing aspects of such a strategy. In most cases acquisitions are screened with financial thoroughness and with some attention to administrative efficiency. However, it is rare to find an acquiring company exploring in depth the quality of the marketing effectiveness of the purchased firm and the level of 'synergy' which the two firms are likely to achieve once the marriage has been consummated.

The Purpose of Acquisitions

Hardly a day passes without some news in the financial papers of one company acquiring another. Sometimes one reads of dramatic takeovers involving very large sums. On other occasions the transactions are small and discreet and manage to escape the headlines. A quick analysis of the reasons offered by the management of the acquiring firms for the decision to adopt such a strategy often leaves many questions unanswered. One wonders whether a sufficient amount of thought was invested in the whole project prior to committing precious company and shareholders' resources in what often proves to be an ill-conceived strategy.

It is always useful to pose to top management the simple question, 'What are your reasons for opting for the acquisition trail?' Some companies can answer this question in a most persuasive way. Others offer a whole range of flimsy and unconvincing arguments. Yet other firms have not considered the question at all. Having decided that an acquisition is the appropriate manifestation of success, growth and manhood they pursue such strategy with energy and vigour without asking too many intellectual questions. Sometimes they succeed, sometimes they fail – this is precisely what happens at the gambling table.

The record of success and failure shown earlier in Table 4.1 indicates what a responsibility top management undertakes in following the acquisition route. It is therefore imperative that when asked the reasons that had motivated them to pursue such a strategy they offer positive and unequivocal defences to any would-be iconoclastic interrogator. It must be remembered that in many cases the decision to purchase another firm is based on a myriad of reasons – some are overtly stated and some are covert. The covert reasons are seldom stated in open forums and are never recorded in writing. They are part of the organisation's cultural and political ecologies which the casual observer would not understand.

The often-quoted overt motivators for acquisitions are as follows:

(a) *To attain 'synergy'* The idea here is that the combined forces of two firms is greater than their individual levels of performance. 'There is strength in unity' is the motto. The word 'synergy' has been chewed, digested and regurgitated for many years now. The idea that $2 + 2 > 4$ has triggered the imagination of many strategists and has formed the justification for many takeovers. Nonetheless, one can quote many examples of marriages that should have generated a powerful 'synergy' and yet have failed to do so.

The idea underlying the concept of synergy is that through the amalgamation of two companies one or more of the following 'pay-offs' might take place: (i) production synergy leading to more effective production and cheaper unit costs through economies of scale; (ii) purchasing synergy leading to some buying leverage resulting in cheaper raw materials; (iii) R & D synergy resulting in better and cheaper innovations; (iv) marketing synergy resulting in a more efficient marketing and selling activities; (v) financing synergy leading to a more effective management of funds.

Where synergy is actually attained many benefits can be derived, leading to increased earnings. Unfortunately synergy often eludes the acquiring company because the information available to it prior to the takeover does not fully match the realities identified after the acquisition has been completed.

One of the areas in which synergy is often missed is in the field of marketing. This happens for two reasons. First, because an inadequate marketing audit normally takes place during the screening and negotiations stage. The tendency is to concentrate one's attention to financial and administrative issues rather than to marketing criteria. Secondly, a thorough understanding of a firm's marketing position in the marketplace is very difficult without having frequent and unhindered access to the acquired firm's internal information. Thus such information as the firm's policy towards specific marketing segments or the productivity level of the sales force or the effectiveness of the firm's communication programmes or the cost of distribution are often not available during the pre-acquisition investigatory stage. During a recent case I came across a company that had acquired a small firm that appeared very attractive because it operated in a similar business as the acquiring organisation but used the direct marketing approach with a vast mailing list. The level of synergy had seemed beyond any reasonable doubt. Nonetheless, very shortly after the acquisition was completed a random analysis of the mailing list yielded very disturbing news: one-third of the persons named on the list were dead, had moved elsewhere or had never existed! The main attraction of the purchased firm disappeared.

(b) *To increase market share*   In strategic terms such a move can be a wise one and can be a useful motivator for an acquisition policy. However, one does encounter many instances where the aim of increasing market share was fully justified – yet during the post-acquisition period something went very wrong and the resultant increase in market share never materialised. The reason is simple: the concept of market share can be a very dangerous pitfall. What appears to be the 'market' for firm A is not necessarily the 'market' for firm B. General Motors has a substantial market share in the US car market. Rolls Royce has an infinitesimal market share of the same market. Nevertheless, they have a very large market share of the so-called 'Rolls Royce market'. Attempting to compare the two market shares would be absurd. In Chapter 8 the question is discussed in some depth. Suffice it to be emphasised at this point that before a firm goes chasing the golden fleece known as 'market share' it must define with great clarity what market it operates in, and also specify as to why an increased market share would give it an enhanced strength in the short or in the longer term. Once again this is a marketing 'input'.

(c) *To eliminate competition*   This sounds a most convincing argument for a takeover. Assuming that one can pass through the net of the Monopolies Commission in the UK or the more demanding rules of the anti-trust legislation in the USA, it always sounds good to get rid of a competitor. But here comes the problem: getting rid of one competitor is seldom a guarantee that other competitors will not become more aggressive or that new competitors will not spring up. The marketplace is dynamic and the elimination of a competitor does not always lead to a more stable and 'cleaner' marketing environment. Moreover, one must always remember that the word 'competition' is multi-faceted. A firm has so-called 'brand' competitors, namely those who offer the same kind of product under different names. At the same time it has 'functional' competitors, those who offer to the customers the same results or cost–benefit relationship but by different methods. The latter often proves a more difficult 'nut to crack'. In the pursuit of a competitor which one does a strategist look for? A bus company that purchases all the competitive bus firms in the area still has to cope with the competition of trains, planes, taxis and cars. To buy them all is obviously not possible. In selecting the elimination of competition as the rationale for a takeover the strategist must consider in depth the marketing implications.

(d) *A defensive strategy* Although there are many situations in which an acquisition can be justified as a defensive measure, this kind of response often hides a multitude of sins. The implication is that having performed badly in our own activities we shall defend our position by purchasing a firm that will mask our inefficiencies. This may sound a harsh statement, especially towards those who perform the strategic planning task intelligently and systematically. It is aimed at the others: those who select a strategy without reflecting sufficiently upon alternative routes for achieving clearly defined objectives. A domestic appliance manufacturer who found that his market share was slipping decided, as a defensive measure, to acquire a group of retail outlets. At no stage did he consider the obvious need to evaluate the quality of his range, the pricing policy, the selling practices and the quality of the promotional mix. Having decided that purchasing retail outlets would provide him with the appropriate defences, he entered the takeover trail with amazing energy and determination. The acquisition, not surprisingly, failed in so far as once the deal went through the manufacturer insisted that his range receive prominent floor space in the acquired outlets. He had hoped to attain synergy but destroyed the firm instead. Of the various functions of an organisation, it is marketing, once again, that should be analysed before, during and after the acquisition.

(e) *Quick and economic entry into a business* During the planning process a firm normally considers a number of alternative strategies for attaining the organisation's objectives. One considers such strategies as 'new product development', namely the introduction of new and better products into the present markets that the firm serves. Alternatively one looks at 'new market development', namely the introduction of the existing products into new markets or segments. Another strategy is 'diversification', which means the introduction of a *new product* for a *new market* (Fig. 4.1). The selection of the most appropriate strategy is the culmination of a very thorough and systematic process. Diversification is normally a very demanding route to choose in as much as the firm is entering uncharted waters in the sense that it knows very little about the 'product' and even less about the 'market'. Nonetheless, there are many situations where diversification is probably the most sensible route to take. Tobacco companies are more or less forced to diversify because it is difficult to see what kinds of new products they can introduce to the ever-decreasing smoking market and even more difficult to identify new markets for cigarettes.

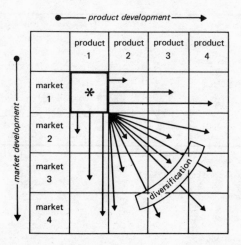

Figure 4.1 The relationship between various marketing strategies. Note that the asterisk indicates market penetration.

Once a strategy has been selected and its appropriateness evaluated in accordance with well defined procedures (example illustrated in Fig. 4.2) the process of implementation commences. Acquisition can often prove a quick and cost-effective route towards implementation. If a tobacco company decides during the strategic planning process that it wishes to enter the frozen food manufacturing business, it will probably be well advised to take over an existing business rather than start from scratch. One buys expertise, a market position, knowledgeable managers and facilities. Starting from a 'green field' approach can be extremely hazardous, although in some cases not out of the question.

An acquisition policy aimed at short-circuiting the entry process into a new business can be a valid motivator. The fact that we are talking about a new business entry implies that the existing management of the acquiring firm has limited knowledge and expertise in this field. It is therefore incumbent upon those responsible for identifying and screening potential candidates to ensure that they are well equipped with all the data which is relevant to the situation in question. Not least is the need to collect, analyse and interpret information about the marketplace and the position which the ideal candidate should enjoy therein. A financial analysis of the various candidates is certainly not enough.

(f) *To achieve tax efficiency* This can be an interesting motivator for firms that operate in a field with substantial tax bills with limited assets to depreciate. The acquisition of a company with a

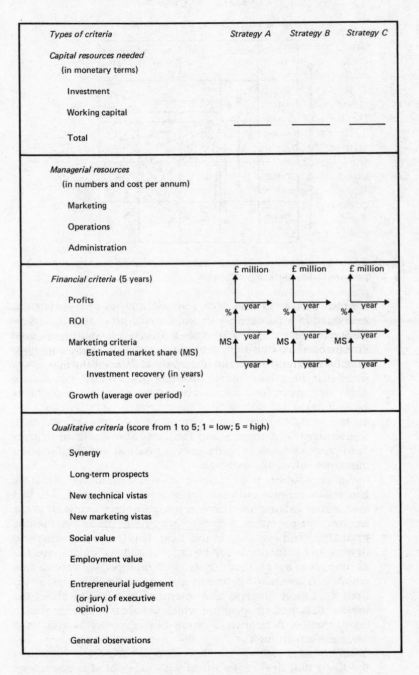

Figure 4.2 Evaluating alternative strategies (an example only).

substantial tax cushion due to past 'tax losses' or operating in an area that enjoys generous tax allowances can be attractive. The caveat is that the acquired firm, despite its tax advantages, does not represent a hot-bed of organisational and strategic problems. It is all very well saving tax on consolidation of accounts, but if the purchased firm is heading for a disastrous performance in the future the game is not worth the candle.

Unless the acquiring company is what is known as an 'asset stripper', and provided that it intends to maintain and develop the performance of the new acquisition, a thorough understanding of the firm's marketing welfare is essential. Saving tax is one thing; having all one's profits absorbed by a lousy company is certainly not very attractive.

(g) *To buy a bargain* This is a frequently quoted acquisition motivator. The question is, 'What is a bargain?' Everything in our society has its proper price. Buying a house at a bargain price may sound attractive. However, if the reason for the low price is the fact that it has been blighted as a result of a motorway planned to run through its living room, it ceases to be a bargain. Purchasing a company at what appears to be a low price is not necessarily an attractive proposition. The firm's products may all have reached the ends of their life cycles. The channels of distribution may be totally ineffectual. The company's image may be poor and the sales force useless. Moreover, the management may be ageing and ill motivated. All one is buying is a decaying organism with endless problems in store for the would-be acquirer.

(h) *To reduce an over-dependence on geographical presence and/or technology* This represents a classical example of the need to move into new fields and/or countries. One of the main motivators for internationalisation is the desire to protect oneself against the vagaries of political and economic swings. Undoubtedly many French companies wished they had acquired an American subsidiary when the going was good and the French franc relatively strong, and prior to the re-imposition of exchange constraints. This is a relatively easy strategy to defend. However, it is also a very high risk area inasmuch as one is attempting to enter a new world with complex commercial, institutional and legal environments. The fact that English is spoken in America and Canada often misleads the acquiring strategist into thinking that the takeover trail is simpler there than in non-English-speaking countries. The number of ill fated marriages that have taken place on the other side of the Atlantic must be a warning to those seeking to indulge in transatlantic acquisitions without a sufficient thoroughness.

Other overt motivators can be listed, such as the desire to improve general efficiency and/or utilisation of assets; to increase purchasing power; to complete product lines; to utilise excess capacity. I have even come across a situation in which a firm was acquired with the sole purpose of acquiring a single manager who enjoyed the reputation of being a creative and imaginative entrepreneur. The acquisition proved a most expensive one in so far as a few months after the marriage was consummated the whizz-kid left for new pastures.

One common denominator seems to run throughout: the need to undertake a thorough and systematic analysis of the marketing aspects surrounding the potential candidates. The interesting point to note is that when a firm acquires a company with the sole objective of adding a number of products or brands to an existing successful range one seldom encounters major failures. The reason is simple – the acquiring firm knows its markets intimately and is therefore likely to appreciate the marketing implications of such an acquisition.

The covert motivators are much more difficult to identify. Some of them are emotional and are best not discussed in an open forum – they can be too embarrassing. I was recently involved in an acquisition where the hidden justification for the whole strategy was the desire on the part of the chief executive to find a suitable job for a close member of his family! Every conceivable justification was put forward as a reason for the acquisition choice except the true one. Millions were spent to buy a company and a few more millions pumped into what proved to be a very ailing enterprise. What a price to pay for a high class unemployment benefit to a dear relative?

Less offensive but equally controversial is the desire to enlarge the firm and its power base in order to attain greater personal prestige, wider horizons and greater remuneration and perks. Obviously, if all this is coupled with better benefits to all the other stakeholders, this is admirable. However, if such a strategy only achieves the enhancement of one person's welfare or that of a small group at the top, the strategy is very suspect.

Even more cynical covert motivators are known in the annals of successful and unsuccessful acquisitions. It has been known for a firm to take over a competitor in order to mete out vengeance upon an old opponent.

This chapter is addressed to those who wish to pursue an acquisition policy with two objectives in mind: (a) to ensure that the risk of failure is mitigated and reduced to a minimum; (b) to approach the whole project with the utmost personal integrity. The emphasis will be placed here on how to achieve the first objective. As far as the second objective is concerned, it is recommended that the strategist reflects upon the covert motivators and, if any of them do exist, that he incorporates them in the various documents that underlie the acquisition process. The aim must be to convert covert motivators into overt ones. Any motivator which cannot be articulated to one's colleagues or other stakeholders must be avoided. If one wants to approach the process with integrity, even the intangible motivators should be considered. Those that are incapable of honest discussion should not form a basis upon which acquisitions are screened. This issue is left to the strategist and his conscience and sense of social responsibility.

Acquisitions and the Planning Process

It is useful to review briefly the role of acquisitions within the context of the corporate planning process. One must remember that an 'acquisition' is only one of the many corporate strategies open to a firm in pursuance of its objectives. It is one of the means for achieving a corporate aim. It is not an end in itself. The planning process presupposes that the firm has undertaken a well proven analytical cycle which falls into distinct but logically interrelated procedures.

Fig. 4.3 shows the process in a diagrammatic form. It is self-explanatory and corresponds in the main to the way most firms carry out their planning cycle. The terms used may differ somewhat from those that some readers have become accustomed to, but the underlying logic of the process is probably universally recognised. Any company which does not carry out a corporate planning process has no right to be searching for acquisitions.

The aim of the planning process is to ensure that the firm defines its

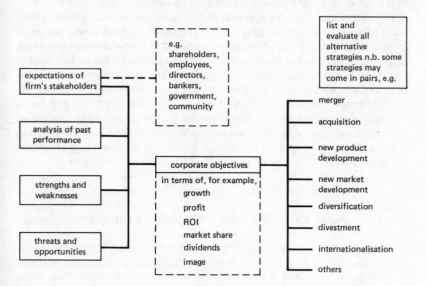

Figure 4.3 A model of the planning process.

goals in a manner which matches its capabilities (hence 'strengths and weaknesses') with potential opportunities (hence an attempt at quantifying 'threats and opportunities'). The ultimate purpose of the whole process is to ensure that the expectations of the firm's stakeholders are met. Obviously the process becomes complex as a result of the dynamism of the marketplace and also as a result of the fact that stakeholders' expectations tend to change at frequent intervals. Moreover, the relative importance of individual groups of stakeholders changes at a dynamic rate.

Until the planner has completed the earlier portions of the process it is irrelevant to talk about acquisitions or indeed about any other corporate strategy. It is only when the corporate objectives have been defined that one can commence the task of exploring ways and means for achieving these goals. Here comes the painstaking task of listing every conceivable strategy and evaluating its appropriateness towards the attainment of objectives. 'Acquisition' is often only one of the possible strategies that the firm can pursue – and is not necessarily the most appropriate one or the most profitable one in every set of circumstances. Other strategies, such as new product development, new market development, diversification, divestment, and internationalisation, may be much more relevant in specific situations and must be looked at with care. Moreover, some strategies may come in pairs. Thus, if a firm's aim is to increase growth and profits, one of the appropriate strategies may be the addition of new products to the existing range. This in turn may be best achieved through the acquisition of a firm with a strong market standing in such products. The rationale here is obvious; through a successful acquisition one can short-circuit the process of developing new products. However, in such circumstances the acquirer must ensure that (a) the management of the acquired company is effective; (b) the management style and culture of that firm is compatible with the acquiring firm; (c) the products of the firm are as good as they purport to be; (d) the level of synergy is high.

The form described earlier in Figure 4.2 illustrates a simple procedure which the strategist should use in attempting to quantify the merits of each of the various courses of action selected for scrutiny. At least he can move to the next step with an easy conscience. This is the point at which the 'acquisition plan' can be finalised and the 'search and screen' process undertaken.

A Systematic Checklist for a Successful Acquisition Project

The rest of this chapter consists of a systematic checklist for a successful acquisition project. It summarises the various steps that one needs to undertake before and during an acquisition and the way the whole process has to dovetail with the corporate planning cycle. A strong bias towards a marketing orientation underlies the various steps because it is felt that one of the major reasons for failure in the past has been the paucity of marketing data.

Activities	*Remarks*

I. THE CORPORATE PLAN

A successful acquisition programme must be dovetailed with a sound corporate plan. It is therefore important that prior to deciding upon an acquisition strategy the following elements are considered:

A   Analysis of the Firm's Stakeholders and their expectations

1.   Who are the main stakeholders and what are their relative expectations?

2.   It is very useful if one can identify a common denominator, such as profits and/or growth, likely to 'please' all the stakeholders' groups. Otherwise one has to strive to identify a set of compromises.

Remarks: This must be carried out and tabulated every time the planning cycle is undertaken.

Covert expectations of powerful groups with an important 'stake' in the business must be identified and expressed with maximum candour.

B   Analysis of the Firm's Past Performance

1.   Ratio analysis of major indicators over a period of (say) five years aimed at identifying performance trends
2.   Key trends in marketing performance
3.   Market status and image
4.   Performance within the competitive environment

Remarks: If 'interfirm' comparison can be obtained it would be very helpful in order to gauge the firm's relative performance vis-à-vis the main competitors.

C   Analysis of Company's Strengths and Weaknesses

1.   Marketing
2.   Management
3.   Operations and/or administration
4.   Financial
5.   Innovation

Remarks: This should include an analysis of every element of the marketing mix.

D   Analysis of the Future Environment

1.   Key trends in economic forecasts
2.   Threats and opportunities in relation to the industry

Activities	*Remarks*

3. Prospects for the marketing environment in which the firm will be operating
4. The anticipated impact of new technology

E   Establishment of Corporate Objectives
1. Quantitative
2. Qualitative

F   Identification and Selection of Corporate Strategies

1. Present businesses
  (a) Internal growth strategies
  (b) External growth strategies
2. New businesses
  (a) Internal development
  (b) External development
	Each strategy or group of strategies must be evaluated per the form illustrated in Figure 4.2 in the main text.

3. Consolidation strategies
  (a) Divestment
  (b) Product rationalisation
	The most promising strategy or strategies to proceed to the next step.

4. Merger and/or acquisition	For the purpose of this paper let us assume that 'acquisition' came at the top of the 'hit parade'.

II   ACQUISITION PLAN

A   Acquisition Objectives

When deciding on an acquisition plan an attempt must be made to ascribe clear objectives thereto. In other words it is important to specify, in some detail, as to what the acquisition aims to achieve:

Includes international expansion.

1. Integrate backward
2. Integrate forward
3. Same products and/or same markets
4. New markets for present products
5. New products for present markets
6. Diversification (viz. new products for new markets)
7. Other special purposes

B   Acquisition Criteria – 'The Profile'

This is a vital part of the whole process. The 'profile' should be sufficiently precise to enable the searcher to identify

Activities	Remarks

fairly quickly which firm falls within the criteria described and which does not. It would contain such items as

1. *Compatibility* with
   - (a) Marketing standing of the acquiring firm
   - (b) Management: style, strength, depth, motivation, culture
   - (c) Location
   - (d) Image and reputation
   - (e) Ownership interests and their expectations
   - (f) The acquiring company's own requirements for success   *Can be quantified*
   - (g) Size and investment in relation to the acquiring company's own size   *Can be quantified*

2. *'Success' criteria*
   - (a) Quantitative
     Profitability
     Return on investment
     Stability
     Capital requirements
     Market share in each operating segment
   - (b) Qualitative
     Risk/reward
     Market maturity
     Product life
     Quality of earnings
     Image
     Channels quality and/or loyalty

3. *Feasibility criteria*
   - (a) Government regulations   This point is particularly important where foreign acquisitions are involved.
   - (b) Institutional codes of practice   Either the acquiring firm or the potential candidate may belong to an industry which is subject to a strong code of practice which may in turn constrain an effective merger. Such codes must be defined.
   - (c) Number of potential candidates   It is never desirable to have to select a company

Activities	Remarks

out of a list of one. It is
wise to specify in advance
as to how many firms one
would hope to see on the
screening list.

    (d) "Willingness' to be acquired
    (e) Degree of dominance by small
        stakeholding groupings
Once the criteria ascribed to the 'profile'
have been defined a process of 'weighing' of
each can be undertaken. This must be carried
out after a thorough debate of the implications to the firm has taken place. A typical
illustration is shown in Figure 4.4 at the end
of this checklist.

**III   ACQUISITION 'SEARCH AND
    SCREEN'**
The ideal approach to a successful 'search
and screen' process is where the acquiring
company manages to combine its own
internal resources and know-how with
those of external specialists such as
consultants, merchant bankers, brokers,
etc. The former possess the 'input' which
helps to match identified prospects with the
needs of the parent organisation. The latter
are able to offer objectivity with an
independent and, if a foreign acquisition is
sought, local analysis of the data available.
This means that the two must work as a
'project team' and communicate at regular
intervals.
A comprehensive search would normally
cover:

Traditionally one uses
merchant bankers in
order to 'search and
screen' prospects. How-
ever, it must be remem-
bered that with all their
professionalism bankers
are anxious to see a deal
take place. It is highly
desirable to add market-
ing consultants to the
'project team' – they are
probably better equipped
to undertake an objective
and thorough 'marketing
audit'.

A   Published Data
    1.   Published lists
    2.   Trade associations
    3.   Other institutions
    4.   Industry periodicals, buyers' guides
    5.   Financial publications
    6.   Marketing publications

B   Internal Information
    1.   The company's own personnel
    2.   Other close contacts, including
        personnel of the company's
        advisers

Activities	*Remarks*

C Field Research

At the end of this phase one should be in the position of narrowing down the field of search to a manageable number of prospects. The 'screening' should be carried out by the 'project team' as a whole and not left to individual managers or to executives of the bankers or consultants assisting the firm.

During the 'screening' two tools can be used to facilitate the process:

1. The 'screening' device described in Figure 4.4 and referred to earlier

2. A 'portfolio management matrix' (Figure 4.5)

Remarks: The choice of questions and/or parameters for the 'matrix' will depend on each particular set of circumstances. The examples shown are purely illustrative and can be modified to suit the needs of specific situations.

IV APPROACH TO 'SHORT LIST' PROSPECTS

The first approach to the would-be seller must be carried out with tact, care and skill. Each situation calls for an appropriate strategy based on a full understanding of the elements likely to motivate the approached firm to consider selling. An approach normally involves the following steps:

Remarks: This is a good test of the firm's skill in marketing itself!

A Preparation

An acquiring company must not forget that a voluntary marriage is better than one attained by duress. It is therefore important that the acquiring firm undertakes the appropriate promotional steps to project itself in an attractive light. The following can be helpful:

1. Description of the firm. An attractive annual report can act as a useful 'aid' in this connection.

2. Description of the firm's aims and growth strategy

3. Reasons for the firm's acquisition interest

Activities	*Remarks*

4. The likely benefits to the acquired company's stakeholders (other than cash)

B   Identification of Decision-Makers
1. Owners
2. Management
3. Directors
4. 'Gatekeepers'

C   Initial Contact
1. A decision must be taken as to who is going to make the first contact.

2. Subjects to be discussed during the first meeting must be listed.

> The first meeting is crucial insofar as a definite impression, positive or negative, is made at this point.

D   Subsequent Steps
1. Schedule of contacts must be listed.
2. Future meetings must be planned
3. A log-book of progress and minutes of discussions is desirable.

> A network showing who is going to contact whom and when is a very useful strategy.

EVALUATION

If the first meetings are favourable, an in-depth evaluation should commence.

A   Matching the Prospect to the Objectives
1. Decision as to whether the company fits into the acquirer's environment and matches the objectives.
2. Is it acceptable in respect of price and other terms?
3. What will be needed to be done to integrate the acquisition with the acquiring firm (unless it is decided to 'leave it alone' for the time being).

B   Elements of Evaluation
1. Marketing audit: marketing standing; products, distribution system, image, promotional and communication methods, selling practices, competitive situation
2. Management capabilities and compatibility
3. Financial status and record
4. Elements of risk

> Figure 4.6 illustrates the kind of algorithm which the evaluating strategist can use. Preparing the questions is a tedious job but the payoff is substantial.

Examples of criteria	Weight	0 – 1	2	3	4	5	6	7	8	9	10	Weighted score
1. Management	0.15											
2. Return on capital	0.15											
3. Growth	0.15											
4. Image	0.10											
5. Distribution channels	0.20											
6. Product innovation	0.10											
7. Location	0.05											
8. Size of investment	0.05											
										Total		

Figure 4.4 Acquisition – a screening method (illustration only).

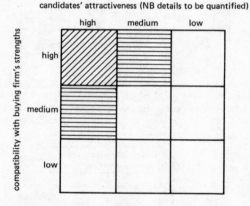

Figure 4.5 'Portfolio management' matrix for the screening of 'candidates'. Diagonally hatched area indicates a prime target; horizontally hatched areas indicate secondary targets; blank areas should be ignored.

In Conclusion

Acquisition is one of the most important strategies that a manager will ever undertake during his career. If successful his image will be of the highest and his progression in the firm's hierarchy assured. If the acquisition proves a failure, the manager responsible will find his standing in the firm greatly diminished. The corollary is obvious: one must ensure that all the necessary steps are taken to reject risky acquisitions and identify the truly promising ones. There are no short-cuts. The rewards normally go to those who approach the strategy in a thoughtful, systematic and well researched way before and during the 'search and screen' activities.

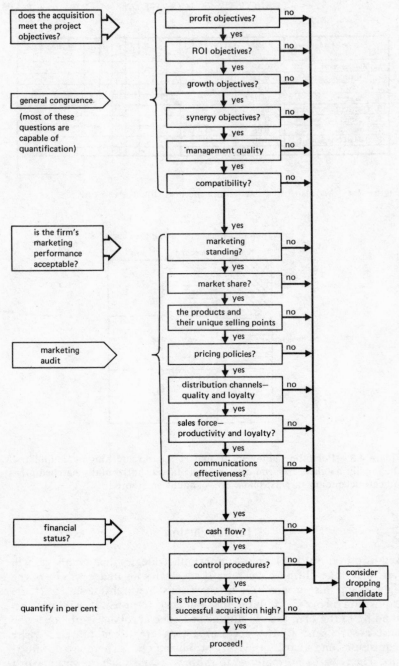

Figure 4.6 An evaluation algorithm. Note that the type and nature of questions will depend on the 'profile' criteria.

This chapter should be helpful to the would-be acquirer who wishes to mitigate the risk that an acquisition strategy seems to entail. It also seeks to emphasise the fact that one of the vital 'inputs' throughout the process is an in-depth analysis of the marketing strength of the potential candidates under scrutiny. Where the marketing effort of the firm under review is effective, creative and compatible with the acquiring organisation the chances of success are greatly increased. The evidence encompassed in the market share analysis of Table 4.1 seems to corroborate this hypothesis.

PART II

Marketing Within its Management Development Context

5
How to Prepare for the Top – A Marketing Perspective

One of the main lessons that I have learnt in my consultancy experience is that high-flyers who reach the top of their organisations fall into three distinct categories: the naturals, the strugglers and the misfits.

Naturals are the managers who slip into the mantle of the chief executive or the marketing director in an easy and natural fashion. These are the managers who carry a general's baton in their knapsacks throughout their careers. They know what the job of a boss entails and they respond quickly to the new challenges of the duties and responsibilities of the appointment.

The strugglers recognise that being at the top calls for a different range of skills and attitudes, but they find it very difficult to wrench themselves from their previous functional affiliations.

The misfits are the managers who should never have been appointed to a top position. They have reached their so-called 'level of incompetence' well before the final appointment was made, but lack the self-awareness that should have discouraged them from accepting the challenge of a top job for which they are clearly not equipped.

Obviously many subtle nuances of the three categories exist. However, one can slot most executives who have reached the top into one of these convenient groups.

My thoughts in this chapter are aimed mainly at the second category. Those who fall into the first group do not need any help. Those who fall into the third category are probably beyond help.

'The top', within the context of this chapter, is reached when a person is promoted to the strategic level of the firm either in the capacity of a chief executive or as the marketing director (or some other functional director). However, it is important to remember that it is not the title that determines whether such a person reaches the top. It is the nature of the job and the responsibilities of the new position which will indicate whether the appointment belongs to the top of the pyramid. The acid test is whether the person in question has acquired the authority to explore and take strategic decisions such as entering new markets or selecting new products or considering a diversification programme.

Equipment for Effective Management

Most managers have participated in management development programmes at one stage or another of their careers. Some of these programmes have been held as tailor-made in-house courses. Others have been public courses open to delegates from a variety of industries and/or service organisations.

The truly professional firm selects such courses with care and with a clearly defined set of objectives in mind. The less professional enterprise selects training programmes at random with little thought as to the true training needs of the individual people it sends on courses. It treats courses as a narcotic; it assumes that the mere fact that the individual has attended a training programme will ensure that his effectiveness at work will improve.

Moreover, the firm that takes management development seriously endeavours to approach the whole process in a systematic and integrated fashion. Courses are selected or structured as a series of logical and cohesive modules. They form a set of interrelated 'bricks' that correspond to the training needs of the various levels of management. In an ideal situation the organisation has a series of developmental 'bricks' appropriate to the needs of specific levels and functions. Such 'bricks' are designed to provide sequential additions to the participant's armoury of managerial equipment and tools. However, it must be remembered that a tacit 'social contract' exists between a firm and its employees: 'We shall provide you with the development aids you require but you must, at the same time, reflect upon and do something about your own self-development in the context of your job'. It is this combination of organised development and self-development that produces 'high-flyers' who reach the top.

In reflecting upon his development needs, the manager must remember that they fall into three distinct areas: knowledge, skills and attitudes. These are the three areas in which a person can improve himself or be helped to develop himself in the context of his firm's environment. Knowledge and attitudes tend to be company- and industry-orientated. The knowledge a manager acquires in a firm marketing machine-tools is hardly appropriate for somebody who wishes to join a company marketing bananas.

Similarly, the attitudes that a manager has acquired in an organisation that places an emphasis on the need to be empathetic to people inside and outside the firm are hardly relevant to an aggressive and results-orientated environment.

Skills, on the other hand, are transferable from industry to industry and from company to company. Once acquired, skills represent an integral part of the personal armoury of the manager. He can apply them to a variety of situations provided that he possesses the appropriate knowledge and has developed the right attitudes towards the new work environment.

Looking at management development from a marketing vantage-point one can illustrate the elements that fall under the three headings. The lists shown in Table 5.1 are not exhaustive and are purely an illustration of the kinds of component that a hypothetical firm would incorporate under each heading. In particular one must appreciate that under the heading 'attitudes' one would only expect to see items which represent the individual firm's deeply felt philosophies and norms of behaviour.

Table 5.1 The equipment of an effective manager – a marketing viewpoint.

Knowledge	Skills	Attitudes (examples)
company and its environment	observing	'marketing orientation'
markets and/or customer environment	reflecting	'consumer orientation'
products and their usp's	fact-finding	'productivity orientation'
competition (brand competition, functional competition and competition for the consumer's PDI)	identifying pertinent facts	'profit orientation
elasticities	analysing	'social responsibility'
law (e.g. EEC regulations)	diagnosing	'We are never knowingly undersold'
institutions	formulating solutions	'we try harder'
human behaviour	deciding	'what is good for the customer is good for business'
customers' motivation	communicating	'we have no problems; every problem is an opportunity in disguise'
sources of information	motivating	
contractual instruments	delegating	
	organising*	
	planning*	

*These skills encompass an amalgam of many of those listed.

Equipment for the Top

When exploring the developmental needs of a person approaching the top, I assume (a) that the candidate in question has been through the normal training 'bricks' that the lower echelons of the organisation are being exposed to, and (b) that he is sufficiently well motivated to work hard at his own self-development, with or without help from the personnel and/or management development departments.

It must be emphasised that I talk here in general terms only. Obviously every manager must reflect upon his own specific needs and in relation to the company, organisational style and industry within which he would be expected to perform his top job. Nonetheless, I have endeavoured to prepare a checklist of development areas for people who have reached the top or are about to reach it.

The checklist is broken down into the three elements listed earlier, namely knowledge, skills and attitudes.

KNOWLEDGE AREAS

As an important preamble to this sub-section it must be stated that a person approaching the top has to undergo a fundamental metamorphosis: throughout his career he went through a process of specialisation; when he gets to the top he has to start de-specialising himself. He needs to understand how other functions think and operate. He must appreciate the way the various departments interact and interrelate. Although his initial entry into the firm was through a functional affiliation, he must learn to appreciate the way other functions contribute to the success of the firm. This in turn involves the acquisition of a vast inventory of new knowledge about functions which he probably only tolerated until this point in his career.

More specifically, knowledge areas for the top fall into two main categories; those that help to manage the 'internal' resources of the organisation and those that relate to the 'external' world. They are both of paramount importance and the new candidate for the top needs to understand and respond to these two challenges.

Internal resources

(a) *Human and managerial behaviour*   A thorough understanding of human behaviour in the context of managerial environments is essential. This area will include
- Patterns of managerial behaviour
- Methods of testing and clarifying managerial patterns (e.g. assertive, responsive, aggressive and non-assertive behaviour)
- How to choose effective patterns in relation to specific organisations
- Theories pertaining to the 'management of conflict'
- Identifying one's own pattern of managerial behaviour
- Main principles of transactional analysis
- The main theories of motivation and job enrichment (this area alone contains a vast amount of knowledge of considerable importance to the person who wishes to manage an organisation in a professional manner).

In this area a lot of reading and a sincere attempt to reflect upon the material read will provide the manager with the 'equipment' required.

(b) *Functional interface*   Here a manager should undergo a process of self-analysis and ask himself the embarrassing question, 'Do I know enough about finance (or production or R & D)?' Nobody can perform an effective top job without a sound grasp of the key principles of the various functions that represent the firm's team'.

In this connection excellent public courses are run on such topics as 'financial knowledge for directors' and 'industrial relations policies for directors'. Such courses, when they are effectively planned and run, not only seek to impart knowledge on the function and/or discipline in question but also create an awareness of the interface among the various functions of the firm. Thus a marketing person who gets to the top must understand not only financial principles but he must also appreciate the way financial and marketing decisions interact.

(c) *Effective communication* An effective manager will be familiar with the various ways in which one can communicate with other people in the organisation. More than likely he will have undergone rigorous training in the skills of communication (listening, report writing, effective presentations, inter personal communication).

When he gets to the top he will need to sharpen and re-orientate his skills of communication. In preparation for such a task he will need to acquire some knowledge as to how to hold effective meetings; interviewing techniques; public speaking and chairing public events.

(d) *Managing 'creativity'* To the extent that the climate for creativity stems from the top the manager will need to read and gather some knowledge about the way the creative process functions. In particular he will need to understand the various blockages that weaken the level of creativity in an organisation. He should also appreciate the methods that can be used to stimulate a more creative style of management, as well as generate ideas throughout the firm. It cannot be over-emphasised: it is the person at the top who is responsible for stimulating the right climate for creativity.

The external environment

This area falls into two groupings:

(a) *The external and/or uncontrollable environment* The following is a brief list of important items:
- Macro-economics and its likely impact on the firm
- An understanding of social patterns development and the effect they are likely to have on the life style of the marketplace
- Developments in the labour market and industrial relations

- Competition (both of the 'brand' type; 'functional' type and for the consumer's disposable income)
- Institutions, both governmental and semi-governmental that have some impact on the firm's strategic decisions. Thus top management of an airline must possess full knowledge of the way IATA functions (or does not function) and the *modus operandi* of the Civil Aviation Authority. Getting to know the senior personalities of such bodies is an important 'knowledge acquisition' process for the person at the top.
- Political lobbies that may affect the destiny of a firm and its products must be also identified and its main protagonists located and met.
- Legal influences must be understood.
- Other regulatory influences such as consumer associations, design and quality approving bodies must be studied.
- Technology development in the firm's manufacturing and operating environment
- Stock exchange(s) and the way they function
- The banking and fund-raising systems.

(b) *The firm as seen by the 'world at large'* One of the major tasks of top management is to respond to attitudes displayed by the external environment towards the firm, its industry, its products and its methods of operation. The person at the top is the ambassador of the enterprise who must attempt to project an image which is consistent with the communication needs of the company as a whole. How can he perform an effective task if he is unaware of the way the world views him and his organisation? Under this heading one needs to acquire an understanding of

- The way the company is viewed by the world in general and the customers in particular (the so-called 'corporate image')
- The firm's image among professional, financial and institutional bodies
- The attitude of the media, especially the business media, towards the firm.

SKILLS FOR THE TOP

Of the many skills of management which were enumerated above, the candidate for the top must attempt to perfect the following:

(a) *Observing* This is a greatly underestimated skill. The ability to notice events, human sensitivities and ideas is a great asset for a senior person. The manager who feels that having reached the top he can isolate himself from observing mundane occurrences will soon find himself isolated from the firm's 'heart-beat'. In this connection an intelligent and sensitive secretary can provide the person at the top with 'eyes and ears' to whom part of the observing task can be delegated.

(b) *Reflecting* This is a skill that every manager at whichever level he happens to be needs. At the top his skill becomes of paramount importance. At the strategic level, one must apply considerable intellect and thought to the formulation of policies and to the allocation of resources. The tasks involved are less operational than those the manager was accustomed to at lower levels. They call for reflection rather than 'doing' things. Many managers find the transition from 'doing' to thinking and planning slightly frustrating.

(c) *Formulating solutions and deciding* I have skipped a number of skills – fact-finding, analysing of pertinent facts, and diagnosing. Of course they are very important, but I assume, firstly, that the manager in question has acquired these skills during his management development process at lower levels and, secondly, that the person at the top will have access to subordinates to whom the collation of facts, their analysis and diagnosis can be delegated. However, the process of formulating solutions and taking decisions remains, to a great extent, the job of the person at the strategic level.

A judicious exposure to complex 'business games' should help the candidate for a top job to improve his skills in this area.

(d) *Communicating* This is a skill which one seeks to develop at every level of management. Yet it seems to take a different perspective as one moves from level to level. For the person at the top effective communication entails first and foremost the ability to listen. As every manager knows, listening is often more difficult than making effective presentations. The person aspiring to become a boss must learn to bite his tongue and listen.

The other aspect of effective communication at the top is the ability to make persuasive presentations to one's peers and/or subordinates. In this area the person who feels that his or her skill is insufficient would benefit from a short and sharp course on effective presentations.

(e) *Motivating* Once again this is a skill that one acquires throughout one's experience at lower levels of management. Knowing how to motivate is a vital skill not only at the strategic level. Nonetheless, the man at the top is totally enmeshed in the motivation game. He has to motivate subordinates, colleagues, shareholders, and representatives of various groups. Provided that he has gone to the trouble of acquiring the knowledge that the vast literature on the subject of motivation has to offer and provided that he allocates enough time to reflect on the implications, he should be able to formulate strong personal concepts as to how the people around him should be motivated.

(f) *Delegating*   It is almost superfluous to say that the person at the top must know how to delegate. Delegating is an important skill for any manager who has to manage through others. However, once at the top the manager must screen very carefully what task he delegates and to whom. He must recognise that his subordinates' time is a scarce resource and when delegating to them a specific task he must ensure that he has considered the importance of such an activity in the context of the person's other commitments. The realisation that the boss has reflected upon his priorities before dishing out work to his subordinates is in itself part of the motivational hygiene of the process of delegating.

(g) *Planning*   This is a skill which encapsulates many of the other skills of management discussed earlier. In this context it is recommended that the senior manager simply learns to 'plan' his own time. Once again, through example he can show the way to others as to how a manager should spend his time in a planned and meaningful fashion.

In this connection I often advise people who get to the top to keep a log-book in which they record, in detail, the way they spend their days. A periodic analysis of such a log-book will highlight for them the relative importance which they attach to specific tasks. On reflection they may find that they devote too much time to one type of activity and not enough to another.

NEW AND OR BETTER ATTITUDES

This is probably the most important and sensitive area in which the person at the top can make an impact on an organisation. The reader must not assume that because I talk about this item last and only briefly that I ascribe less value to this topic. The development of attitudes for the organisation is the basis upon which a firm's style and mode of conduct is structured. Attitudes must be planned and developed and people persuaded to adopt them; they do not just happen.

The people at the top, like leaders of a nation, are responsible for selecting attitudes and indoctrinating the system in their wholehearted application. On approaching the top the manager must ponder the list of attitudes which in his judgement will make the firm a modern, efficient, confident and successful enterprise which is 'pleasant to work in'.

Through a series of comprehensive debates with colleagues, subordinates and possibly external resources, coupled with a considerable amount of thought, he must attempt to crystallise a cluster of attitudes, a philosophy, a charter of behaviour for all to follow. In so doing he must seek to identify (a) the various attitudes which imparted strength to the firm in the past and (b) his own deeply felt principles and attitudes upon which he believes that a positive style of management and relationships can be structured.

6
The What and How of Creativity

A full page advertisement placed in the *Financial Times* on 20 July 1978 by the advertising agency J. Walter Thompson posed a very challenging question to the readers: 'What the hell is an advertising agency for?' The question was not as daft as it may sound. It referred to a published survey organised by Wood, Brigdale and Company, which sought to identify advertisers' perceptions of the role of advertising agents. One of the findings of that survey was that fifty clients, responsible for 103 advertising accounts, *put 'creativity' as an agency's most important quality.*

Many of the respondents ranked J. Walter Thompson as the leading 'main creative agency'; Collett, Dickenson, Pearce was a close second and Saatchi & Saatchi Garland-Compton third. The survey therefore provided a good platform for J. Walter Thompson's advertisement, the content of which was devoted largely to another finding of the survey. This was that *nobody seemed to know what creativity was.* The most generally agreed description was 'an ability to produce memorable advertising'.

The advertisement shattered some of my own confidence. Having been deeply involved in the process of training managers in the need to be creative, and having sought for over a decade to elevate the quality of creativity in many organisations, I found myself asking the question: Do I know what creativity is? The *Shorter Oxford English dictionary* (1978 printing) has no entry for the word, so presumably its compilers found the word indefinable too, even though it does define the words 'create' and 'creative'. So anybody who cannot provide an instant definition can be forgiven. Perhaps one can possess creativity without being able to define its meaning.

It may be useful to explode a few popular myths surrounding creativity:

(a) *Creativity is the sole prerogative of advertising agencies* Advertising agencies would have us believe that they are the custodians of the creative process. Indeed, most agencies have a so-called creative director, though it is not clear whether this process of delegating creativity to a well defined focal point means that everybody else in the agency can relax and abdicate from contributing to the creative process. It is almost like appointing a director of efficiency in a manufacturing company, which would obviously be quite absurd.

(b) *Creativity's most important role is as an ingredient of successful advertising* There is little doubt that creativity can help to develop an effective and memorable advertising campaign. However, this is only one area among many in which creativity can help to generate new and better solutions to problems. Creativity has a vital role to play in every aspect of the managerial process and not only in advertising. In fact creativity is the raw material for new and better solutions to problems in any sphere of human endeavour. Creativity helps us to develop new and better products. Pricing policies can be more creative. Channels of distribution can be identified and developed in a highly creative way. Market research projects can be creatively designed. It is to be hoped that one day we shall tackle national problems in a creative fashion. Presumably this is where the government's so-called Think Tank comes in. The sooner we recognise that creativity has an all-embracing role to play in the development of a better future for an organisation the better.

(c) *To be creative one must look creative* An inexplicable tradition seems to exist in our industrial society that a creative person must look creative. For example, people purporting to be creative often grow their hair long, and bald people often find it difficult to get invited to brainstorming sessions. On one occasion I had the pleasure of helping the chief executive of a well known public company to select a senior person for a job entailing an important fashion element. The idea was to recruit a creative person. The person in question who appeared to me as the best candidate for the job was turned down by my client. 'Anybody who dresses in such a conservative fashion cannot be creative' was the chief executive's irrevocable verdict.

(d) *You need to be intelligent to be creative* General intelligence bears about the same relationship to on-the-job creativity at the managerial level as weight does to ability in American football. You have to have a lot of it to be in the game at all. However, once you are a member of a team your weight has little bearing on your performance. Similarly, it is necessary to have a certain level of intelligence to join an organisation, but once there one's IQ does not necessarily bring with it a corresponding level of creativity.

Enough has been said to impress upon the reader that creativity is not the prerogative of a few long-haired, specially trained, highly publicised members of an élite. It is an ill-defined gift which many more members of our society possess than we realise, provided that certain conditions prevail.

Creativity and Innovation Defined

For the purpose of good communication, I ought to say what I personally understand when I use the terms 'creativity' and 'innovation'. I find that very often people use these two terms interchangeably, thus adding to the confusion.

(a) Creativity is the thinking process which helps us to generate ideas.
(b) Innovation is the practical application of such ideas towards performing a task in a better and/or cheaper way.

Creativity is the raw material; innovation is the commercial or technological outcome. Creativity can be eccentric, extravagant, even 'way out'. Innovation is practical, commercial and capable of yielding results. In talking about 'better' we must of course include aesthetic improvements and not only functional ones. To that extent improved design (provided it is seen as such in the marketplace) is an innovation.

According to my perception of the two terms, therefore, a task which has been performed in a manner which is neither better nor cheaper does not constitute an innovation. Novelty *per se* is not necessarily innovative in character. A manager must avoid pursuing an idea just because it appears creative in its original thought. If it costs more to do the same job or if the results are less satisfactory, the idea does not lead to innovation and must be avoided. An electric shaver which performs the task of shaving in an identical way to the previous model cannot be classified as an innovation simply because it is packed in a more extravagantly designed box. On the other hand, a shaver which shaves better or is smaller or is more aesthetically pleasing would meet our criteria.

Innovation may result from *normative creativity* or *exploratory creativity* or *creativity 'by serendipity'*.

(a) *Normative creativity* Creativity is said to be normative when ideas are sought to provide solutions for identified and detailed needs, problems or objectives.
(b) *Exploratory creativity* Exploratory creativity occurs when ideas are generated which are not necessarily related to known requirements or recognised demand. Exploratory creativity highlights opportunities which are not always exploitable in commercial terms.
(c) *Creativity 'by serendipity'* Creativity and the innovation that may result from it are said to take place 'by serendipity' where the idea underlying the innovation is discovered by happy but unexpected accident.

All three styles are valid in the overall quest for ideas. Normative creativity is more closely aligned to a predictive marketing model of future needs. To that extent it is often considered more cost effective. At the same time one must recognise that normative creativity, by its very nature, may act as a constraint on the full fertility of human imagination and idea generation. The ideal combination is the synthesis between the normative and exploratory approaches – the normative approach provides the goal, the exploratory approach the richness that only an unconstrained human brain can generate. Creativity by serendipity is the windfall that a perceptive mind endowed with imaginative potential can sometimes grasp.

The Creative Individual in Organisations

Thus far the behavioural scientists have not been able to claim that scientific tests and other techniques have been developed for identifying in advance those persons who will perform creatively. Identifying the highly creative person in advance of his creative production is as difficult as identifying a leader before he is actually exposed to the task of demonstrating his power of leadership.

A person's creativity is therefore best judged by what he has done, but a person who performs creatively in one firm may fail abysmally in another organisation. There is therefore little doubt that organisations influence creativity. There are some organisations in which creativity flourishes and others in which the creative process dies. The ideal situation is one in which a compatibility is attained between the creative person and the creative or innovative organisation. The characteristics of these two interrelated elements must therefore be examined.

The Creative Individual

It is very difficult to generalise as to what constitutes a creative individual. It is important to emphasise at the very outset that except for a few outstanding historical examples the most creative people in one field are not necessarily likely to be the most creative in another. Thus Einstein, who by every possible criterion was a most creative man in his particular field, might have proved to be a dismal failure had he joined J. Walter Thompson as a creative director. In other words it is virtually impossible to talk about general creativity. Nevertheless, the creative individual is a person who manifests a few, or possibly all, of the following attributes:

(a) *Conceptual fluency* The ability to generate a large number of ideas rapidly. Thus, if asked to list novel uses for a paper-clip, the creative individual can spurt them out at a rapid rate.

(b) *Conceptual flexibility* The ability to 'shift gears', to discard one frame of reference for another.

(c) *Originality* The ability to give unusual answers to questions, responses to situations, interpretations of events.

(d) *Suspension of judgement* The willingness to avoid early commitment and the willingness to treat every solution as feasible until the contrary is proved. The creative person spends more time in analysis and exploration before committing himself to a course of action.

(e) *Attitude towards authority* People of low creativity are more apt to view authority as final and absolute. Creative persons are more likely to think of authority as conventional or arbitrary, contingent on continued and demonstrable superiority. This is why creative people are often assumed to be more difficult to manage.

(f) *Impulse acceptance* Creative individuals are more willing to entertain and express personal whims and impulses. People of low creativity stick closer to realistic and conventional behaviour.

(g) *Tolerance* The creative person is tolerant of other people's ideas. The less tolerant person can raise many reasons as to why an idea is impractical. 'We have tried it before,' 'It is against the code of practice of our profession', 'It may be illegal', and so on.

It is evident that a few of these characteristics represent personality traits which the individual cannot alter. Some of the others are capable of change and improvement. An intelligent man can discipline himself towards a greater level of tolerance to other people's ideas. Similarly, most people can train themselves to 'suspend judgement' when a flow of ideas is generated around them.

The conscientious manager who wishes to improve his contribution to the creative process of his organisation certainly has the power to do something about it. Most individuals are capable of honing their innovative edge.

The Creative Organisation

The most important element for successful innovation is the climate of the firm. Creative people can behave in a more creative way in an organisation in which ideas are encouraged. A firm in which the boss discourages ideas is obviously less likely to be innovative. Such discouragement can take an overt form or can be subtle, in the form of a non-verbal communication. The boss can stifle creativity simply by looking bored when an idea is presented to him. Alternatively, he can dampen the enthusiasm of his subordinates by asking for a written report instead of going to the trouble of listening to the idea exposed. Suggesting to a person that he ought to discuss the idea with a third party is another way in which a creative manager can be demotivated.

Creativity can best thrive in a firm where ideas are solicited and encouraged. Every person in the organisation must feel that his ideas are wanted and that a receptive ear is always ready to listen to what he wants to say. It is very important that the climate is supportive throughout the firm. It must transcend all levels of management and exist in every functional area. Pockets of creativity in limited areas of the company, for example in product management, advertising or in some specific country, do not add up to a creative climate.

The dilemma which confronts most organisations is how to cope with the conflict between two countervailing forces. On the one hand, in the interests of efficiency, a firm seeks to develop a rigid routine for its operations, inevitably leading to conformity and the inhibition of the more creative members of the group. On the other hand, most firms recognise that innovation is an essential ingredient for survival and success. The effective boss must try to find a *modus operandi* between these two contradictory pressures.

Three factors in organisational functioning help to determine whether the climate is a stimulant to creativity:

(a) *The availability of organisational 'slack'* When an organisation has little slack in human and material resources the climate is less favourable for innovation. The tightly run ship may be very effectively run, but it can seldom sustain the distractions and costs involved in innovative experimentation. Managers are more or less forced to introduce impediments to creativity.

This may sound like a paradox, but it needs to be stated. A firm struggling to survive needs creativity. On the other hand, the pressures to remove organisational slack lower the firm's innovative capability. It has been suggested that the best way to cope with this paradox is to resort to *ad hoc* groups to deal with the need for innovation. Special task forces performing brainstorming or synectics exercises may close the self-imposed gap.

(b) *Centralisation or decentralisation* A decentralised structure is likely to provide more scope for innovative behaviour. Solutions to problems are normally handled at a divisional or departmental level, thus offering greater decision-making latitude to those at intermediate and lower positions. In a centralised organisation many decisions are taken at the top of the authority structure, thus narrowing the scope for creativity at lower levels in the hierarchy.

(c) *The system for communicating ideas* An effective system for communicating ideas is a vital catalyst for innovation. To increase the relevance of the creativity of the individual, the communication system must work well in both the vertical and the horizontal dimensions. Large firms often miss excellent opportunities simply because good ideas are lost as a result of poor communication procedures. This is particularly important in firms operating in more than one country. If a manager encounters a good idea during his travels he must communicate it to the appropriate person who may benefit from it. However, if the communication system is ineffectual, he may find the process of passing the idea on to an unknown recipient much too troublesome.

Techniques for Generating Ideas

Many techniques have been developed over the years and the literature is rife with many variations on a number of basic methods. The person who seeks to use these techniques must not be over-awed by their ostensible intricacies and must not be afraid of modifying them to suit the style of his company and the specific requirements of a given situation. The most helpful techniques for generating a large number of ideas are brainstorming, synectics and morphological analysis.

Critics of all three are abundant, and one should not expect miracles from any of them in isolation. The real value of these methods is not always measurable in concrete terms, but the mere fact that they are used contributes to the development of a suitable climate in which creativity can thrive.

BRAINSTORMING

This is a frequently-used technique. It is based on assembling a small group of eight to ten individuals and giving them a specific problem to solve. A few general rules normally apply:

(a) The group must suspend temporarily any judicial thinking. In other words it must learn to suspend judgement.
(b) Uninhibited thinking should be encouraged. The wilder the idea the better; it is easier to tame down than to think up.
(c) Quantity is wanted: the greater the number the higher the probability of good ideas being generated.
(d) Combination and improvement should be encouraged. In addition to contributing ideas of their own, participants should be encouraged to suggest how the ideas of others may be combined to yield yet another idea.

A long list of ideas should emerge from a brainstorming session, and a thorough screening and evaluation process should follow for each idea, however absurd it may at first appear. It is important to remember that an apparently absurd idea can stimulate and lead to useful ones. And two apparently absurd ideas can make sense when put together.

SYNECTICS

The word 'synectics' means the joining together of differently and apparently irrelevant elements. It aims at the integration of diverse individuals and disciplines into a problem-stating and problem-solving group. Members of a synectics group should ideally represent as many functions or activities as possible. A person who has held a number of jobs and had diverse experience is usually better equipped than a person whose career has been concentrated in one area.

The essence of the synectics process revolves around the participants' ability to generate metaphoric analogies based on the respective disciplines of the members. Thus, if the subject matter of the discussion is camouflage, the zoologist can easily draw parallels from the animal world, such as the way the chameleon changes his colours and the way other animals place themselves in backgrounds which hide them from sight. This kind of analogy can be a very fruitful source of ideas and viewpoints.

In the business world solutions to problems can be evolved by seeking to draw parallels with other commercial environments, however different they may be. What is to stop an insurance company from attempting to develop a communication programme based on the well proven methodologies of religious or political creeds? And Chairman Mao's 'little red book' has proved its communication effectiveness on a massive scale. Perhaps something can be learned from that. The constraint is psychological: most managers are reluctant to accept that one can learn from other industries and/or disciplines. The ability to rid oneself of the self-imposed mental ghetto that characterises our thinking is one of the greatest steps that a creative manager can undertake.

MORPHOLOGICAL ANALYSIS

This technique is also known as morphological method. It aims to single out the most important dimensions of specific problems and then examine all the relationships among them. Morphology means structure, and the technique seeks to explore all the possible alternatives which a multidimensional matrix may yield. Thus, a firm operating in the immensely competitive packaging field might develop the three-dimensional matrix shown in Figure 6.1. One dimension is the shape of the new pack, another dimension its contents and a third the materials (or combination of materials) from which the pack could be made.

Assuming that these three dimensions define fully the problems, there would then be 7 × 7 × 9 = 441 cells, and each cell represents an idea.

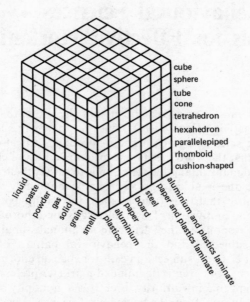

cube
sphere
tube
cone
tetrahedron
hexahedron
parallelepiped
rhomboid
cushion-shaped

liquid
paste
powder
gas
solid
grain
smell

plastics
aluminium
paper
board
steel
aluminium and plastics laminate
paper and plastics laminate

Figure 6.1 A morphological matrix for a new package.

In Conclusion

This is a vast subject and all I have tried to do is to provoke some food for thought. Knowing what creativity means is less important than knowing how to be creative and to respond to the creativity of others. It is useful to remember that creativity in an organisation can thrive only when the climate allows the creativity of the individual to spawn, and the various techniques associated with the process of generating ideas are potent stimulants for improving that climate.

7
The Behavioural Sciences – A Basis for Effective Marketing

A marketer must always remember that the ultimate objective of all marketing activities is to satisfy consumer needs in such a way as to increase the sales of a given brand or product. It is also important to remember that the word 'needs' encapsulates a host of elements – some tangible and many intangible. The aim is to satisfy them all, provided of course that one is able to do so in an economically viable way and provided also that one understands the complexities of human behaviour and motivation. This in turn calls for a thorough study of the way people respond to the various motivational stimuli to which they are being subjected and the behavioural pattern of their buying decisions. It is a vast subject and calls for such an enormous amount of knowledge that the practically minded marketer prefers to relegate the whole concept to a low priority level. It is a great pity because some of the concepts drawn from the behavioural sciences – psychology, social psychology, sociology and anthropology – are extremely valuable as an input to creative and effective marketing strategies.

Considerable damage was inflicted upon the cause of the behavioural sciences in marketing as a result of Vance Packard's book *The hidden persuaders*. The book, first published in the late 1950s, brought to light a number of disturbing and almost sinister examples of how the consumer gets manipulated and is persuaded to buy goods which he does not really wish to buy. It described the kinds of effort which marketers and advertisers resorted to in an attempt to channel the consumer's unthinking habits and thought processes by the use of insights gleaned from psychiatry and the social sciences. Vance Packard felt that the most serious offence that the many depth manipulators committed was that they sought to invade the privacy of the citizen's mind. In writing the book he wanted to alert us to the dangers and strive to protect this privacy.

Packard's book is a fascinating volume and has contributed an enormous amount towards the development of the various legislative and institutional codes of practice which seek to protect the public from unscrupulous manipulative processes. Many of the so-called 'hidden persuaders' are either banned by the legal systems of various countries or considered as unprofessional by the advertising industry itself in others. To that extent Vance Packard has made a most laudable contribution towards protecting the consuming public. Nonetheless, his powerful indictment of motivation research and other behavioural methods acted as a brake on the interest and enthusiasm which marketing organisations had shown in the whole concept. Understanding human behaviour and acting thereon is not necessarily a bad practice. It deserves criticism when it becomes manipulative and 'hidden'. On the other hand, it can be a very potent tool in the process of providing full consumer satisfaction and indeed, as we shall see later, can be an instrument of enhanced productivity in one's marketing effort.

Marketing and Human Behaviour

Marketing always involves dealing with people. Where there are no human beings there is no scope for marketing. Man is a complex creature and his behaviour is stimulated and motivated by a host of cultural, sociological, economic and pyschological factors. Unfortunately it is not possible to analyse each individual customer in depth with the view of identifying what 'makes him tick'. First, there are too many of them; secondly, not many consumers would be prepared to lie on a psychoanalyst's couch and be analysed. Obviously, if the marketing company only had one solitary customer and the purchasing power of this one person was therefore vast, the company could employ a full time behavioural scientist with a view to ensuring that every behavioural factor of the person in question was observed and tabulated. The company could get to know its single customer in as much depth as Pavlov got to know his dogs.

In most situations, however, the marketing company has to work with a large marketplace consisting of a large number of human beings. Human beings differ considerably one from another. However, it is useful to realise that they can be slotted into fairly distinct 'typologies'. The ability to do that can be extremely helpful inasmuch as it can offer a basis for a segmentation strategy. Normally one associates segmentation policies with a socio-economic classification or with demographics or with geographic divisions of the marketplace. As we shall see later, the ability to stratify a market by behavioural typologies can be a very exciting and efficient approach.

It is important to emphasise a fundamental point: very few firms can afford nowadays to be 'all things to all men'. The aim of satisfying every consumer regardless of size, wealth, location, habits, tastes and attitudes is a gargantuan task. The main aim of a sound marketing planning process is to enable the organisation to target its effort on the most promising audience group. This can only be achieved if the audience is well defined and conforms to a homogeneous and clearly identified 'typology'. Such a typology can conform to a myriad of criteria such as usage rate, income, interests, education, personality, etc. In this chapter a strong case will be made for the value of developing 'typologies' based on behavioural factors. It is not possible within the context of this chapter to cover every aspect of human behaviour and its appropriateness to marketing decisions. Nonetheless, if the reader finds some of the thoughts propounded here sufficiently provoking so as to want to learn more about this vast subject, the main aim of this chapter will have been met.

Before leaving this introductory note a brief message must be added to those readers who belong to organisations offering industrial goods. I often encounter among them some resistance to wanting to acquire knowledge pertaining to the understanding of human behaviour. They feel that this is an area which affects consumer marketing personnel only. This is certainly not so. Marketing industrial goods is also directed to human beings. Companies as such do not buy anything; it is the people who man companies that buy goods or services. They are also human beings and are subject to the normal behavioural and motivational stimuli. The only major difference between consumer marketing and industrial marketing is the fact that in the former we collect data which enables us to *generalise* about the behaviour of the so-called 'decision-making unit' whereas in the latter we have to be *detailed and specific* about each customer and his much more complex unit. Table 7.1 illustrates these differences and the impact which they have on the marketing tasks. In other words most of the ideas developed here

Table 7.1   The decision-making units

Industrial goods	*Consumer goods*
buyer	buyer
decider	decider
influencer	influencer
user	
'gatekeeper'	
others	

The main tasks

to acquire knowledge about each customer and understand his decision-making unit in detail	to 'generalise' about the target group with the view of achieving 'the greatest happiness of the greatest number'
to record and monitor this information at regular intervals	to develop a homogeneous strategy of communication with a well defined marketplace
to plan for a complex and multi-faceted communication programme aimed at satisfying the needs of many stakeholders	

should have some relevance for the industrial marketer as well, and he must resist the temptation of rejecting them just because they first saw daylight on the other side of the fence.

In addition to exploring the role of human behaviour as a basis upon which to develop typology segments, we shall consider how a better understanding of human behaviour can assist the marketer in developing more creative policies pertaining to specific elements of the marketing mix.

The Nature of Needs

Marketing aims to identify, anticipate and satisfy consumer 'needs'. One often forgets that the word 'needs' includes a large number of elements – some rational and some emotional. Some needs are tangible, others intangible. Needs are dynamic in the sense that they change with cultural and societal changes and also with the individual's own progression through his own life cycle. Various attempts were made to divide human needs into a hierarchical sequence. Notable among the scholars in this area is Maslow, who talked about the 'hierarchy of needs'. He postulated that a person undergoes a sequential progression through a series of needs. Obviously when he is hungry his main need is a physiological one, namely the need to feed himself and his family. Once this need has been satisfied other needs are awakened, and the desire to satisfy them increases in intensity. Maslow's theory was based on the idea that human needs are based on the following hierarchy:

1 *Physiological needs,* e.g. for food to alleviate hunger; for drink to remove thirst, for clothing to protect from the weather etc.
2 *Safety and security needs:* protection from loss or danger.
3 *Belonging and love needs:* the sense of being part of a group.
4 *Recognition needs:* the need to feel respected by others.
5 *The need for self-actualisation,* namely the need to feel that one has achieved personal fulfilment.

People have a requirement to satisfy all these needs, but the level of intensity changes with age and with one's ability to climb up the material ladder. Inevitably marketing to people who are still in the process of satisfying their physiological needs is a totally different game from trying to market products to those in the more advanced categories! The concept has received many face-lifts by many writers and academics. Nonetheless, it still represents an important landmark in understanding the dynamism of human motivation and behaviour. The important practical lesson to have emerged from all these writings was the fact that in trying to identify *needs* the marketer must go beyond the measurement of physical, physiological, rational and tangible needs.

When a person buys a Rolls Royce or a Porsche it is not only the need for transportation which he tries to satisfy! Similarly, when a person invests in a new solar-powered digital watch it is not only a time-keeping device that he buys.

Let us review a number of behavioural concepts which, together with Maslow's hierarchy of needs, may provide the marketer with a fresh perspective as to how to communicate with the consumer in accordance with his specific pattern of behaviour.

THE 'ADOPTION' PROCESS

It has been realised for a long time that those who purchase an innovative product at the beginning of its life cycle are very different people from those who buy the same product at the end of its life cycle. The former are more venturesome and willing to take some risk. They often buy the product not because it is good but because it is new. The latter are reluctant to accept risk. They tend to avoid products that smack of change or appear to be unproven.

Table 7.2 Adoption categories and their characteristics

Adoption category	Size (%)	Typical characteristics
innovators	2½	venturesome; prepared to experiment; often people of higher social status; higher income group; urban
early adopters	13½	same as 'innovators' but less venturesome
early majority	34	display less leadership than previous two; avoid risk; rural rather than urban types; active in community life
late majority	34	conservative; imitators; extra cautious; dislike change; older; lower income groups; less prestigious occupations; more orientated to local contacts
laggards	16	'isolates', stubbornly resist change, unimaginative

E.M. Rogers, in his interesting book *Diffusion of innovation* (New York: Free Press, 1962) classified customers into five categories on the adoption scale (Table 7.2). The percentages shown in Table 7.2 are based on the logical assumption that the adoption process takes the shape of a normal distribution curve. In statistical terms one expects few people to adopt the new product at first; the subsequent categories build up demand towards a crescendo and, finally, the laggards fall in line towards the end of the product life cycle. This is demonstrated in Figure 7.1.

The whole concept is capable of further analysis and development. It opens new vistas for creative marketing based on a better appreciation of how people behave in the face of innovation. It enables the shrewd marketer to adjust his marketing and communication programmes to the behavioural make-up and typologies of each one of the categories described. When the 'Concorde' entered into service it was obviously the innovators that British Airways sought to satisfy. It was not just transport that they were purchasing. They paid a lot of money for the excitement of being 'firsts' to use an exciting new product. They also wanted to gain the admiration of their social peers. They were venturesome and risk-takers. The only tangible bit of the product they had bought was transport. The rest were intangibles matching the higher echelons of needs on the Maslow hierarchy.

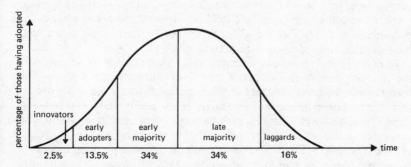

Figure 7.1   The adoption process as a distribution curve.

Similarly, one can assume that an 'innovator' in the medical profession is more likely to prescribe new drugs that come to his notice. The 'laggard' would avoid the same drugs like the plague.

Industrial buyers working for a modern and progressive firm are more likely to manifest the characteristics of innovators than their counterparts in a conservative and change-resistant organisation. The industrial marketer can easily capitalise on this notion when launching a new and innovative product. All he must do is list the firms among his clients which deserve the title of 'innovators'. Trying to sell new products to the laggard organisation is hardly a formula for productivity.

LIFE-STYLES AND CULTURAL VALUES

No marketer can afford to face the future without a better understanding of trends in thought in relation to the concept of life-style and the general behaviour of people towards the allocation of time, money and effort in the pursuit of personal interests and activities.

The literature is rife with discussions about the life-style of the consumer of the future. Many scenarios have been described and many predictive models developed suggesting that we are moving towards a so-called "ME-culture" where the consumer will be seeking personal and selfish self-gratification. Many of these scenarios have been developed in the USA (Stanford Research Institute; Yankelovitch, Skelly & White and others). In the UK, Research Bureau Limited, a marketing research agency, reported a few years ago about consumer life-styles in this country. Some of their findings will be summarised later.

The more recent research projects seem to suggest that people will be turning away from the materialism of the 1960s and the 1970s. This in turn will mean that leisure and cultural and physical recreation activities will grow at a very substantial rate. The work ethic that dominated our lives for many decades will decline. People will feel less guilty about taking time off for leisure activities and holidays. Loyalty and/or respect for old institutions will decline. (Indeed, who has respect for politicians today?) Declining belief in the 'system' will mean that considerable individualism and extreme self-expression will develop.

In behavioural terms one normally talks about two main segments in the marketplace: 'outer-directed' and 'inner-directed' consumers. The former buy products with an eye to appearances and what other people think. The latter buy goods to satisfy inner needs and personal self-expression. Such consumers wish to meet their own inner wants and pleasures as opposed to the process of responding to the norms of others. The 'inner-directed' consumer is still in a minority, figures being suggested place their number at around 15% of the adult population. However, the trend seems to indicate that their number will increase rapidly during the 1980s and may reach between one-third and one-half of the European marketplace towards the end of the decade.

The 'inner-directed' consumer will be typified by a number of traits: he will be (a) fiercely individualistic; (b) slightly impulsive; (c) experimental; (d) socially conscious and anti-pollution; (e) aesthetically conscious; (f) a health and physical welfare enthusiast.

If this trend continues and the number of the 'inner-directed' consumers increases to the level anticipated, major opportunitites (and threats) will develop. A significant segment based on behavioural criteria will be emerging, calling for imaginative marketing strategies. No marketer in the consumer goods field can afford to let this development take place without monitoring its far-reaching implications.

Before leaving this subject it is appropriate to refer again to the study carried out by Research Bureau Limited (T. Lunn, S. Baldwin and J. Dickens, 'Monitoring consumer life styles', *Admap,* November 1972). Through a combination of factor analysis and cluster analysis based on a sample of 3500 housewives under the age of 45 eight groups were identified.

(a) *'The young sophisticates'* (15%)   Characterised as extravagant, experimental, non-traditional, young, A, B and C1 social classes, educated, affluent, sociable, cultural interests, owner-occupiers, in full-time employment, interested in new products.

(b) *'Cabbages'* (12%) Conservative, less quality conscious; demographically average, but more full-time housewives. Middle class, average income and education; lowest level of interest in new products. Home-centred; indulging in little entertaining.

(c) *'Traditional working class'* (12%) Traditional, quality conscious, seldom experiments with food, enjoys cooking; middle-aged, D and E social groups, less educated, lower incomes, council house tenants; sociable; husband and wife share activities; betting.

(d) *'Middle-aged sophisticates'* (14%) Experimental, not traditional, less extravagant; middle-aged, A, B and C1 social classes, educated, affluent, full-time housewives, owner-occupiers; interested in new products; sociable, cultural interests.

(e) *'Coronation Street housewives'* (14%) Quality conscious, conservative, traditional and obsessional; D and E social classes, live relatively more in the Lancashire and Yorkshire ITV areas, less educated, lower incomes, part-time employment; low level of interest in new products; not sociable.

(f) *'The self-confident'* (13%) Self-confident, quality conscious, not extravagant; young and well educated, owner-occupiers, average income.

(g) *'The homely'* (10%) Bargain seekers, not self-confident, houseproud; C1 and C2 social classes, Tyne Tees and Scotland ITV areas, left school at an early age, part-time employed; average level of entertaining.

(h) *'The penny pinchers'* (10%) Self-confident, houseproud, traditional, not quality conscious; 25–34 years, C2, D and E social classes, part-time employed, less education, average income, betting, saving, husband and wife share activities, sociable.

The reader may object to some of the descriptions and to the terminology ascribed to the various groups. However, it was a very refreshing attempt at finding a new basis for segmenting markets on a behavioural typology as against the very antiquated social class system that most marketers are still working to. Marketers should be vigilant for other studies of this nature because they may pave the way for exciting and novel bases for segmenting their markets.

THE SELF-IMAGE AND PERSONALITY TRAITS

There is no escaping from the fact that human beings develop perceptions of themselves which lead them to actions designed to protect their self-image. Some people are much more prone to this process than others. Ask a person what car he drives (assuming of course that he has the freedom to choose) and you can diagnose the self-image which that person is trying to protect. If this statement is correct, a car manufacturer should reverse the process and try to identify the various key 'self-image typologies' that exist and design cars for the most promising of them. Obviously one cannot attempt such an exercise without the help of competent and knowledgeable behavioural scientists.

The situation is complicated by the fact that a person's self-image is to a great extent the result of his interpretation of how those he has been associating with regard him. This interpretation may in fact be erroneous. It often happens that a person's reading of other people's perception of him does not match the reality. In such circumstances that person is trying to protect his self-image, believing that by doing so he is matching the behavioural expectations that others have ascribed to him. He behaves, dresses, shops and buys products that in his opinion match the illusory image that his own self-perception has imposed upon him. If he believes that others regard him as a bohemian he will develop a behavioural pattern commensurate with a bohemian way of life. If he feels that others consider him as a tycoon he will adopt a life-style that matches his own idea of how a tycoon behaves: he will buy a Rolls Royce, eat in expensive restaurants, shop at Harrods, indulge in exotic holidays and acquire an opulent wardrobe. From time to time he may encounter some self-doubts as to whether he is meeting all the criteria of being a tycoon. At this point he may derive some encouragement and reassurance from well designed advertisements in the appropriate media targeting on people of his own ilk.

The self-image concept is an important factor that affects a person's behaviour in many areas and not only in relation to marketing activities. It normally influences his interpersonal relationships in many directions. It affects the way he reacts to his family, friends and colleagues. In connection with the latter it often creates interpersonal organisational problems which in turn have some impact on the smooth functioning of the organisation. This is a notion well understood by those responsible for managing the organisation development activities of a firm. They often resort to the behavioural sciences for help in the form of setting up so-called 'T-groups' or 'sensitivity training' sessions. On the other hand, inadequate attention has been devoted to the subject among marketers. Somehow marketers shy away from a concept that entails an overt appeal to emotions that one normally prefers not to articulate openly. Obviously one does not go shouting from the rooftops that one is seeking to satisfy the needs of the self-image-building personality freaks. The process can be designed to achieve the same objective in a subtle, indirect and creative way. The fact remains that a marketing opportunity exists in relation to such a segment, especially where the product conveys image-boosting characteristics. Flying by 'Concorde' may be a useful self-image prop for many customers: why not trade on such a marketing opportunity?

ATTITUDES AND BEHAVIOUR

Attitudes have a very important role to play in the field of marketing, and especially in relation to the communication mix. In general people are more likely to respond to any kind of communication (advertising, sales promotion, publicity or personal selling) if their own attitudes are congruent with the message transmitted. In other words, a message is more likely to be effective if it tells people what they want to hear – or is consistent with their past beliefs. Attitudes can vary between latent ones that can be awakened to those that are live and ready for immediate response.

Attitudes represent a very complex part of an individual's behavioural pattern and deserve an in-depth study of the whole subject. For the purpose of this brief summary it suffices to list a number of important elements:

(a) *Attitudes are fairly enduring in nature* As most readers will know, one of the most difficult areas in our society is the change of attitudes. As governments have found out, it is easier to talk about the need to change attitudes than to achieve results.

The level of change in attitudes that a person is likely to undergo will differ from individual to individual. Some people are more set in their attitudes than others. Thus more extreme attitudes are more likely to resist change. An isolated attitude, as against one which forms part of a consistent set of a value system, is probably easier to change.

(b) *People tend to be influenced by the opinions of 'reference groups'* A 'reference group' represents the kind of group that an individual aspires to belong to. A person need not be a member of the reference group. He simply respects its values and aspires to be counted among its silent supporters. Furthermore, a person may be influenced by a number of reference groups in relation to different activities and products. He may follow the attitudes of one group in respect of food products yet follow a totally different reference group when it comes to buying a car.

(c) *Social class, demography, geography, race and religion all have an impact on people's cluster of attitudes.* In this connection it is important to emphasise that the stronger the bond between a person and his class or affiliation group the more likely he is to stay within the attitudinal boundaries of the class he belongs to.

(d) *In general the older the person the more conservative are his attitudes* However, succeeding generations are better educated and more travelled. In consequence today's young person is likely to be less conservative when he is sixty than were his parents at the same age, but less tolerant than when he was young himself.

People's attitudes represent a significant factor upon which buying behaviour is based. Considerable work has been invested in this area and the literature on the subject is valuable. Nevertheless, very few companies have made full use of this valuable knowledge. What is to stop an insurance company researching the market with the view of defining the typology of the 'perfect customer' for their life policies. The 'perfect customer' meaning in this area the person who displays the kind of attitudes which are totally congruent with the need to buy a substantial life cover! Among the appropriate attitudes one would probably find the following: positive attitude towards security and protecting one's family; positive attitude towards saving; positive attitude towards 'nest-egg' building; some conservatism; etc. Once these attitudes have been identified and tabulated the task of designing an 'identikit' of the perfect customer can commence. What an aid to selling productivity such a tool could be for an imaginative organisation! Instead of calling on every consumer irrespective of his personality and inventory of attitudes, the salesmen of that company would concentrate their selling effort on individuals who better match the characteristics of a well researched and well designed typology.

COGNITIVE DISSONANCE

The theory of 'cognitive dissonance' first emerged in the fascinating work of Leon Festinger as far back as 1957 *(A theory of cognitive dissonance,* Stanford: Stanford University Press). The term translated into simple layman's language means 'after-purchase doubt'. Cognitive dissonance occurs when an individual develops dissonance, a state of disharmony, tension and frustration following the purchase of a product. According to Festinger the level of the post-purchase dissonance occurs in a direct ratio to the importance and/or cost of the decision and also of the relative attractiveness of the rejected alternatives.

Thus the buyer of a motor car may develop a post-purchase anxiety because (a) the level of expenditure was high; (b) the qualities of the rejected alternatives came to his notice (either through advertisements or through comments made by some good friends); and/or (c) the product itself started to manifest some faults. The buyer is unhappy with his purchase and unless his post-purchase doubt is alleviated may become an awkward customer, demanding constant attention from the vendor under the after sales service agreement. Moreover, if the cognitive dissonance continues to persist the buyer will make up his mind never to buy such a product again. This in turn may destroy any hope of continuing loyalty towards the selling firm and its products.

Cognitive dissonance, as stated earlier, is more likely to occur when the product is relatively expensive. It is likely to be quite intense when one purchases a house or a motor car. Insurance companies suffer from this problem. Purchasers of life policies often terminate the contract as a result of having developed a dissonance. The booking of expensive holidays may cause some anxiety. On the industrial front managers that have committed their firms to an expensive computer installation may easily manifest after-purchase tension.

This is not a problem that should be dismissed too lightly as an amusing albeit unimportant conversation piece. Cognitive dissonance is a phenomenon that calls for an imaginative process of alleviation. A vigilant marketer will attempt to build into his advertising programme an element of reassurance and post-purchase communication objective. Unbeknown to the casual citizen, one of the objectives of car advertisements is precisely to attain an alleviation of the doubts that have developed or still linger as a result of a recent purchase. The buyer often derives considerable post-purchase satisfaction as a result of perusing an advertisement that extols the virtues of the very same product that has been giving him some anxiety. This is the moment at which doubts are dispelled and the cognitive dissonance alleviated.

Cognitive dissonance can be reduced by other creative methods. A car manufacturer has instituted a mandatory system for his dealers to phone the customer after two weeks to find out if the customer is satisfied with his new car. The psychology is obvious: the garage is showing personal interest in the buyer as an individual. A friendly relationship is forged between the vendor and buyer and that in itself is a source of reassurance! One of my clients, a house-builder, introduced a simple device for attempting to reassure his customers: shortly after the buyer had moved to his new home the manager of the estate was made to arrive at the buyer's house with a bottle of champagne and a bunch of flowers. What can be a more friendly and reassuring sign of confidence than such a gesture? Many of the customers were so touched by this simple gesture that they only complained about serious and genuine problems instead of submitting vexatious items purely to manifest their own personal frustration at the thought of having made the wrong buying decision.

TRANSACTIONAL ANALYSIS

Every enlightened marketer must familiarise himself with the rules of transactional analysis. The two prominent writers in this field are Eric Berne (of *Games people play* fame) and Thomas A. Harris, the author of the bestseller *I'm OK – you're OK.*

Whilst transactional analysis is the outcome of work carried out in the field of psychotherapy, it soon transpired that people do not have to be 'sick' to benefit from it. It has helped many people to improve their relationships and communication ability with other individuals or groups. To that extent it has practical applicability to managerial and marketing environments.

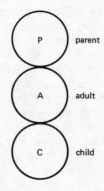

Figure 7.2   The three personality states in transactional analysis.

Briefly, transactional analysis is based on the theory that every person is an amalgam of three personality states: *'parent', 'adult'* and *'child'* (see Fig 7.2). Continual observation has supported the assumption that these three states exist in all of us.

The *'parent'* represents the huge collection of attitudes built into an individual as a result of observing what parents did and said between his birth and the age of five. These are 'recordings' of imposed, unquestioned external inputs. All the admonitions, rules, laws, cuddlings, affections that the child heard and observed from the earliest communications, verbal and non-verbal, have become part of the *parent* 'recordings'.

The *'child'* represents the 'recordings' of internal events and responses of the little person to what he saw and heard once again between birth and five. The child is helpless. There are endless and uncompromising demands upon him. The *child* state is an aggregation of all the feelings and frustrations of the child during that period which he was never able to communicate. It stems from the *situation of childhood* and *not* the intentions of the parents that produced that state. A *child* (as indeed is the case with the *parent* state) is a state into which any person may revert at almost any time in his various transactions.

The *'adult'* state commences development at 10 months. It develops as a result of the child's ability to find out for himself what is different and is the consequence of the emergence of a thought process. It is the accumulation of data gathering and processing, exploration and testing. This inventory of experience is constantly updated.

Thus the average person is like a juke-box which contains three sets of 'recordings' called *parent, child* and *adult.* Each comes into play in a given set of circumstances and affects the communication relationship that the person would have with other individuals.

Normally one can tell which state a person is retrieving from his 'computer' by a number of physical and verbal clues. For example, *parent* clues include furrowed brow, pursed lips, the pointing of the index finger, hands on hips or a statement like 'I am going to stop all this nonsense'.

Child clues include baby talk, 'I wish', 'I want', use of superlatives, the 'mine is better' game.

Adult clues include tilting of the head when listening, use of such words as why, what, when, who and how. Phrases like 'It is my opinion'.

Many other clues have been identified to determine which state of the personality one is dealing with. Any textbook on the subject would provide a whole checklist of the various clues which help to identify each of the three states described.

A number of communication rules apply to the concept of transactional analysis:

(a) *When stimulus and response on the P-A-C (parent, adult, child) diagram make parallel lines the transaction is complementary and can go on indefinitely.* This is described in Figure 7.3.

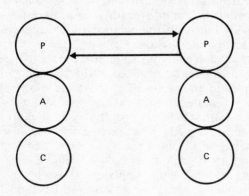

Figure 7.3 *Parent–parent* transaction.

Example:
Stimulus: 'You can never trust one of those people' *(parent).*
Response: *'Exactly!* Their kind are all alike' *(parent).*

(b) *When stimulus and response cross on the P-A-C transactional diagram, communication stops,* as shown in Figure 7.4.

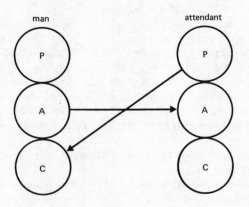

Figure 7.4   Crossed transaction.

Example: Man standing with friend in a petrol station:
Stimulus: 'We were trying to get this gas cap unlocked and dropped the key behind the bumper. Could you help us to get it out? *(adult* to *adult* stimulus).
Response: 'Who did it?' *(parent* to *child* response).

An individual must try to understand the *parent* and *child* elements in himself. This will help him to strengthen his *adult* responses and this in turn will provide him with the competence of communicating more effectively in any given situation.

This is transactional analysis in a minute nutshell. The rest one must glean from the two books mentioned at the beginning of this section.

The principles of transactional analysis are most valuable in the training of salesmen, demonstrators and merchandisers – all of whom have to communicate with lots of people. It is also useful in developing a better communication inside the marketing department with the view of improving management integration. It can also help in training personnel of service organisations such as airlines, banks, restaurants and stores how to deal with complaints. It is obvious that when a complaint is communicated on an *adult* to *adult* level and the response is on a *parent* to *child* level the balloon, not surprisingly, goes up!

The Application of Behavioural Theories to Marketing Decisions

There is hardly a corner in marketing practice which cannot make use of the ideas propounded by the behavioural sciences. In fact each ingredient of the marketing mix can be enriched through the incorporation of ideas stemming from one behavioural theory or another. Let us explore each one of them in turn.

THE PRODUCT

Colour

Research has indicated that the colour of the product has considerable bearing on its ability (a) to please the customer and (b) to gain attention when on display.

Warm colours (yellows and reds) are better attention-getters than the cool colours (blues and greens). On the other hand, where the product needs to convey a clinical and clean image pale cool colours are to be preferred.

Considerable information is available on the subject but the marketer must seek advice and demand evidence of appropriateness in each situation.

In international marketing one must watch the cultural angle pertaining to some colours. Black is a colour of mourning in some countries in the Far East and must be avoided.

Shape

People communicate with certain shapes of products better than with others. Should a bar of soap be rectangular, circular or in the shape of a sphere? Obviously there are ergonomic considerations as well as behavioural ones. Nonetheless, the marketer will find that the majority of his customers will relate better to the traditional rectangular shape. The more artistic and venturesome consumer will be prepared to experiment with less traditional shapes.

Other questions can also be answered by behavioural research.

Should a pack contain six, ten or twelve units of, say, chocolate, carbon ribbons or some other product? Once again there may be some production considerations, but the marketer must remember that the consumer may have his own ideas on the subject.

Is a hatchback car as satisfying to the customer as present-day car manufacturers seem to believe? The marketplace tends to be highly imitative, as the 'adoption process' described earlier implies. Is it possible that we are approaching the 'late majority' and 'laggard' stages for this kind of vehicle? Maybe not, but without reference to the consumer and his range of attitudes and motivational responses we do not know.

The classical story of the 'Mary Baker Mix' taught marketers an interesting lesson. The product was a cake mix designed to be so simple that even congenital idiots were capable of producing delicious cakes by following the very simple instructions. The product failed because the average housewife felt that the simplicity of the product derogated from her personal cake-mixing virtuosity and self-image. It represented almost an insult to her perceived culinary skill. The firm redesigned the product and its instructions. It made them more complicated, added a variety of subtle nuances calling for some decisions regarding extra optional ingredients. The product in its new metamorphosis was a great success.

Many firms ignore the impact of new packaging devices upon the consumer. The consumer knows how to open and close traditional packs. He is less conversant with new packaging ideas, with the result that on many occasions he has to struggle for a long time with unfamiliar devices. Such a struggle can generate dissonance in him and reduce the level of satisfaction in the product itself. This is an important area for imaginative behavioural research as well as the development of an effective communication system in relation to the new packaging. A marketer must never forget that if new methods of packaging are designed to improve the firm's own logistics system they must also be integrated with the customer's needs and level of satisfaction.

A high level of homogeneity is creeping into our clothing industry, especially for ordinary daily wear. Jeans, for instance, are worn by a very large number of people irrespective of their social class. Nonetheless, many consumers manage to preserve their own self-image by acquiring jeans with a more prestigious label and in stores with a high class personality. They pay two or three times more than they need to, but what they buy is a prop for maintaining their own self-image and that in itself is a useful product in certain behavioural states.

PRICE

We have all encountered the so-called psychological pricing of retailers. £9.99 somehow sounds cheaper than £10. We all know it, yet the 1p difference often seems to do the trick.

Recent research into consumers' attitudes to house prices was conducted by my firm. The results were most enlightening: a house buyer seems to enter the marketplace with a positive price tag in mind. Such a price is partly determined by his present and potential means and partly by his perception of the kind of house he ought to have in order to preserve his status, social acceptability and self-image. The margin of deviation which he is prepared to accept from his self-imposed price will range between -10% and +10% and seldom outside this psychological barrier. The interesting point is that if a house is offered to him at above this benchmark he will reject it as too expensive. If the house is below the lower limit he will also reject it. He assumes that something is wrong with the house offered. In either case he will tend not to bother to look at the property!

Many consumers will spend £40 on a dinner for two without batting an eyelid yet flinch at spending half that amount on a book. Obviously they have their own priorities as to how their personal disposable income ought to be spent. It is incumbent upon the marketer to identify the motivational stimuli that make people behave in such a manner.

Many companies are happy to pay a fortune every year for renting photocopying equipment based on a few pence per copy made. If they were to purchase a photocopying unit they would probably attain a payback on the investment within 12–18 months. How does one explain such a behaviour? If one could understand the psychology better, one might be able to emulate this strategy in relation to other spheres of activity.

The most expensive perfume is often the most prestigious and sought-after brand. This is what one calls 'reverse elasticity'. The same manufacturer may find that a reduction in price will entail a drop in sales. The same phenomenon often applies to professional services. It is seldom the cheapest consultancy firm that gets the assignment!

'Derived demand' is an area which causes marketers considerable trouble. For example, the demand for razor blades depends on the firm having managed to sell a quantity of razors. In pricing the two products one has a vast number of permutations available. Does one sell the razors cheaply in order to make them very attractive and then make the margin on the blades? Or does one aim to make the same amount of margin on both? This problem can be looked at purely from an economic point of view but surely the determinant factor is a behavioural one: what kind of combination offers the consumer the highest motivational stimulus to buy? This is not a question that can be answered without some in-depth probing into the customer's behavioural pattern.

One is always intrigued by the fact that most car dealers offer around 10% off the list price. There is hardly a consumer who pays the full price. Why not reduce the price list by 10% and adhere to it? Presumably this practice is so well ingrained in our system that a new attitude has developed among customers who expect to get a reduction at all times. We have in fact developed an attitude which is familiar to buyers and sellers in the Far East and the Middle East. As intimated earlier, attitudes are difficult to change, in which case we have to live with this new system rather than attempt to change back to the rigid price pattern of the past. The only advice to the marketer of motor cars: try to formalise the system in such a way that your price structure and margins build the special discounts into the costings.

PROMOTION

This is a most fertile area for behavioural analysis.

What is the attitude of one's audience to large or small advertisements? It is much too tempting to assume that a large advertisement is by definition a more effective one. What about the position of advertisements in a magazine? Colours versus black and white? Busy copy as against a cryptic message? Media advertising versus direct marketing? These and many other questions carry behavioural undertones of some importance. Obviously competent advertising agencies possess data based on experience and/or research that may throw light on these topics. Nevertheless, one must remember that each situation and each product raises different behavioural relationships and responses.

A few years ago I came across an advertising campaign for an airline which failed to achieve its objectives in terms of image and 'attitude' building. The airline sought to create better 'liking' for its new jets and livery. In-depth projective techniques were used to measure the level of 'liking' after the campaign. Alas the results were disastrous. Considerable heart-searching and research was undertaken in an attempt to identify the offending bits of the campaign. Eventually it transpired that the main culprit was the steep angle at which the aircraft was seen to catapult itself into the sky. It generated insecurity and fear among many of the viewers of that advertisement. They were not able to articulate these fears and probably were not even aware that the advertisement had created such emotions in them. Nonetheless, their response was negative. This is how fickle human behaviour can be. The campaign generated dissonance rather than an effective attitude which it had sought to achieve.

Chapter 9, dealing with sales aids, records a number of examples based on how firms have responded to a sound understanding of consumer and customer behaviour.

It is worth remembering that effective communication depends on the ability to transmit messages that are understood and remembered by the customer. Moreover, it is useful to recall that some methods are more efficient than others. Research into learning and retaining processes has shown that there is a great disparity in the effectiveness of our various senses:

We learn	We retain
1% through taste	1% of what we hear
1½% through touch	2% of what we read
3½% through smell	30% of what we see
11% through hearing	50% of what we see and hear
83% through sight	

The marketer who wishes to improve his communication strategies must remember these figures. They point strongly towards the need to attempt communication methods which encompass 'seeing and hearing'. The level of improvement in effectiveness is pretty eloquent.

It is also worth remembering that consumers, like all humans, prefer to see an optimistic and cheerful face: like the old story about the pessimist and the optimist who compare notes in relation to a glass of wine on the table. The former says that the glass is half empty; the latter says that the glass is half full. The message is the same yet the second one is more acceptable to the listener. A friend of mine was recently told by his doctor that 5% of all those who undergo a certain operation die. He was most upset until I rephrased the message by telling him that 95% survive! Somehow he was much happier with the new message.

Marketers must remember that people respond much better to the cheerful portion of the story. Rather than say in the instructions that the product fails in 1% of the cases it is better to say that the success ratio is 99%.

SELLING

This too is an important area for a better understanding of human behaviour. After all a salesman deals with people and the more he knows about the way they behave the easier he will find selling to them.

Just a few useful ideas. How many salesmen realise that the greatest barrier to communication is the desk that lies between them and the customer? The desk is a territory which belongs to the customer. It gives him a positional advantage vis-à-vis the salesman who sits on the wrong side of the desk. A creative salesman would try to find a way of taking the customer away from his advantageous position or find a way of positioning himself on the same side of the barrier. Obviously this has to be done in a subtle and tactful way. A sales aid that assists him in this direction is a true sales-aid.

The principles of transactional analysis can be of great help in improving the communication skills of a salesman. They can alert him to the kind of messages that create an obstacle to effective communication and the type of response that alleviates tension. I am always amazed at how badly aircraft crew normally handle potential conflicts. If their training had encompassed a basic understanding of human communication under pressure they might have coped with such situations in a more effective way. Or maybe they forget that they represent an integral part of the marketing mix.

Another important element in a more effective selling process is a better understanding of body language and bodily communication. People transmit a vast number of messages without uttering a word. Indeed some of these non-verbal communication messages can convey emotions, attitudes and personality traits. One transmits messages through facial expression, gaze, gestures and bodily movements, posture, body contact, general appearance and spatial behaviour. Many of these signals correspond to a fairly well established 'language' in a given society. The rules of the language change from culture to culture and therefore one needs to learn a new body 'language' when one operates in new environments. The Englishman transmits a totally different sign when he is furious with a driver on the road than the Italian.

Understanding body language is particularly important when dealing with customers who visit one's own marketplace; for example receptionists in opticians' practices can learn a lot about patients through observing body signals, as can bank officials and salesmen of their clients. It is a fascinating subject and readers who wish to learn more about it are advised to read Michael Argyle's book *Bodily communication* (London: Methuen, 1978) – a most valuable contribution to understanding human behaviour through non-verbal communication.

DISTRIBUTION

Last but not least is the impact of human behaviour on distribution policies. Many creative strategies were based on a thorough appreciation of what motivates customers.

Avon Cosmetics and Tupperware built thriving businesses on the notion that many housewives would enjoy the combined process of making money and having a social activity at home. To the two companies the idea offered a most successful and cost-effective distribution system.

The Wine Society has established a successful wine distribution system based on a club-style membership. Only members can order and obtain wine from the organisation. In order to become a member one must buy a share at a fairly nominal amount. Nonetheless, a fairly exclusive aura has been established around this membership. I do not know whether this strategy was developed on the basis of some behavioural input or not. Nonetheless, it is an idea which carries useful motivational connotations and the creative marketer may find other areas in which a similar approach can be profitably emulated.

Some insurance brokers have branches in airports in order to sell policies to travellers. What a superb marketplace for insurance products. Air travel still generates some trepidation in many passengers. By taking a heavy insurance cover the traveller's subconscious gains some reassurance. 'After all insurance companies seldom lose money', rationalises the passenger in the depth of his complex brain, 'and therefore I shall reach my destination safely'.

In Conclusion

Understanding human behaviour is not a luxury. It is an essential part of a marketer's armoury. The main aim of this chapter has been to alert the reader to the great variety of knowledge that is available in this area. The literature is vast and the topics covered, on the whole, fascinating. Through a judicious assembly of data, based on observation, experience and reading, the marketer will find that his future strategies will be greatly enriched in one of the most important aspects of marketing practice.

PART III

Tools of Marketing – A Creative Approach

8
Market Share: Deception or Diagnosis

It is widely suggested by marketing-orientated companies that one of the main criteria of business success is the market share that a firm is able to achieve and maintain. The assumption is made that the attainment of a high market share indicates an effective marketing effort. By the same token, a poor market share suggests that the enterprise has performed badly. If this is true, one cannot escape from the simple axiom that in order to be successful a firm needs to direct its full attention to the maximisation of market share.

In a very interesting article in the *Harvard Business Review* (January–February 1975) – 'Market share – a key to profitability', a group of American academics reported on an on-going project involving fifty-seven companies sponsored by the Marketing Science Institute and the Harvard Business School. The main purpose of the project was to determine the profit impact of market strategies. In the article the authors come up with a positive correlation between market share and return on investment (ROI). The authors go on to discuss why a high market share is profitable, listing economies of scale, market power and quality of management as possible contributors to such results. They specifically suggest that as market share increases, a business is likely to have a higher profit margin, a declining purchases-to-sales ratio, a

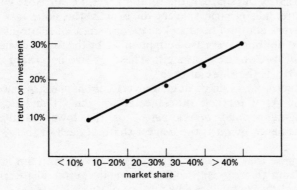

Figure 8.1   Market share and pre-tax return on investment.

decline in marketing costs as a percentage of sales, higher quality, and higher priced products (see Fig. 8.1).

The findings of the team are obviously dramatic and cannot be ignored. Nonetheless, to the more practical marketer they present major problems. Are the companies in the sample successful because they have attained a high market share or do they have a high market share because they are successful? Moreover, the implications of the conclusions are quite alarming for small and medium-sized firms – are they all doomed to a poorer performance simply because they are unable to muster an important share of their respective markets? Finally, when we talk about 'market share' we inevitably assume that we always know what market we are in. This latter point presents the biggest pitfall of the market share concept.

Share of Which Market?

On the face of it market share is an uncomplicated concept. I manufacture electric shavers; the annual market for new electric shavers is around one million units a year; I sell 100 000 units a year and therefore my market share is 10%. I can now also investigate my performance during the last five years and monitor changes in my share of the market during that period. I can attempt to plan the future after analysing my strengths, weaknesses and general resources and specify new objectives including a market share objective for the future. This may be more than 10% or less than 10%, depending on my assessment of my capabilities and the potential market environment. All this is fine and logical, but, it might be asked:

(a)　What is the share in terms of money?

(b)　What is the share of shavers for men and shavers for women?

(c)　What is the share of the total market, i.e. all those who shave? After all, electric shavers do exactly the same task as other razors and you need to know your share of the total business.

(d)　No doubt shavers are bought either by the future owner himself for his own use or as a gift. These are two important segments. What is the share of each?

(e)　Shavers are sold through a myriad of channels. A few cater for the A, B market; others cater for the C1 and possibly C2 segments, and others cater for the lower socio-economic segments. What is the market share of each of these?

I recognise that these are fairly valid questions but I am thoroughly confused and am very tempted to abandon the market share criterion. If it is so multifaceted it looks like a tool of doubtful value.

Let us now explore two other examples to illustrate the danger of selecting a market share criterion without sufficient thought about which market is the most relevant for the purpose of gauging company performance. Whilst the facts and figures are hypothetical they are both based on real-life studies.

CASE 1: STANTON PHARMACEUTICALS

Stanton manufactures an ethical drug which alleviates the discomforts of asthma. Its performance has been good in terms of profit and return on investment. However, the firm's marketing personnel fear that aggressive competition may place pressure on the performance of their product. In an attempt to lay down criteria of performance for the future they undertook a thorough study of the drug's share of the market in terms of a variety of parameters. The following results emerged:

(a) The market for anti-asthma drugs is around £5 million (in terms of retail prices). Stanton's share of this market is £1 million, i.e. 20%.

(b) Recognising that the main decision maker in the field of drugs is the doctor who prescribes specific preparations, they measured the firm's share of the total number of prescriptions issued for anti-asthma drugs. Here Stanton's share appeared to be much higher at 30%. In other words, whilst Stanton's share of the 'prescriptions market' is 30%, its share of the 'turnover market' was only 20%.

(c) A further complication was that the number of doctors who actually prescribed Stanton's brand represented only 18% of the total number of doctors in the market.

(d) At the specific request of the marketing director some research was conducted to measure how many people suffered from asthma and how many of them had been treated by Stanton's brand. Here the results indicated that 40% of those suffering from asthma were being treated with Stanton's product.

This brief case illustrates how misleading the market share analysis can be. Four ways of measuring the firm's market share in a specific and

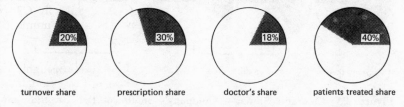

| turnover share | prescription share | doctor's share | patients treated share |

Figure 8.2 Stanton Chemical's shares of the market for anti-asthma drugs.

well defined market yielded seemingly contradictory and confusing results. The findings are summarised in Figure 8.2, which sets out the various market shares.

Each one of the pie-charts shown is valid, but the second chart shows a market share of 30% and represents good news in accordance with the Harvard Business School project, whilst the third chart is bad news by the same reckoning. Yet both charts represent the identical company, the identical product and the identical market.

CASE 2:   ELDORADO SHIPPING COMPANY

This case is a highly simplified version of a fairly typical situation in service organisations such as transport, banking and insurance. It is very easy to measure market share in relation to the most misleading parameter. Eldorado operates a regular shipping service between the UK and Eldorado (a fictitious island in the Pacific). The firm is quite successful in terms of profit, growth, return on investment and, as the management optimistically believes, in terms of market share. Whilst the company's capacity represents 60% of the tonnage of that route, its market share in terms of tons carried is respectively 67% of the tonnage carried from Eldorado to the UK, and 59% of the tonnage carried from the UK to Eldorado. The management considers such a performance fairly satisfactory, although some pressure is being placed on the sales force to increase the market share of the UK outward cargo to represent at least 60%.

Now comes the crunch: an in-depth analysis of the firm's market share in terms of revenue indicates that it is only 48% of the inward business and 46% of the outward route. Once again, a number of pie-charts (Fig. 8.3) helps to illustrate these significant disparities.

Was the management unwise in selecting tonnage as the parameter of market measurement, or should you always seek to measure market performance in a number of different ways?

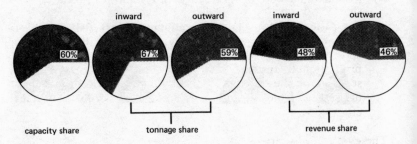

Figure 8.3 Eldorado Shipping Company's shares of the UK–Eldorado freight market.

Market Share as a Diagnostic Tool

These two cases seek to illustrate how dangerous it is to base objectives on the nebulous criterion known as market share. In spite of this, market share has a very important role to play in the management of a firm's marketing activities. Its real value is seldom recognised or used. The market share approach to measuring levels of performance represents one of the most potent diagnostic tools available to a good marketer. If used correctly it can alert the imaginative manager to areas of weakness in marketing strategy of a specific product or service. The best way to illustrate the principle is to cast our minds back to the cases we have already discussed.

We saw how Stanton Pharmaceuticals could identify different market shares in relation to different markets. On the face of the facts the conclusion that one comes to is that the market share findings are of doubtful value, but let us look at the diagnostic implications of the four market shares identified.

(a) The fact that the 'turnover share' is only 20% and the 'patients share' is 40% suggests that Stanton's product is either under-priced, or much more effective in use than competitors' products, or both. The facts can be verified, but the basic conclusion is that something is wrong with the firm's pricing policy. This is undoubtedly an important area for diagnostic investigations.

(b) The disparity between the 'prescriptions share' and the 'doctors share' is of course puzzling and needs further examination. Nonetheless, it seems to suggest that the firm has managed to 'convert' too few doctors to its preparation, but managed to turn these few into very 'heavy users' of Stanton's product. This indicates a patchy penetration of the general practitioner market. If this is correct, the market share analyses have yielded a most useful pay-off in so far as the firm is diagnosing an important weakness in its overall penetration strategy.

(c) The enormous difference between the 'those treated' market share and the 'doctors' share points to another significant conclusion, namely that a large number of asthma sufferers are treated by a relatively small number of doctors. If this conclusion is correct it would suggest that the company must reconsider its promotional strategies and re-orientate them to a smaller segment of the 'doctors' market. Obviously this will help to utilise available promotional and selling resources more effectively.

These reflections are examples of the kinds of readings that a multidimensional market share analysis can yield. They are much more useful than a single market share study. And in the case of the Eldorado

Shipping Company once again we saw the dramatic difference in market share between the 'tonnage' market and 'revenue' market. An analytic approach reveals vital clues about this firm. Having concentrated its marketing effort on the acquisition of tonnage, the firm has lost sight of the fact that some types of shipping tonnage are less valuable in terms of revenue per unit of capacity than others. In other words, Eldorado got landed with the cheaper freight, whereas its competitors were content to carry a smaller tonnage of the more revenue-orientated cargoes. This is a very useful insight: Eldorado must now increase its revenue share of the market. All cargoes must be segmented in terms of the revenue to space ratio. Such analysis can form the basis of promotional and selling concentration. In other words, salesmen can be redirected towards the attainment of sales to specific types of customers with the right cargoes. They can be alerted to what represents an attractive cargo and what does not.

The examples given above were very simple. More complicated studies can be undertaken by the creative diagnostician. He can ring the changes in a variety of ways; he can measure market shares in accordance with a large number of unusual, albeit logical, parameters and manipulate the results to identify relevant strengths and/or weaknesses in marketing variables. In some cases marketing results could be improved whilst ostensibly reducing market share.

Market-orientated Share

We saw how markets can be defined in many ways and how the measurement of market share in relation to each market thus defined can yield different results. Unfortunately it is not always easy to measure a firm's market share in relation to a given parameter. The information required to undertake such a study is either not available or is too costly to obtain. Obviously it is necessary to be selective in the kind of market share exploration attempted, and there is absolutely no point in spending a lot of time and money measuring the firm's market share in relation to a market which is simply not measurable.

There are also instances where all the variables measured indicate a constant market share. This is particularly true of oligopolistic industries, such as cement, where a small number of manufacturers dominate the market and where price leadership is strongly adhered to. In such cases one normally finds that the market share in terms of tons, turnover or bags will be more or less the same. Yet with some imagination one can find useful disparities in relation to specific segments of the market served. Whilst the market share of the total market may be constant, variations may exist in relation to specific segments. This, of course, is extremely valuable to the marketing strategist.

Markets must always be identified in a marketing-orientated way. We must recognise that we are moving towards an era when the cost–benefit to the customer or the consumer is the criterion that will matter. Thus a carpet manufacturer whose carpets last longer than his competitors' products and has only 10% of the carpet market could specify his market share in terms of 'year-square feet of floor covering' and this is likely to be more than 10%. After all this is what people buy carpets for and this is how consumer satisfaction is gauged. Moreover, this is how the *Which?*—type analysts evaluate the product. By simply saying that the market share is 10% of the total yardage sold one is being highly production-orientated. Surely it is wrong to assume that the firm that sells 50% of the yardage produced in the country is automatically a successful company. This is what the Harvard study seems to imply.

Referring once again to the Stanton Pharmaceuticals case mentioned earlier, we can now ascribe some marketing relevance to the various market shares listed. The 'turnover' share is, of course, production-orientated. The 'doctors' share is slightly more marketing-orientated, but does not relate directly to the real market, namely to those who suffer from asthma. The 'prescriptions' share is useful but once again is not truly consumer-orientated. Let us imagine that as a result of over-prescription the average patient gets 100 tablets, uses 70 and throws the other 30 away. This may be good for business, but to the firm that believes wholeheartedly in the marketing concept such an arrangement is anathema. To the marketing perfectionist the starting point for measuring market share in such circumstances is the identification of how many people suffer from asthma and how many of this well defined segment derive solace and health from his product, and, in the most cost-beneficial way to them and to society. This sounds idealistic, but the firm that follows this simple path wins in the end.

9
Back to First Principles on Sales Aids

Sales aids are a bonanza – but more often for the designers and printers who produce them than for the companies that buy them. Vast quantities are produced every year and their total cost represents a substantial annual budget. Catalogues, brochures, leaflets, general handouts, product specifications, testimonials, article reprints and gifts are produced every year in vast quantities and given to salesmen as part of their communication armoury. Some of these handouts are very well designed and produced in very expensive formats.

Every time one goes to a car dealer, for example, one picks up a number of brochures describing the range offered by that dealer. Again, medical representatives calling on doctors leave behind a myriad of leaflets and samples. They are all classified as sales aids and they certainly cost a lot of money, but how many of them really aid sales? Surely the material that is dumped in the doctors' waste bins can hardly be described as sales aids.

Many examples can be given of similar material which is classified as a sales aid but which in reality fails miserably in fulfilling the aiding task. It is sufficient to look at the literature some insurance companies and banks distribute to realise how little thought has gone into developing effective aids to selling. On the contrary, some of these so-called aids demonstrate an amazing lack of sensitivity on the part of their compilers towards the layman reader who is simply unable to comprehend the intricacies of the tax system and the fiscal implications described in the printed material. It would be an interesting project to try to identify how many contracts have been lost as a result of non-decodable sales aids rather than seeking to measure the level of success.

Unfortunately sellers often approach the potential buyer with the notion that the latter is well informed about the company's offering. In such situations it is inevitable that communication suffers and unless the sales aid used rectifies this gap in knowledge and understanding in a simple, logical and well planned step-by-step approach the aid may prove more of a hindrance than a help to effective selling.

Let us consider the simple example of a person who walks into a shop distributing hi-fi equipment. He knows very little about hi-fi, but the first thing the salesman does is to produce an avalanche of sales aids from various drawers. They are all complicated specifications, full of the jargon and the mumbo-jumbo that characterises the hi-fi industry. The salesman adds to the customer's confusion with talk of the wow and flutter qualities of the various systems. He refers to woofers and tweeters, dBs, colouration and impedance. The customer is alarmed and his initial interest soon wanes.

Surely a sound sales aid strategy would help the salesman to adapt his sales pattern to the needs of each individual case. The salesman could be taught to identify the knowledge level of the prospect. And having done so he should be able to pull out a sales aid in the shape of a diagram, a booklet or a demonstration model designed to match the level of knowledge, interest and expectations of the potential buyer. A tool that assists effective communication is what constitutes a good sales aid.

Confusion With Other Material

Some confusion exists between the term sales aid and other types of promotion material and handouts. The average marketer tends to ascribe the same meaning to both. He normally considers any item left with a client as a sales aid. It is true that both seek to facilitate the selling process, thus helping the firm to meet its marketing objectives. Nonetheless, in qualitative terms there is a fundamental difference between the two. Sales aids, as the term implies, must be designed to facilitate the face-to-face selling transaction; promotional aids are much more peripheral to the actual selling process.

Sales aids are designed for use in the selling interview itself and are intended to overcome carefully identified obstacles to a successful sale. The latter are meant to communicate the product's merits, or the firm's standing, or some other communication objective that will ultimately help to sell. Promotional tools seek to encompass in a single package all the information the marketer wishes to place in the hands of the potential buyer. Such a package may be perused at a leisurely pace either before or after the face-to-face selling activity. Sometimes it even replaces the personal selling relationship, when it is sent by mail, for example.

The difference may seem subtle, but in practical terms it is a very important one inasmuch as different inputs are required for the design of sales aids than for the preparation of other promotional tools. In order to design effective sales aids it is necessary to understand in detail what happens when a salesman meets a buyer. When designing promotional aids the need is to know the communication objectives of the firm. A good sales aid seeks to help the salesman to clinch a deal by overcoming well defined obstacles to a sale. A good promotional device aims to inform, to advise, to stimulate a positive attitude to the seller's products. It seldom goes beyond attempting to achieve a series of general communication objectives which ultimately will facilitate a sale. Effective sales aids can be measured in terms of sales achieved. Good promotional aids can be measured only in terms of the communication objectives they have attained.

A number of short case studies are described below to show what constitutes an effectively designed aid.

CASE 1: AN INTERNATIONAL AIRLINE

A well known international airline has recognised that airfreight, on the whole, is more expensive than surface freight. Nonetheless, as every transport manager knows, there are many instances where it is advantageous to send goods by air. The speed of delivery often outweighs the cost. Moreover, there are situations in which the total cost of the logistics process by air is cheaper than the total cost by sea, in spite of the fact that the sea module *per se* is considerably cheaper than the air module. It is the total logistics cost that needs to be compared.

The total logistics process includes a myriad of items, such as packing, insurance, documentation, transport to the point of departure (seaports, or airports), loading, unloading and trans-shipping, customs duty and storage. Obviously the cost of each one of these items may be higher or lower when air transport is involved than in other methods of transportation. What must be considered is the total cost.

The situation is more complicated inasmuch as one must consider also the comparative indirect cost of sending goods by air and by sea. The fact that airfreight is faster helps to reduce the re-ordering lead time, and this in turn reduces the inventory carried in the firm's warehouse, thus saving money on inventory carrying costs. In other words, airfreight may have some attraction for cash flow management.

The airline realised that carrying out the comparative computation of the total cost of sending goods by air and by sea is often very intricate and therefore many customers do not undertake such an important study. It therefore decided to set up in its central computer a data bank of the comparative total costs of sending each commodity and product in relation to each country of market, both exported and imported. A most imaginative booklet was designed to explain how the computer model worked and the kind of information that was needed by the company's computer personnel to make it possible to compare the total costs of sending the merchandise by air with other means of transportation.

This service, which was free of charge, can be called an aid to selling. The salesman could use it as a door opener when calling on clients. Moreover, where the computer was able to demonstrate an unequivocal cost advantage in favour of air transport the availability of the computer printout was probably decisive.

CASE 2: FROZEN FOODS

A manufacturer of frozen foods carried out a study of a number of supermarkets to establish the product mix which a successful unit should carry in order to optimise its profits in relation to the space available. The study sought to highlight both the average return per linear foot that each product could earn, and the sales elasticity in relation to the space allotted to each product.

The study showed that frozen foods were among the most profitable items that a supermarket carried when measured in terms of space utilisation. At the same time they were the most responsive to an increase in the space allocated to them. In other words, the evidence showed that the more space a supermarket allotted to frozen foods the better. What could be more helpful to salesmen?

The investigations highlighted other valuable ideas which every supermarket manager would find very useful. A very attractive brochure summarising the results of the study was prepared. The brochure contained a large amount of valuable information, supported by diagrams, about the dimensions that a successful supermarket should endeavour to develop. Whilst frozen foods were shown as the most attractive product range for a supermarket operation, the brochure did not mention the company's own products in any way. Professionalism was maintained throughout.

This brochure could be described as a sales aid. It offered clients a professional input to the way they ought to run their business. It gave them a useful insight into the industry's competitive environment. At the same time it helped the salesman to improve his communication with his customers. It provided him with a tangible tool that enabled him to discuss the real value of his products to the overall profitability of the customer. It placed him in a unique position vis-à-vis his competitors. He was elevated from the position of a salesman–merchandiser to the more prestigious role of adviser–consultant.

CASE 3: A ROAD HAULAGE CONTRACTOR

Effective aids to selling can be met in industries which are not, on the whole, renowned for their virtuosity in the area of creative promotion or sales aids development. A large firm in the road transport and physical distribution business was disturbed by the fact that price constituted the major factor in the way buyers placed their business. In an attempt to escape from this price sensitivity the firm explored many ideas for enriching the product with a number of unique features that would raise its overall attractiveness to the point where price would cease to be the main ingredient of selection.

On the various ingredients explored it was felt that the best one was the setting up of a free packing advisory service. If it were possible to help clients to increase the load per truck through more efficient packing it could certainly represent an exciting and unique selling proposition. A 10% extra load per truck means a cheaper rate for the cargo and this is what matters.

A packing advisory service was set up, but unfortunately most customers were extremely sceptical about its value. They regarded it as a gimmick. The company therefore designed an ingenious selling aid. It took the form of a miniature toy truck bearing the name of the firm together with the address and phone number of the packaging advisory service. Inside the truck were packed a dozen or so wooden blocks. At the appropriate moment the salesman opened the truck, emptied its contents on the buyer's desk and invited him to fit them back into the truck. Invariably, the buyer found that without the necessary specialist knowledge he was left with two or three blocks outside the truck. The salesman was then able to demonstrate the correct method. This helped to clinch many sales.

Developing Effective Sales Aids

Creative and effective sales aids must be based on research that tries to identify the behavioural and interpersonal relationships that take place in the face-to-face selling environment. Figure 9.1 summarises the various steps that must be taken.

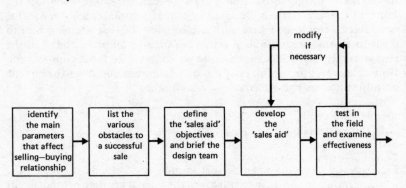

Figure 9.1 Creating a new sales aid by objectives.

IDENTIFICATION OF THE MAIN PARAMETERS

A study of the various elements of the customer's environment must be made and systematic research, observation and general discussion must be used to develop a full understanding of the stimuli which motivate the customer to behave in a certain manner. In the case of consumer goods, a generalised perception of how the majority behave is needed. In the case of industrial goods, the need is to acquire more specific knowledge about the major types of customers and their respective behavioural patterns. And in the industrial situation it is also necessary to understand the relationship and roles of the different members of the decision-making unit, such as the buyer, the decider, the influencer, and the user. Similarly, the perceived cost–benefit value to the average customer must be identified and evaluated, plus the rate and speed at which a new product is likely to be adopted by the various segments of the adoption process. Again, brand and functional competitors must be considered and their relative unique selling points explored, and the sensitivity to pricing policies has to be measured. In brief, the marketer who wishes to design good sales aids must know as much as possible about his marketplace.

LISTING THE OBSTACLES TO A SALE

The essence of all research and investigations is to determine with some precision the various obstacles the salesman is likely to encounter when trying to effect a sale. Such obstacles may be of a rational or of an emotional nature. They may be based on a true appreciation of the facts or on a long-standing prejudice against the seller's product or the company's image. The obstacles may stem from an inadequate understanding of the benefits that the product may bestow upon the buyer or the user. They sometimes originate from the fact that the buyer is unable to comprehend the technicalities of the product and does not wish to demonstrate his lack of knowledge or technical experience. Again, a sale is often lost for the simple reason that the buyers or other decision makers are very busy people and any presentation that imposes an additional mental load on them is not welcome. This is the kind of obstacle most medical representatives encounter when addressing members of the very busy medical profession.

In this connection it always pays to discuss the matter with members of the sales force. After all, they are the ones who have an intimate knowledge of what happens during the face-to-face selling relationship. They are the ones who have to cope with the various obstacles that the potential buyers project, either openly or through non-verbal communication and behaviour. Any marketer who ignores this valuable input is likely to miss a very important dimension to the sales aid.

DEFINING THE OBJECTIVES

Once the selling situation is fully understood, and the real obstacles to a successful consummation of a sale are identified, the objectives of the sales aid programme can be defined. It must be defined in terms which are capable of being understood by those who will have to undertake the physical design of the appropriate aids. The brief must include details of the product and the background to the selling environment. It must list the obstacles likely to occur, if possible in the sequence in which they are likely to arise. Ideally the brief should be described in a flow diagram-type model which normally helps to communicate the situation in a logical manner. In other words the recipient of all this information should be aware of the various steps likely to occur when a salesman faces a typical customer of a well defined segment.

Thus, for instance, a person applying for a life assurance policy behaves differently from a person who is being approached as a cold contact. The mere fact that he has applied means that a large number of potential obstacles have already been overcome and the salesman can safely move to a different level of communication. An experienced salesman will, of course, appreciate this point. The less experienced salesman may fall into the trap of discussing obvious details which the applicant may well appreciate, such as tax advantages or the savings aspects. A good sales aid in this connection will help the salesman to avoid such obvious pitfalls by simply directing him to the most appropriate communication path. He will move to the heart of the matter.

DESIGNING THE SALES AID PACKAGE

The design calls for a very skilful interpretation of the data submitted into a package which truly reflects the realities of the selling environment. This means that the designers must allow themselves to be deeply involved with the sales team with the view to producing an aid to selling which is accepted by the sales force as a real aid. Working closely with the sales manager and members of the sales force can help to ensure that they feel committed to the whole programme. It is normally a good idea for the designer or members of his team to spend some time travelling with a number of salesmen in order to see for himself what actually happens in a selling-buying relationship.

TESTING THE SALES AID

A sales aid must be tested in the field before one can reach the final conclusion that it is an effective one. If all the steps described earlier have been followed conscientiously, the likelihood is that the resultant aid will function well. Yet unexpected problems may arise. Thus in one instance the sales aid proved to be extremely useful, but the buyer felt that he was being manipulated into giving answers to a rigid programme of questions and resented the process. The aid was redesigned to give a less efficient flavour and this new obstacle was thus eliminated.

In another case the aid was based on the use of a computer program seeking to help the client to maximise his profit out of a mixture of raw materials available in his warehouse. The calculations were based on a simple linear programming model and the resultant printout was extremely valuable to most customers. The aid misfired a bit inasmuch as some customers were reluctant to provide the appropriate details out of fear that their competitors would find out all about their activities through the supplier's indiscretion. This obstacle was overcome by a judicious use of portable terminals where it was possible to hand over to the customer on the spot the printout that the terminal produced. The feedback from the marketplace was thus acted upon swiftly and with considerable creativity.

10
Improving the Productivity of the Sales Force

The need to improve a firm's productivity is a well recognised challenge for the 1980s. It is becoming evident that in order to maintain an acceptable profit and return on investment in the current economic climate it is essential to refocus one's attention on and productivity of each cost component of the enterprise. Some managers assume that the words 'increased productivity' imply a mandatory reduction in costs with a resultant diminution in the workforce. This need not be true: productivity can be increased in some circumstances without firing a single person. Increased productivity means a greater level of 'output' from each unit of cost in the enterprise, whether it is labour, machine or money. If the firm has been accustomed to generating a level of return of x per unit (in terms of say turnover and/or profits), an increase to $x+20\%$ per unit means an improved productivity. The organisation may in some cases manage to achieve such an improved performance without closing factories and without shedding people. This would occur where the company manages to sell more with the existing infrastructure. Obviously increased sales with the same level of costs mean improved productivity.

It is true that we live in a period of considerable economic stagnation and many companies appear to be facing declining markets. Nonetheless, one does encounter 'winners' in terms of enhanced productivity even in these difficult marketing conditions. Some of these winners have achieved their goals without reducing the level of employment. In some cases they had probably started with a lean and effective team. In other cases they have managed to prevent the cancer of restrictive practices penetrating the firm. In yet other cases they have managed to identify the key to a more productive marketing strategy through better products or a better service, or through better communication, or by a smarter selling effort or in some instances through a combination of all these ingredients. The fact remains that in the most turbulent market conditions one meets firms that have managed to produce outstanding results in accordance with whatever criterion of success one cares to choose – including productivity. Whilst BL is fighting for its existence, BMW announces fresh records despite some decline in their domestic market. Whilst ICL is in the process of considering large redundancies, IBM are still going from strength to strength. In every industry one encounters one or two names who have managed to come on top without massive blood-letting. Success in difficult market conditions is a far better test of good management than success during periods of growth and relative prosperity.

Productivity is a notion which is fairly well understood by production personnel. Considerable effort has been invested over the years in improving production processes with the view of obtaining a higher level of productivity. Far less work has been undertaken to improve the productivity of other activities in the firm. Whilst I intend in this chapter to concentrate my attention on how to improve the productivity of the selling effort, I wish to start by postulating a much broader philosophy: 'management by productivity' is taking over from where 'management by objectives' has left off.

If management accepts the notion that the great challenge that it will face in the future is the need to improve the firm's productivity, it must undertake a systematic, in-depth analysis of each activity of the organisation, starting at the top and working its way downwards. The chief executive officer of the company must be productive. All other Board members must fulfil standards of productivity. The R & D department must seek to improve the valuable and commercialisable output of its efforts, i.e. become more productive. The personnel department must become more productive in such terms as reduced personnel turnover, better and cheaper training and so on. Every individual in the organisation, whether he belongs to the strategic level, management or operational level, must be able to place his hand on his heart and say, 'I have generated a greater output per unit of my time and/or cost this month as against last month or this year as against last year'. To many managers this idea may sound anathema inasmuch as it may sound like the end of a happy, easy-going, undemanding work era. To others the notion may present great difficulties because they belong to staff functions which in their opinion are not capable of measurement or productivity quantification. The bitter truth is that every task in every organisation is capable of some measurement and quantification. The best acid test is 'How much would this service cost us if we used outside resources?' An internal lawyer can measure his performance and productivity by comparing his output to that of a self-employed solicitor in relation to his own earnings. A trainer can measure his productivity in terms of course-days that he conducts and the cost thereof as against the cost of sending the same number of participants to outside training centres.

A word of warning for people at the top of the firm's hierarchy: avoid at all costs conveying the impression that productivity is a notion for others and not for those at the top. Many excellent concepts and techniques have floundered through this kind of hypocrisy. The boss who turns up at work at 10 a.m. every day would have great difficulties in insisting that everybody else arrives at 8 a.m.! The senior man who treats the firm as a personal playground in terms of extravagant and lavish living would find it almost impossible to preach parsimony and results orientation to his subordinates. Leadership means giving a good example. If the new motto is to adopt a more productive style of management, the people at the top must be seen to adhere to all the rules of the new game. In other words *productivity is an attitude* and, as explained in an earlier chapter, attitudes take time to develop in' an organisation. If one chooses productivity as the new way of life for the total organisation, every member of the company must become aware of the meaning of this philosophy, must learn how to apply it to himself and must become vigilant of areas of enhanced productivity around him. It calls for a lot of work, a lot of thought and persistence. However, if applied consistently to every nook and cranny of the organisation, it may yield very rich pickings.

The rest of this chapter is devoted to the exploration of how a firm can plan for a more productive sales force. After the fairly long introduction regarding productivity in the organisation as a whole, it should become plain to the reader that where the company has accepted the tenets of 'management by productivity' for the total firm the chances of developing a more productive selling effort are greatly enhanced. Let us assume that it is within such a receptive environment that some of the ideas propounded here will be applied.

The Sales Force – its Role and Objectives

The sales force is one of the most precious resources of the firm. It takes many years to build and develop, and an effective sales organisation is the envy of any competitor. However, it must be emphasised that the sales force can only be effective where the other ingredients of the marketing mix are sound. To expect the salesmen to become more productive in isolation is hardly fair. Every ingredient of the mix must be placed under the microscope with the view of having its productivity improved. The product itself, the pricing policy, the promotional mix (advertising, sales promotion and the publicity effort) and the distribution system all have an indispensable contribution to make to the overall success of the marketing programme. Each of these ingredients, in turn, can have its productivity improved. Let us assume that all the relevant homework will have been carried out in this direction and that the sales force is in the happy position of knowing that they are selling within an environment in which the marketing mix as a whole is healthy, constantly improving and truly customer-orientated.

The sales force is the infantry that has to visit customers and/or channels of distribution with the view of either imparting information and knowledge (as is the case with medical representatives) or actually obtaining orders from specific customers or ensuring that existing customers are happy with the firm and its service. A host of other objectives may be ascribed to the firm's selling effort. Later on we shall explore the kinds of objectives that can be given to salesmen and the basis upon which they should be determined. At this point it is important to discuss three aspects relating to the formulation of selling policies.

THE SALES FORCE AND THE PLANNING PROCESS

The role and objectives of the firm's selling effort can only be specified after the initial steps in the planning process have been taken. It is impractical to define the objectives of the sales force and its various constituents without having defined the objectives of the marketing effort as a whole and also the objectives of the other ingredients of the mix. This subject has been covered in some depth in Chapter 2.

Moreover, before defining the objectives of the sales force and determining the way in which the force should be organised and developed the strategies and resources of competitors must be studied and understood. It is impossible to develop a reliable working plan for the sales force without understanding competitors' strengths and weaknesses.

THE NEED FOR OBJECTIVES

In a well managed and productive sales force one must specify objectives for the overall effort, for the regions (if the force is organised geographically) and for each individual. Each salesman is entitled to know what level of performance and productivity is expected of him. The attainment of objectives not only represents a tool for measuring results, it also offers a very potent motivational stimulus to the individual performer. To that extent the practice that some sales managers indulge in of giving salemen enormous and unattainable targets in order to 'keep them on their toes' is hardly a clever thing to do. The danger of such a strategy is twofold: the salesman can get totally demotivated when he sees that his objectives are incapable of attainment in spite of hard work on his part; what is even more serious is the fact that the firm's plans may get into total disarray as a result of inflated published sales budgets. Sales managers beware!

In defining salesmen's objectives one must remember that three major conditions must be fulfilled if they are to represent an effective standard of performance:

(a) *Measurability* (as far as it is possible) Ideally the salesman should be able to finish a day's work and be able to evaluate his own level of productivity in accordance with the standards ascribed to him. Thus, if his objectives are specified in terms of units sold, he can easily determine whether he met the day's or week's or month's quota, depending on the nature of the business.

(b) *Relevance* The objectives given to an individual must be relevant and appropriate to his job. A person selling aeroplanes would find a 'number of calls a day' a totally irrelevant standard of performance. The fulfilment of such a standard of performance and a subsequent increased productivity could not be translated into better results. The first principle of effective sales management is the ability to identify and define the most relevant criteria of measurement to each selling task. Being relevant and not measurable is as bad as being measurable and not relevant. Both conditions must be considered and met.

(c) *Fairness* In an organisation seeking to conduct its affairs in a supportive and decent manner it is important that objectives given to individual members of the team are fair and capable of being attained by well trained and hard-working people. Where these objectives are overstated in relation to the area of operational performance one might as well double, treble or quadruple these objectives. Unfairness in this regard is synonymous with the non-existence of standards of performance.

As an aid to reflecting upon and selecting the most appropriate criteria of performance and/or productivity for a sales force, Figure 10.1 sets out a long list of options. The list is not comprehensive and other items can be added thereto. However, the person responsible for deciding upon the most appropriate set of criteria of performance in a given set of circumstances should run through this list and attempt to evaluate each item on a simple screening device provided at the right-hand side of the form. Any item that earns a high score (say '3' or '4') after a thorough discussion with everybody concerned will probably need to be incorporated in the salesman's terms of reference and measurement of performance system.

THE CHANGING ROLE OF SELLING

It is appropriate to review briefly the nature and scope of salesmanship and also to exlore the changes that this function is undergoing in a modern marketing environment. A full understanding of these changes may help to consider methods of improving the productivity of the selling effort. The word 'to sell' covers a great variety of activities ranging from the salesman who actually delivers the product (e.g. a milkman) to a salesman who sells a sophisticated 'turnkey' nuclear power plant. They both 'sell', yet they are as different as chalk and cheese. Between these two extremes one encounters a wide range of

Figure 10.1 Standard of performance and/or productivity of salesmen and saleswomen (example only). The relevance of an item should be indicated by placing a value from 1 to 4 in the appropriate box according to the following scale: 1, not relevant; 2, fairly relevant; 3, relevant; 4, extremely relevant.

I. MEASURES OF ACHIEVEMENT

A. OBJECTIVES UTILISING VOLUME OF SALES

Relevance

1. Sales volume by salesman by value ☐
2. Sales volume by salesman by units ☐
3. Sales volume by salesman by number of customers ☐
4. Sales by product lines ☐
5. Sales volume by salesman to new accounts and old accounts – ratio clearly prescribed ☐
6. Number of sales related to number of calls ☐

B. OBJECTIVES UTILISING MARKET AND/OR CUSTOMER PENETRATION

1. New accounts secured ☐
2. Number of customers sold to compared with number of customers assigned ☐
3. Number of customers sold to compared with number of customers in area ☐
4. Accounts lost ☐
5. Share of market achieved in area ☐
6. Towns sold or not sold to ☐
7. Number of customers served among the 20% who represent 80% of the business in the area ☐

C. OBJECTIVES UTILISING MARGINS

1. Gross margin or contribution secured (especially where salesmen exercise some discretion in quoting prices) ☐
2. Amounts of high and low gross margin products sold ☐
3. Gross margins secured per call ☐
4. Gross margins secured per day (week, month) in relation to salesman's costs ☐

D. OBJECTIVES UTILISING EXPENSES

Relevance

1. Salary (or salary plus expenses or total emoluments) related to sales or to number of units sold ☐
2. Salary + travel expenses + a proportion of overheads (directly related to selling effort) related to sales or to number of units sold ☐
3. Sales cost : sales ratio ☐
4. Cost per day ☐
5. Cost per call ☐

II. MEASURES OF ACTIVITIES

A. Daily calls ☐
B. Days worked ☐
C. General demeanour, tact, judgement, etc. ☐
D. Planning of work ☐
E. Conduct of interviews ☐
F. Number of quotations ☐
G. Use of sales aids and/or equipment ☐
H. Procurement of prospect lists ☐

activities known as 'selling', varying enormously in level of complexity and scope. Nonetheless, as we shall see later they all have something in common, namely an effective 'selling' skill. A milkman could not sell a computer not because he lacks the skill but because he does not possess the appropriate knowledge of the product, the technology and the information industry.

Salesmen fall into a number of distinct groupings:

(a) *The salesman who delivers the product* (milk, fuel, papers, etc.) He needs to spend very little time on communicating or persuading. The customer is almost pre-sold. The main effort is to provide a punctual, cheerful, friendly face at all times.

(b) *The salesman who functions in a well defined marketplace* (shops, travel agents, offices, government departments) The role of 'selling' here is to ensure that the customer's needs are fulfilled quickly, efficiently and with a smile. In certain circumstances he can apply some skill in ensuring that a deal does take place and that the customer does not leave empty-handed (a car salesman).

(c) *The salesman who is expected to build goodwill or impart knowledge* (the medical representative) The salesman's task here is first to make sure that the customer agrees to see him and secondly to make an effective presentation which is instructive, interesting and meets the needs of the recipient of all this communication.

(d) *The salesman who sells on the basis of excellent technical knowledge* He is expected to sell and in fact to obtain orders but seeks to achieve these goals through a well informed counselling service. He almost acts as a consultant to his client companies. Obviously to be able to do so he needs considerable knowledge and must be equipped with excellent sales aids. Whilst his productivity can be measured in terms of results, it depends to a great extent upon the productivity of the training methods invested in him and the quality of the tools placed at his disposal (e.g. sales aids, specifications, promotional handouts).

(e) *The salesman who sells tangible products to the ultimate consumer* (e.g. washing machines, vacuum cleaners and encyclopaedias) He must be creatively persuasive and very often can only achieve a sale by 'de-marketing' the old product in the eyes of its owner.

(f) *The salesman who sells intangible products* (e.g. insurance or banking) The salesman of such products must possess thorough product knowledge yet must know how to communicate this knowledge in terms that the customer is able to understand. Many sales in this area are lost for the simple reason that the customer is incapable of decoding the messages transmitted to him by the salesman and/or the firm's literature.

This is a fairly comprehensive list of selling activities. Each has its problems and each requires its own skills and knowledge. The productivity of each would be measured and enhanced in accordance with different rules. Yet they all require something in common: the ability to communicate in an effective and empathetic way with a customer or group of customers who have needs, tangible and intangible, and want them fulfilled in an efficient and honest way. Within such a well defined framework a good salesman of diesel engines should be able to perform an admirable selling job in a local grocery. This is not meant as an insult. On the contrary it is meant as a compliment to a person who knows how to relate to and communicate with other fellow human beings.

The role of the salesman, especially in the more advanced technological industries and/or service organisations, is undergoing a radical change. It was suggested that 'salesmanship' in the 1950s meant 'tellmanship'. The job of the salesman was simply to knock on doors and *tell* the customer about 'our wonderful product'. The customer felt honoured by the opportunity to buy the offered product.

In the more competitive world of the 1960s salesmanship graduated to its proper role. *'To sell'* meant communicating details of the product and its benefits and unique selling points, persuading, dealing with objections and striking a deal. A more challenging and creative task.

The 1970s saw the emergence of the concept of *'counselling'*. The salesman virtually became a consultant, a walking *'Which?'* report, In trying to sell his product he needed to communicate to the customer the cost–benefit relationship of using that product as against competitive offerings. The aim became to assist the customer in taking wise, cost-beneficial, result-orientated decisions. This meant that the quality of salesmanship hinged around the quality of the information that the firm's marketing department was able to impart to him. Many firms equipped their sales forces with tools that enable them to communicate to their customers reliable and up-to-date information about the wisdom of a certain course of action. Obviously the credibility of such counselling activities depended on the quality of the advice offered, the methodologies used in reaching the various conclusions, and in addition the standing of the firm and its image in the marketplace.

The challenge for the 1980s is referred to as *'joining'*. To sell will mean *'to join'*. The winner of the battle of the 1980s in the marketplace will be the selling organisation that recognises that a relationship with the customer is not a hit and run affair. Selling will entail a long term relationship with one's clients: 'The client may not require my products or services this year or next but one day he is bound to return to the market. I must be ready for him, and if I invest in this special relationship I shall be the first supplier whom he will approach when the time comes. Meanwhile I shall make a point of keeping myself up to date with his problems, opportunities and developments in his marketing environment. I shall endeavour to be as knowledgeable about the goings-on in his marketplace as he is'. This may be a tall order. Nonetheless, the rewards may be substantial. Obviously productivity in this kind of challenging selling environment assumes a very different perspective than just counting daily calls, measuring the number of units sold or measuring the level of expenses per call. In this new environment a salesman will become an 'account executive' with a long term relationship with the client, and the *quality* of his work will assume as important a role as the *quantity* of his short term achievements.

Key Areas for Improved Productivity

There are many areas in which the productivity of the sales force can be improved. Sales managers are familiar with many of these areas and I am aware of a number of organisations that have taken radical and imaginative steps in this direction.

My aim here is to highlight a number of important areas which often escape the attention of those responsible for increasing the productivity of the selling effort.

DEVELOPING A TYPOLOGY OF THE 'PERFECT CUSTOMER'

May I refer the reader to Chapter 3. A strong case was made in that chapter for looking at 'products' from the vantage point of the consuming segments or user groups rather than from the perspective of the physical product that the firm manufactures. Ball bearings should be viewed as anti-friction devices that help to reduce friction in machine-tools, extraction machinery, etc., and not as a batch of spherical metal balls that come in a plethora of sizes. The main purpose of such a perspective is to be able to allocate areas of attention towards which the selling effort can be directed. Through careful analysis and planning one can place degrees of attractiveness against each market vector and present such a list to the sales force. The salesman would know that any user group designated as 'A' is a star target market and 'B' is somewhat lower down the scale and so on. Obviously any segment which has been designated as 'E' will receive no selling attention at all. This means that the sales force will be equipped with an aid to deciding in which direction their attention should be targeted.

As a further suggestion the marketer was reminded of the usefulness of the Standard Industrial Classification (revised 1980) as a tool for analysing the marketplace. Against each item – whether it is a 'division', a 'class', a 'group' or an 'activity' (to use the nomenclature of the SIC terminology) – one can append the appropriate letter that would designate the relative commercial attractiveness of each sector. It is self-evident that by doing so one has taken the first step towards ensuring that the selling effort becomes more productively directed. If ammunition is a scarce resource, it must be aimed at the target most likely to yield results within the aims of the military organisation. The same rationale applies here.

Not every business can plan its marksmanship on an SIC-based target. Other classifications may be more compatible with the firm's needs and must be considered. A few important principles must be borne in mind:

(a) Very few firms can afford to target their sales force on every potential customer, large and small. Some selectivity is essential, especially if one aspires to be more productive and run the sales force as a tight and effective crew. The planning process in this respect aims to identify and list the most promising opportunities within the firm's own strengths and opportunities.

(b) What is an opportunity for firm A is not necessarily an opportunity for firm B. With this important thought in mind the planner can identify the targets that should be avoided because by doing so one does not expend valuable selling energy on customers that competitors are more likely to penetrate.

(c) In classifying customers into typologies one can use a large number of varying criteria: size of firm and/or its consumption level; the segments that potential customers serve; the nature of the firm's products, technologies and production processes; the personality of the 'decision makers' and/or their motivational stimuli (e.g. wanting to buy from large firms or from small firms only); the geographical location of the customers; levels of expenditure on specific areas (e.g. 'Our ideal customer is the one who spends 8% of his turnover on R & D' or 'Our ability to sell to firms spending over 7% on physical distribution seems somehow favourable'); personal foibles of members of the decision-making unit.

Many other criteria can be identified and considered. It calls for a painstaking analysis of a lot of data. However, if one can emerge at the end of this exercise with a profile of the 'perfect' and 'next to perfect' customer or group of customers, one has acquired a dramatic aid to a more productive selling organisation.

A BETTER UNDERSTANDING OF THE CUSTOMER'S DECISION-MAKING UNIT

In a previous chapter we explored the complexity that a 'decision-making unit' can assume, especially in relation to industrial goods and/or services. A salesman seldom sells to one individual. He has to deal with a number of stakeholders. One normally talks about 'deciders', 'buyers', 'influences', 'users' and 'gatekeepers'. Each one of these has a role to play, sometimes supportive and sometimes obstructional. A good salesman must understand the way the 'unit' functions and the respective roles of each member thereof. This is particularly relevant in a sales environment which the salesman is seeking to 'join', as described earlier.

The situation is further complicated by the fact that in large firms there are many members in the decision-making unit. Each one of them needs to be communicated with in some form or another and it is impractical, inefficient and often positively imprudent for the salesman to contact them all. One uses other ingredients of the marketing mix to communicate with the less important or less accessible members of the 'unit', e.g. through literature, direct mailings, exhibitions, conferences, etc. This is an excellent example of an exercise in integration of the marketer's promotional mix. A large number of people in a customer's organisation must be communicated with and the objectives must be that: (a) the total communication programme is achieved in the most cost-beneficial way; (b) every member of the decision-making unit receives the right amount of information; (c) all the bits communicated must be integrated into a cohesive 'package' and (d) the sales force must concentrate their efforts on the most important and decisive members of the customer's buying team. The total weaponry available to the marketing organisation must be directed upon the customer's buying organisation in a planned way. This in turn will ameliorate the productivity of the effort.

In this connection the following ideas may be of help to the conscientious sales manager or whoever else is in charge of planning the sales effort:

(a) Assemble a dossier about every one of your more promising customers. This dossier should contain such information as annual reports and published accounts; a scrapbook of material published about the firm in the financial press and/or other publications; the firm's literature and product specifications; organisations charts; a 'Who's Who?' of personnel in the organisation; if possible an interfirm comparison of the firm's performance vis-a-vis their competitors. Such a dossier takes time to build, but one must ensure that it is kept up-to-date.

(b) Prepare a comprehensive list of the members of the 'decision-making unit' and together with other departments of the marketing function design an integrated communication programme. An example is shown in Table 10.1.

Evidently one can afford to undertake such detailed analysis only in situations in which the marketer has a fairly small number of large potential accounts. One cannot expect to carry out such an exercise

Table 10.1 A scheme for an integrated communication programme with members of the decision-making unit.

Members of the decision-making unit	Communication method to be applied					
	Trade press	Technical press	Salesman	Direct mail	Exhibition	Others (specify)
Internal						
managing director						
marketing director						
production director						
finance director						
R & D director						
other board members						
buyer or purchasing chief						
chief engineer						
quality controller						
the user of the product						
others (specify)						
External						
consultants						
financial advisers						
advertising agents						
other appropriate persons and organisations						

where the marketplace consists of thousands of customers or more. Nevertheless, it is surprising how many firms do not bother to collate the most rudimentary information about their client companies, even where the total catchment market consists of no more than a couple of dozen firms. This kind of input is a most valuable basis upon which to improve a firm's selling and communication productivity. First, it helps to ensure that changes in personnel do not affect the quality of subsequent contacts. Lack of information and records is always a source of deterioration in productivity in firms that suffer from personnel turnover. Secondly, an in-depth understanding of a customer's environment is one of the most effective ways for improving one's contact with him and selling to him. People do like buying from friends.

CAPITALISE UPON INTERNAL INFORMATION

This section should be of particular interest to large firms operating as many decentralised units. The nature of the structure and the relative independence of its various units implies that the communication level among these units is slender. This in turn means that the information available in one unit is seldom available to others. This is a great pity inasmuch as the totality of the data locked away in separate, quasi-autonomous, operational activities can be of value at some time to one unit or another. Many firms do not realise what wealth of intelligence is scattered around the organisation. This is particularly true of decentralised organisations operating on a multinational scale. I have recently come across a large British company operating as a highly decentralised organisation in the field of engineering, electrical equipment and turnkey plants where five senior managers representing separate subsidiaries embarked on fact-finding or selling trips to the Middle East. None of the five knew of the existence of the others. Two met on the plane; two of the others bumped into each other in a hotel. It so happened that somewhere in the organisation there was a gentleman who possessed a wealth of knowledge about the Middle East and the kinds of customers that at least three of the five travellers were attempting to contact. If ever there was a case for a selling 'synergy' this represented one! The trouble was that no system or procedure existed for retrieving the names of people who might possess the appropriate know-how. The problem was overcome by a very simple device: every manager in the entire organisation, above a certain level, was asked to complete a brief questionnaire in which he listed the countries which he had visited during the previous five years, the contacts he had developed and the nature of business that he managed to transact with each. All this information was cross-indexed and placed in the firm's computer. Once the system was completed managers were expected to keep it up to date by sending in new information at the end of each foreign trip. The result was dramatic: before embarking on a trip to a new territory the traveller could consult the data bank in order to identify those individuals in the company who had gained useful experience in that part of the world. The computer would list a number of names and their location and the traveller could contact them for advice and guidance and possibly useful contacts to approach. The system worked well and certainly ameliorated the productivity of the firm's managers in relation to their international selling effort. An unexpected fringe benefit emerged from this strategy. Managers belonging to different units operating in a variety of locations got to know each other and forged close relationships. A system that was designed to improve international selling productivity helped, albeit indirectly, to improve communication among the disparate units. Two birds were killed with one stone.

Great benefits can be derived through the tabulation of 'who knows what?' in any company. A sales force consists of many people. In industrial marketing the number of salesmen can be fairly small. In consumer goods marketing the sales force often consists of scores or even hundreds of salesmen. It is inevitable that among all these people someone knows something which can be of great benefit to the others. It is the job of an effective manager to develop a system capable of catching the gems which normally get lost. The traditional reporting system which most salesmen have to complete should contain a section soliciting data about snippets of information which the salesman believes might be of value to other members of the sales force. The quality of this kind of cross-fertilisation will improve with time, experience and as soon as members of the team recognise the benefits which they can derive therefrom. Undoubtedly once this system becomes operational great benefits towards improved selling productivity can be attained.

LEARN FROM YOUR 'STAR' PERFORMERS

A sales force consists of a myriad of personalities. With all the training in the world one cannot expect to achieve total homogeneity of behaviour, attitudes and performance. It is simply contrary to human nature. The team normally consists of high-flyers at the one extreme and 'sloggers' at the other extreme. The former are enthusiastic, creative and effective. The latter may work hard but results do not come easily to them.

It should be possible to adapt the Pareto law (the so-called 20:80 rule whereby 20% of any activity represents 80% of the results) to a sales force, although it would be a very sad day for a sales manager if the full rigours of this law apply in practice. It would be a shattering revelation if in practice 20% of the sales force achieved 80% of the sales! If this were the case one could simply increase productivity by firing 80% of the force. This would of course be complete nonsense. It is possible to adapt the Pareto law into a qualitative framework rather than a quantitative

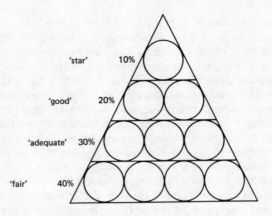

Figure 10.2 Sales force classified by performance quality.

one. Let us decide arbitrarily that the 'star' performers represent 10% of the sales force: the 'good' ones 20%, the 'adequates' 30% and the 'fair' ones 40%. This can be illustrated, as in Figure 10.2, in the shape of a pyramid.

Different descriptions can be attached to each of these qualitative groups. In fact different percentages can be ascribed to each as long as the total is 100%. The important point is to recognise the various levels of performance which exist in the sales force. Excellence is quite easy to identify in a selling environment which carries quantitative criteria of performance. In any event it is rare for a sales manager not to know who his 'star' performers are. Equally it is unusual for him not to know who his poorish performers are.

Once the sales force has been categorised into clearly defined groups one can ask a very legitimate question: 'What does the "star" do which the "fair" performer does not do?' If one could identify in some detail how the 'star' behaves in front of a customer, the way he communicates the message, the way he plans and manages his time, the way he uses sales aids, etc., one would acquire most valuable information. One would know how to develop new training methods for the rest of the force. One would gain an insight into the selling and buying environment and this should help one to perceive areas in which productivity can be improved.

In order to find out what the 'stars' do which is different from the pattern of behaviour of the lower quality echelons one should simply escort a representative sample of 'stars' and 'fairs' and observe in detail the way they behave and perform. Spending a week travelling with 'stars' and another week with members of the other extreme can be a most enlightening exercise! Moreover, it is a very useful project for a sales manager. It gives him an opportunity of renewing his knowledge of the marketplace. There is no better way of understanding the problems that a sales force has to contend with than spending some time in the selling arena.

In some circumstances it is difficult for the sales manager to escort members of the sales force and derive the kind of benefit that was described above. The reason is simple: salesmen cease to perform in accordance with their normal pattern and behave in a contrived manner. This would defeat the whole purpose of the study. In such situations one can either attach a trainer to them during their travelling schedule or employ a training consultant. At least the hierarchical shadow has been removed.

I have participated in many such projects and have discovered that this approach is a most fruitful source of ideas for improving the productivity of the non-'stars'. On occasions I was staggered by the quality of creativity which the 'star' performer generates in order to improve the quality of his presentation and persuasion tasks. Moreover, on a number of visits I discovered a salesman using 'do-it-yourself' sales aids without the knowledge of his superiors. I once met a 'star' medical representative who had produced at his own expense overhead projector transparencies incorporating the main features of the product as contained in the firm's literature. Whenever the opportunity arose he would ask the doctor for permission to use his illuminated X-ray panel. These transparencies always looked impressive on such a unit. The doctor invariably agreed to such a suggestion and at that point the presentation took place in front of the X-ray unit. To me, the casual observer, the presentation that followed was reminiscent of two consultants discussing a case in a hospital rather than a salesman and a doctor talking. Only afterwards did I discover that the salesman's main objective was to remove the barrier that always exists in these situations, namely the desk. He had read that a desk is an impediment to communication and decided to find a creative way of getting rid of this barrier. The man's superiors were totally unaware of this superb bit of creativity. That case vindicated in my eyes the value of the procedure recommended here for improving sales force productivity.

SALES FORCE SIZE

Ideally a sales force should not be too large nor too small. If it is too large it incurs unnecessary costs. If it is too small it may not be capable of covering the marketplace effectively with a resultant loss of sales. Somewhere along the line there is a size which is capable of achieving optimum performance. The ability to pinpoint this size is a most valuable tool in the productivity game.

A few obvious and well-trodden principles may help in determining the optimum sales force size:

(a) *Some* increase in sales volume can always result from the addition of a salesman. It is very rare for a new salesman to achieve zero results. On the other hand, a salesman who costs say £17 500 per annum (including car, travelling, subsistence, insurance and other direct costs) and who only generates an annual volume of £50 000 with a gross margin of 30% has not earned his keep! Clearly one has to ensure that he was given a suitable territory size with a fair potential and that he was adequately trained. However, if this is the best he can achieve after all the support given to him, then his value to the firm is doubtful.

(b) Sales volume hardly ever increases in a linear relationship to an increased number of salesmen. Life would be very cosy for sales managers if they knew that an increase of 30% in the sales force would generate a 30% increase in sales volume. Unfortunately the practical reality is less helpful. The so-called 'law of diminishing returns' sets in at a certain point and the addition of salesmen after that would generate an ever-decreasing sales volume.

(c) The law of diminishing returns is reached by different sales forces at different rates. Some firms can afford to increase their sales forces for quite a while before 'diminishing returns' start taking their toll. Others find that the level at which the diseconomy of increasing one's sales force occurs at a fairly early stage. This point is illustrated in Figure 10.3.

One of the tasks of the manager is to try to understand the relationship that exists between growth in sales force size and sales volume in his own selling scene. It is absolutely impossible to extrapolate from one marketing environment to another.

(d) In designing territories for individual salesmen one must strive to give each one of them a territory of equal potential. Thus if the market is estimated to be worth £10 million and one employs 100

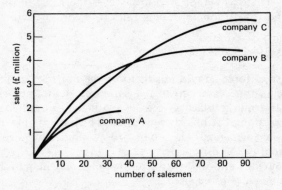

Figure 10.3 Relationship between sales volume and sales force size in three companies.

salesmen the country should be divided, as far as is possible, into 100 territories worth a potential of £100 000 each. Obviously many factors such as mix of accounts in the territory, geographical structure and economic developments must be brought into consideration. However, one must attempt to give every salesman a comparable challenge.

(e) The minute the cost of every additional salesman is not matched by commensurate profits (gross margin minus direct costs) one ceases to increase the size of the force. This is of course based on the assumption that the existing sales force is efficient and is operating at a fairly acceptable level of productivity. It is also assumed that the rest of the market mix is reasonably effective. The last principle is illustrated in Figure 10.4.

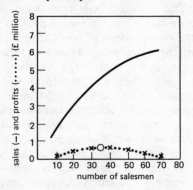

Figure 10.4 Relationship between sales force size and sales and/or profits.

In Figure 10.4 a hypothetical situation is illustrated whereby sales continue to grow with an increase in the sales force size. On the other hand, profits struck a peak at the point where the sales force reached around thirty-five salesmen. If profits are the main criterion of success, the need to stop enlarging the sales force at thirty-five individuals becomes obvious. A similar exercise can be undertaken in relation to other parameters, such as return on investment and market share. A sales force might have reached its law of diminishing returns in relation to profits at thirty-five individuals, yet it may reach the point of diseconomy in relation to return on investment at an earlier point.

This kind of analysis is pretty demanding in terms of time and data collection. It can be greatly facilitated if the firm possesses accurate and comprehensive information about past performance. Nevertheless, it is a most valuable exercise to undertake inasmuch as the determination of the most suitable sales force size can be extremely helpful in one's endeavours to improve the overall productivity of the team.

THE SALESMAN'S 'PROFIT AND LOSS ACCOUNT'

Most salesmen realise that they represent a cost and that their efforts must yield a result. They also recognise that the output must exceed the input. How far they are actually aware of the quantitative details depends on the firm for which they work and the style of management that prevails therein. In some firms the data is blurred. The salesman knows very vaguely what cost he represents and knows even less what net revenue his sales have generated. In other firms the data is comprehensive, open and well tabulated. There is very little justification in the modern and competitive world we live in for concealing such important information from people who have to produce results which ultimately make the attainment of the corporate objectives possible. I hereby appeal to those who run their sales organisation in a secretive and non-participative style to mend their ways. To attain productivity one depends on the co-operation of one's team. Co-operation can be best achieved where the relationship is frank and the information freely available. Admittedly every firm has a number of secrets of great commercial importance which one is reluctant to transmit to every employee in the organisation. I am not referring to such information. These must be kept secret. I am referring to more mundane data such as contributions per product, gross margins, production load, cost of logistics, inventory levels, etc. The salesman who possesses all the appropriate information which enables him to formulate a simple 'profit and loss' account at the end of each call or at the end of a working day is the kind of person who is capable of motivating himself towards a higher level of productivity.

Equipped with the appropriate data regarding cost, margins and selling time required it is possible to work out a simple profit and loss account for each customer, group of customers, typology of customers, segments, etc. This kind of calculation can be worked out on the basis of historical data and also as part of the firm's planning process, in which case the information will be based on forecasts and estimates.

Table 10.2 illustrates a profit and loss account for five customers. For each customer the figures show sales, contribution, marketing cost and selling costs, net contribution towards profit and overheads and percentage of contribution in relation to sales. The figures are self-explanatory. They show which customer yields the best return in terms of contribution as a percentage of sales, namely customer C, who yields 24.5%. This is a result of a combination of factors: low production costs, relatively low credit terms and also low selling costs. In the productivity pecking order it is the most attractive customer, although in absolute terms other customers generate higher contributions (A and E have higher contributions, yet E is the least productive in relation to the effort invested therein.)

Another example is shown in Table 10.3. Here the analysis is based on

Table 10.2 Profit and loss accounts for five customers – a comparative study.

	Customer				
	A	B	C	D	E
sales during year	£180000	£130000	£145000	£170000	£240000
cost of goods supplied as a percentage of sales	70%	70%	67½%	72½%	75%
cost of goods in £s	£126000	£91000	£97875	£123250	£180000
contribution	£54000	£39000	£47125	£46750	£60000
marketing costs (direct costs attributable to customer plus a portion of total marketing expenditure)	£9000	£6500	£7250	£8500	£12000
cost of money (based on credit taken by each customer at a cost to the company of 15% per annum)	£4500	£1625	£2720	£2125	£9000
selling costs (based on time spent and expenses)	£2200	£1200	£1500	£750	£3000
total marketing and selling costs	£15700	£9325	£11470	£11375	£24000
net contribution towards profits and overheads	£38300	£29175	£35655	£35375	£36000
percentage of sales	21%	22½%	24½%	20.8%	15%

Table 10.3 Net contribution made by three products (an example).

	Product A	Product B	Product C
price per unit	£600	£800	£1,450
cost of sales (%)	68%	71%	72%
cost of sales (£)	£408	£568	£1,044
contribution	£192	£232	£406
marketing costs per unit	£48	£64	£72
selling costs per unit	£42	£80	£72½
total marketing and selling costs	£90	£144	£144½
net contribution	£102	£88	£261½
percentage of sales	17%	11%	18%
contribution : selling costs	$\frac{102}{42}=2.43$	$\frac{88}{80}=1.1$	$\frac{261.5}{72.5}=3.60$

the profit and loss account of three products which the sales force have to sell. The analysis shows the prices of the three products, their relative costs, contributions, marketing costs and selling costs, contribution per unit as a percentage of the selling price per unit and the efficiency of the selling effort as a ratio between net contribution and cost of selling per unit. The higher the figure the more productive it is in relation to the selling task.

Other combinations and permutations can be worked out in respect of other cost elements and/or other divisions of the marketing/selling activities of the firm. The aim of these examples is to illustrate how an analysis of the costs that go into generating a sale can help to understand the relative productivity in a multiproduct, multicustomer environment.

THE STIMULATION OF CREATIVITY

Ideas are normally a scarce resource in most companies. Furthermore, the number of ideas that actually get implemented is extremely low. If one believes statistics the rate of exchange between ideas and commercialisable innovations is 58 to 1. This means that a firm must catch every idea that floats in its atmosphere because ideas are as precious as gold dust.

A sales force can be a very useful source of new ideas. Salesmen travel around. They visit a large number of customers in a variety of industries. Somewhere along the line a salesman is bound to come across an idea which may help his firm to perform its work in a better, cheaper or more efficacious way. Salesmen must be encouraged to use their observing skill in order to detect useful and interesting things. Futhermore, the firm must motivate them to seek out such innovations. Everything that was said so far about productivity can be easily surpassed in an organisation that knows how to motivate its salesmen to look and search for novel ideas. This can be a most fertile source of productivity. However, the manager responsible for the sales activities of the firm must remember that three conditions must exist if the salesmen are to become a useful source of ideas:

(a) The climate in the organisation must be such that ideas are allowed to spawn therein.
(b) A system for communicating ideas must be developed. Many excellent ideas are often lost because of the simple fact that the originator of such ideas does not know to whom to transmit such ideas.
(c) A system for screening and evaluating ideas must exist.

More information on the subject of creativity is contained in Chapter 6.

It is important to remember that whilst productivity is normally associated with facts and figures capable of quantification it would be a very poor sales manager who forgets that a firm's operational tasks can also be enriched by qualitative and innovative methods. To that extent, in the quest of ideas for productivity improvement we must harness all the creativity that rests in the sales force as a whole.

11
Advertising by Objectives

The famous statement that 'I know half the money I spend on advertising is wasted; but I can never find out which half' has been attributed to at least two great sellers and advertisers, the first being Lord Leverhulme and the second John Wanamaker, the nineteenth-century American merchant. Whoever first said it, the quotation is understandably popular among advertising men, who must continually search for methods of measuring the effectiveness of advertising. This long-standing problem has been preoccupying an increasing number of marketing executives and company chairmen alike. Advertising is a major resource area in many companies, and it is inconceivable for no heart-searching to follow the deployment of such substantial sums. In Britain close to £1600 million is spent on advertising – 1.4% of the gross national product; in the USA this expenditure exceeds 2.2% of the gross national product. To spend these vast amounts without wanting to see results is the sort of mindless extravagance which the modern manager can hardly afford.

Not surprisingly, the subject has stimulated considerable interest among academic researchers and businessmen. Management literature abounds with lengthy and interesting studies on how advertising results can be measured and how the advertising effort can be made more effective. Panaceas grow and die by the dozen; methodologies and techniques fill volumes; and, like alchemists, a new breed of specialists has emerged ready to turn advertising budgets to gold dust. Techniques for measuring effectiveness have sprung from all directions. Some are simple and naive; others are sophisticated to the point of incomprehensibility. Some are highly qualitative and conceptual; others are quantitative and mechanical. The whole subject has become so riddled with methodologies that most marketing managers prefer to steer clear of this overwhelming battery of 'aids', developed to help them. They treat them as the bear-hug that should not be trusted.

A modern enterprise rarely fails to measure the effectiveness of its human resources. Similarly it is quite normal for a company to analyse carefully its raw material content and utilisation. But how many companies measure systematically, if at all, the results of their advertising effort? How many companies are able to express in quantitative terms the impact that a specific campaign has achieved? This, of course, leads one to ask the logical question, How many companies know precisely what they are trying to achieve through advertising?

A few years ago I had the opportunity of undertaking a comprehensive survey among British and Continental companies with the objective of anwering these questions (survey conducted by the author and Urwick Orr & Partners Ltd in 1971). The search was for a clearer picture of how companies on this side of the Atlantic treat their advertising effort in general and, specifically, how they measure the attainment of their advertising objectives.

Whilst the findings of the survey may not entirely represent present-day conditions, the results were so enlightening that it is worthwhile to summarise them again. The perceptive reader should be able to derive the appropriate lessons from this chapter.

Most of the companies approached, in a wide cross section of industries, showed interest in the survey and felt challenged by the implications of what was for many the first opportunity to consider these questions in depth. A simple questionnaire was used which sought the following information, in jargon-free language: (a) historic data on the relationship, over a period of five years, between two ingredients of the marketing mix – advertising and sales turnover; (b) whether the company had actually formulated advertising objectives and, if so, the details of such objectives; (c) how the company measured its advertising effectiveness, and details of the methods used to do so; (d) how the company decided on its budgets.

Replies to the last question, although slightly away from the overall theme of the survey, helped to throw light on the companies' general attitude to advertising and its objectives. Such answers as 'we select an advertising budget in accordance with what we can afford in any given budget period', or 'percentage of budgeted sales', helped to indicate a company's state of enlightenment towards advertising as an effective tool of the marketing process. These replies usually come from companies which slash their advertising appropriation the minute that turnover shows a tendency to decline. Thus, the questionnaire was simple but fairly comprehensive. It was designed to remove the obfuscating mystique that surrounds the subject in the minds of most managers.

The answers revealed that a surprisingly large proportion of British and Continental firms claim that they formulate advertising objectives. This claim was made by 70% of the sample. Nearly all consumer goods firms select objectives for their advertising effort, or say they do. Most answers make it evident that the process rarely goes beyond a very basic and almost crude description of objectives. Many companies declared that they had advertising objectives, but seemed to confuse them with overall marketing objectives.

The survey showed, however, that companies which formulate an 'advertising by objectives' strategy fare better than those which do not.

While most respondent companies in the sample reported increased sales during the five-year period previous to the survey (whether or not they formulated advertising objectives), only 35% of the total sample also reported *increased market share* during the same period. Of these high-fliers no less than 85% believe in and actively pursue an 'advertising by objectives' philosophy. This indicates that firms which formulate their advertising objectives clearly (and more than likely also have a total 'management by objectives' approach to business) enjoy a marked competitive edge. However, although 70% of the sampled companies formulate advertising objectives, only 55% of the total sample actually reduce these objectives to a written form.

The majority of the companies which admit to having no advertising objectives at all market industrial goods. Most of them spend relatively small amounts on advertising. This, of course, is predictable – the less a manager spends on advertising, the less he is preoccupied by its effectiveness. Nevertheless, the replies suggested that even these companies have become aware of the need to evaluate the results of their advertising appropriation. Banks and hire purchase companies in the sample seemed to occupy a unique position. Their advertising budgets are on the increase; but none could point to clearly defined goals.

The question, what are the actual advertising objectives of companies, yielded the following list (in order of frequency of mention):

1   Increase or support sales
2   Create or increase product or brand awareness
3   Improve image of company's products
4   Improve company's image
5   Sales promotion
6   Influence attitudes
7   Inform or educate the consumer
8   Introduce new products

The wording is extracted from the forms with minimum changes in order to reproduce accurately the general impressions gained.

On methods used for measuring effectiveness the survey aimed to unearth two aspects:

(a)   What methods are being used by British and Continental companies which actually purport to measure the effectiveness of their advertising effort?
(b)   Are the methods disclosed by the companies used effectively? More specifically, are the individual measurement techniques used appropriate to the selected advertising goals?

The methods used, again in order of frequency of mention, can be summarised as follows:

1   'Sort and count' techniques, such as consumer mail or coupon
     response
2   Group interviews or panel discussions
3   Recall tests
4   Comparison of sales results (monthly, quarterly or annually)
5   Psychological depth interviews
6   Folder tests
7   Salesmen's monthly reports
8   Annual survey by market research department
9   Reports from dealers
10   Mathematical models

The number of companies using fairly sophisticated mathematical models was small, and even such companies were not entirely clear about what precisely they were trying to measure.

An analysis of the questionnaires indicated a common failure to dovetail the measurement methods with the specific objectives; for instance, the psychological depth interview method is used by one company to measure attitude changes, although the advertising objective it gave on the questionnaire is 'to inform the public of a product's availability' – which is like using a thermometer to measure the humidity. Many similar instances were observed; in other words, the impression is inescapable that even progressive companies which have formulated clear advertising objectives do not always use the most relevant measurement methods to evaluate results.

The rationale behind the enquiry about methods used to determine appropriations was an attempt to establish whether a strong 'advertising by objectives' approach helped in the task of determining the size of the advertising budget. The survey revealed that most of the companies in the sample used slightly dated methods for determining advertising budgets. 'Percentage of past sales', 'as much as we can afford', 'matching competitors' expenditure' and so on are phrases that recurred frequently. Only 25% of the companies claimed, in so many words, that their advertising budgets were regulated to correspond with predefined advertising objectives. They set objectives and only then determined the advertising resources required to carry out the task to be performed. Thus size, shape and function of the edifice are determined before allocating the bricks and mortar needed for building. That this is the sole logical course is, unfortunately, only understood by a small minority of enlightened companies.

Most businessmen would declare that the basic objective of advertising is to aid sales, and that the only criterion of effectiveness is the 'cause and effect' relationship between advertising and sales volume. This is a practical approach, but it does not always correspond to the true state of affairs. An extreme example of an advertising objective which is not set in action terms (e.g. to increase sales), but in communications terms (e.g. to impart information, or to change attitudes) is that of eliminating 'cognitive dissonance'. That technioal phrase means the post-purchase anxiety or doubt which the buyer, especially the buyer of an expensive product, sometimes develops after acquiring the product. This doubt may be a partial carry-over from the pre-purchase period, when the customer had trouble making a choice. If, for example, the product was a car, each possibility had attractive and unattractive qualities: the customer chose a specific product because, after careful consideration, he decided that the attractive qualities outweighed the unattractive ones. Once the product is in his possession, however, the less attractive qualities start bothering him and doubts set in.

Dissonance is common among purchasers of homes, motor cars, major appliances; it is also common among investors in shares and unit trusts. The tension caused by dissonance leads the buyer to seek its reduction. He may wish to rid himself of the offending product through its return to the seller, or its disposal, or its concealment in the attic. He may, on the other hand, try to resolve the nagging doubt by seeking proof that he has made the right choice. The manufacturer's aim is to provide the doubting purchaser with reassurance and confirmation of the product's excellent properties. Unless the seller makes some positive effort to dispel the dissonance he may lose the purchaser as a future customer. If this effort is the main objective of the advertising, it should be clearly spelt out, and a method of measurement should be provided. The effectiveness of the campaign can then be monitored. The measuring of such results may admittedly require the use of complex techniques (such as the 'projective technique' or the 'thematic apperception test'), but measurement is nonetheless possible.

Most managers, however, see advertising's main objective as 'increasing sales' or 'increasing market share'. But these aims describe the total marketing objectives, not the objectives of one element of the marketing mix. It is hardly reasonable to expect advertising to shoulder the full burden of attaining basic marketing objectives, unless it is the single variable in the marketing mix used. So what is really the basic goal of advertising? The subject is full of controversial notions which have stimulate a voluminous and fascinating literature. There are two main opposing schools of thought, basically either that (a) advertising should be stated in terms of sales objectives or that (b) advertising, together with other forms of promotion, aims to accomplish clearly defined communication objectives. Thus advertising succeeds or fails depending on how well it communicates predetermined information and attitudes to the right cost. This philosophy is often referred to as DAGMAR (defining advertising goals – measuring advertising results).

What happens when these two concepts are applied to specific situations? Where advertising is used to alleviate 'cognitive dissonance', or post-decision doubt, especially in relation to expensive items,

DAGMAR supporters carry the day. Again, advertisements aiming at the creation of primary demand, say, for wool or steel or aluminium in their generic forms, are often mounted by or on behalf of a large number of manufacturers acting collectively, in order to enhance the general awareness by readers or audience of the excellent properties of the product – irrespective of a specific manufacturer. The rationale is that once public awareness is generated, the wide demand for the product will facilitate the promotional efforts of individual manufacturers. The success of such a campaign cannot be measured in terms of sales; the time-lag between the campaign and the possible purchase of a specific brand ('selective demand') is too prolonged to be of measurable significance. DAGMAR wins the day again!

Another example is financial. Unit trusts advertise heavily nowadays: and each advertisement carries a coupon, clearly identified with a 'key' or code and ready to be used. The effectiveness of each advertisement or each campaign in each medium can be evaluated by reference to the number of coupons returned. The DAGMAR protagonists may have some difficulties here. Sales are the real target, and sales volume can be readily measured.

In another case, two large detergent manufacturers advertise their respective brands; both extol the many virtues of their splendid products – they both wash 'whiter than white'; both claim to be God's gift to housewives. Each company would like to increase sales and raise its market share at the expense of the other.

If the firms are of comparable efficacy, it is difficult to see how advertising can help them to achieve this aim; yet if one manufacturer were drastically to reduce his advertising effort, the other would obtain some market benefits.

If both companies were to reduce their advertising expenditure simultaneously, if not by agreement then by some telepathic intuition, it is likely that they would gradually both lose part of their market shares to smaller and hitherto less successful competitors and/or own-label brands. We are thus dealing here with a defensive type of promotion, designed to maintain brand loyalty at all levels of the marketing process. Measuring sales attainment after each campaign or even at the end of the year is not a valid yardstick of advertising effectiveness. The advertiser's objectives must be clearly defined if the results are to be meaningfully measured; and the objectives here would be expressed in DAGMAR communication terms rather than in action terms.

A bank advertises the many services it is able to offer to the public. The advertisement is specially worded to appeal to young students – potential clientele for the bank: the bank considers that the student of today is the tycoon or the professional man of tomorrow. Here advertising fulfils a communication function in the sense that it attempts to create awareness of what the bank can offer; it can also improve the reader's attitude to banks, to bankers and to the advertiser. If the bank tried to judge the effectiveness of its advertising effort by counting how many students rushed to one of the bank's branches to open an account, it would be very disappointed; but in communication terms the advertisement may have attained significant results – another good example of a DAGMAR-based campaign.

A large electronics firm advertises in order to make the market generally aware that the company is in the electronics business; it wishes to convince people that this is a company capable of bringing out new or improved electronic products. Ideally the company would wish to create a level of awareness among readers which would result in their associating anything which is good in electronics with its name. This is a perfectly legitimate ambition, and it can be couched in measurable terms such as: 'We wish to raise awareness of Proposition A from its present level of 20% of our target group to an appreciably higher level'. DAGMAR once again.

A synthetic fibre manufacturer runs a very substantial campaign emphasizing the excellent qualities of the product incorporated in finished garments which the firm does not manufacture itself. It is inconceivable that readers will respond by dashing out to the nearest store and buying the garment made from this wonder fibre; so it is pointless to measure the effectiveness of such a campaign in action terms. Underlying the campaign may be this type of 'advertising by objectives' reasoning:

(a) 'We recognise that our product is in no way superior to that of our major competitors.'

(b) 'Our major strength is the fact that our range of colours and textures is modern in appearance and conforms to the taste of a specific market segment' (the segment, or the target group, being clearly defined).

(c) 'We therefore wish to communicate this message to the market with the view of increasing the level of awareness among the following groups:

(i) *Customers*   Here we wish to increase the level of awareness of our brand and its attributes from its present level, which is known to us, by 20%.

(ii) *Manufacturers of finished garments*   Here we wish to increase the level of awareness of our special range of colours from its present level by 40%.

(iii) *Members of the channels of distribution*   Here we wish to increase the level of awareness of the fact that our brand is synonymous with fashionable colours from the present level by 25%.'

These are clear, simple and measurable communication objectives which support the DAGMAR theory.

On the other hand, a mail order firm advertises a special offer. A coupon is provided at the bottom of the advertisement soliciting orders accompanied by a remittance. It would be impossible to find a simpler example of advertising effort that can be measured in action terms: the larger the number of responses, the more successful the campaign.

All these examples have been taken at random from recent advertisements appearing in well known media; they show clearly that while sometimes advertising can and should be measured in terms of sales achieved, there are other occasions when communication objectives are more relevant. The DAGMAR versus SALES controversy is futile: each situation should be taken on its merits. Whichever way one looks at it – in action terms or communication terms – clearly defined objectives are needed, and their attainment can be measured. Conceptual controversy as to what advertising is all about in no way detracts from the basic fact that an effective advertising effort needs pre-set goals.

An 'advertising by objectives' approach can yield considerable benefits. The following are, briefly, some of the specific advantages:

(a) It helps to integrate the advertising effort with the other ingredients of the 'marketing mix', thus setting a consistent and logical marketing plan. In the absence of advertising objectives there is every danger that the advertising appropriation will fail to maximise the contribution of advertising to the marketing effort. The mental exercise of preparing objectives and reducing them to a written form is in itself effective stimulus to the clear thinking and consistent reasoning which are so badly needed in any planning task.

(b) It facilitates the task of the advertising agency in (i) preparing and evaluating creative work and (ii) recommending the most suitable media. The chances of an advertising agency performing successfully in both creative work and media selection are greatly enhanced when a well formulated set of objectives is presented. These objectives can, of course, be formulated with the agency's help, but it is neither wise nor fair to leave the setting of advertising objectives entirely to the agency. To do so resembles leaving the selection of your meal to the chef or the head waiter; it can be done, but there is no guarantee of satisfaction.

(c) It assists in determining advertising budgets. It is easier to decide upon an appropriate budget with a specific task in view: without objectives the determination of budgets is a highly pragmatic affair.

(d) It enables marketing executives and top management to appraise the advertising plan realistically and approve or disapprove. It facilitates the control of advertising expenditure: in the absence of such control criteria, top management tends to be suspicious of the validity of the advertising effort and often presses for drastic cuts, especially during cost-reduction drives.

(e) It permits meaningful measurement of advertising results. This is probably one of the greatest benefits of the 'advertising by objectives' approach. This aspect alone can justify the time and effort spent on formulating the objectives of a company's advertising effort in general and of a specific campaign in particular. The reward stemming from performance measurement cannot be over-emphasized.

Before any useful work on setting advertising objectives can begin, all relevant information on the product, the market and the consumer must be available. Of prime importance is a thorough assessment of consumer behaviour and motivation, with particular reference to the company's target group. A full appreciation of the overall marketing plan and its objectives is an essential part of input information. The advertising planner can now consider which of the marketing objectives can best be achieved through advertising. 'Best' here implies a combination of effectiveness and minimum cost. Advertising objectives can then be formulated and should be consistent with the overall marketing objectives and with the objectives of the other ingredients of the marketing mix.

Whenever possible they should be expressed in quantitative terms: for communication objectives, clearly defined and accurate 'benchmark' bases should be incorporated in the plan. (If an increase in 'awareness' from 20% to 50% is sought, and the basic 20% figure is suspect, the whole exercise could be futile.) The help of the company's advertising agency in the important task of formulating objectives can be called for; whether this is done depends on the experience and degree of sophistication of the company.

A detailed plan can now be prepared to show how the objectives can be attained. It will incorporate details such as (a) budgets (funds required to attain the set task); (b) the message; (c) media selection; (d) scheduling. The next step is to obtain management approval. This will be more readily provided if evidence can be produced to show that the hypotheses put forward in the plan are tenable. Successful pre-testing of an advertisement (both as to message and media) and a favourable response from a representative sample of the target group are useful proofs that the plan is soundly conceived and structured. With the campaign under way, with the budget being spent, with objectives clearly defined – whenever possible in quantitative terms – the company can measure results and evaluate the performance of the advertising plan. This is not always simple; there can be difficulties in finding a representative sample of the target audience; the cost of evaluation can turn out to be excessive. Yet without objectives there cannot be so much as an attempt to measure results.

An example of the 'advertising by objectives' approach at work comes from the Common Market. A Continental domestic appliance manufacturer recently added a novel type of hair-drier to his range. The marketing department collected a wealth of information about the market and the potential customers. The marketing plan envisaged a market share of 7% within three years, with the upper middle class segment as a target group. Successful launching of this new product depended, according to the marketing plan, on the following conditions: (a) that 30% of the target group should become aware of the existence of this hair-drier and of its novel properties; (b) that a strong association should be found in the mind of those becoming 'aware' that this hair-drier was the product of this acknowledged leading manufacturer of top-class appliances; (c) that there should be effective communication with the target segment of the outlets where the drier could be seen and purchased; (d) that encouragement should be provided to the stores selected as distributors to stock the new product and display it conspicuously.

The advertising manager realised that the main brunt of achieving the above aims would fall on his shoulders; he studied the information available and translated it into a plan which set out the following objectives:

(a) To create among our 'well defined target group' an awareness (currently nil awareness) of the following: (i)   availability of new hair-drier – 30% awareness at the end of the campaign; (ii)   the brand – 30% awareness; (iii)   special features of the product – 20% awareness; (iv)   stores where available – 20%.

(b) To generate enough interest among the target audience to produce further enquiries about the new product, either directly or through appointed distributors. The objective is to stimulate 5000 direct enquiries and 10 000 enquiries through distributors. The plan is that attractive brochures will be available to those showing interest.

(c) To instil in the mind of the target audience a strong link between the new brand and the company's corporate image – 60% of those 'made aware'.

The advertising manager could now work out his plan and the budget required to reach his basic objectives. To eliminate residual doubts he was in a position to pre-test his plan, trying out both message quality and media effectiveness. Following the campaign he was in a strong position to evaluate the results of his department's work in relation to the campaign. He knew what the advertising objectives were and thus could measure the extent to which they were achieved. He could further measure the contribution of his work and effort to achieving the marketing objectives and hence the firm's overall objectives.

In this way the 'advertising by objectives' approach can be a valuable tool in the effort to cut the waste out of advertising. It can help companies to obtain better results from their advertising effort, often at lower costs. It can go a long way towards making the effectiveness of advertising measurable – and that in itself is an aid to, as well as a consequence of, better management.

12
The Application of the 'Business Portfolio' Concept to Marketing Decisions

One of the problems that has always confronted corporate and marketing planners is the task of deciding on an optimum product mix in relation to the firm's inventory of resources, strengths and weaknesses. One fairly simple methodology is the use of the 'Pareto curve' which seeks to identify the 20% of the firm's products which may yield 80% of the company's sales or profits or some other criterion of success. The logic of such an analysis is simple: if we can determine which are the company's breadwinners as represented by results, we should know in which area of our activities to invest more resources, both human and material. The so-called 20:80 rule, with all its simplicity, gave planners an opportunity to measure the relative performance of the product range and determine the 'star' products on the one hand and the 'troublesome' products at the other extreme.

The value of Pareto analysis has proved limited in so far as it has lacked the dynamism which the planning process requires. It enables us to measure the relative performance of products or sales territories or fields of activity *as they stand today*. It does not tell us what may happen in the future. Essentially it is a diagnostic tool which assists us in placing activities in their proper performance slot. Many firms have abused the value of this tool by using it as an instrument of decision making. The planner who decides to drop all those products which fall at the bottom of the Pareto curve, namely the last 20% that generate a minuscule level of return may well run the risk of obliterating the only bit of profit that the firm has ever achieved. Obviously such a situation is not healthy, but the fact still remains that some firms achieve an overall break-even point with 80% of their products and the minute profits produced by the 'troublesome' 20% represent the only bit of profit that the firm achieves above its break-even level. Furthermore, the planner who takes a radical decision to drop all the 'troublesome' products is left with 80% of the range. If he continues to apply the Pareto curve and continues to drop the bottom 20%, he will gradually have a range which vanishes into statistical oblivion.

The other problem confronting the planner is the fact that the analysis of performance can only tell him what the firm achieved in the past. In reality the past has no bearing on the future. The only relevance of past data and its analysis is the diagnostic statement that, if the firm managed to achieve certain levels of results and performance in the past, there is a level of probability that similar attainments could be reached in the future. This is the only reason why planners analyse the past. However, when one reflects upon this statement one soon realises that it contains serious elements of danger. The change in the commercial and technological environments may be such that the picture presented by the past is totally misleading. In fact some of the products in the 'star' category may move into the 'troublesome' category and vice versa.

At this point the planning philosophy has directed us towards the task of trying to match existing fields of activity and their relative results to a fundamental assessment of future environmental opportunities and/or threats. In other words the process entails matching highly quantifiable and diagnostic measurements to futuristic and sometimes controversial forecasts.

The 'Boston Effect'

An exciting tool emerged a few years ago as a result of work carried out by the Boston Consulting Group. This tool started its life as the 'Boston effect' and it is probably better known nowadays as the 'product portfolio' or more broadly the 'business portfolio'. Like most effective tools of management it is a very logical and simple concept to apply. In analysing the relative performance of clients' products and activities mix the Boston Consulting Group sought to categorise such products into four groups, as described in Figure 12.1.

Each quadrant of Figure 12.1 represents the relationship between the *market share* that the product and/or activity has achieved and the

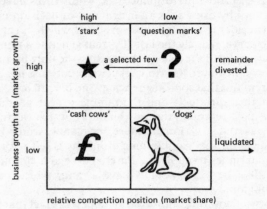

Figure 12.1   The business portfolio or growth-share matrix.

market growth rate that the market itself enjoys. For convenience the market share level has been divided into 'high' and 'low' and so has the market growth rate. The theory is that most products and/or activities are capable of being slotted into one of the four boxes depending on their performance in the marketplace vis-à-vis the behaviour of the marketplace itself. Obviously the basic concept is simplistic in the extreme. However, it does not need too much imagination to perceive that when designating the terms 'high' and 'low' one can ascribe well defined and highly quantifiable criteria to each of the dimensions. Thus 'low' market share may be defined as 'less than 10%' and 'high' a figure in excess thereof. Once again 'low growth ratio' can be defined as 'up to 10% growth per annum' and 'high' as a figure in excess of 10%.

Thus the four quadrants that emerge are *'high/high'*, indicating products enjoying a high market share in a high market growth business; *'high'/'low'*, namely a situation where a high market share exists in a low growth market; *'low'/'high'*, where the market share is low but the market is growing fairly fast; and *'low'/'low'*, when both the market share and the market growth are low. This is all a bit of a mouthful. For ease of communication quaint titles were given to the four groups: *'stars'* for the *'high'/'high'* category; *'cash cows'* for the *'high'/'low'* category; *'dogs'* for the *'low'/'low'* category; and *'question marks'* for the *'low'/'high'* category. Other descriptive titles were given to the last-mentioned quadrant, such as 'problem children' and 'wildcats'. For the purpose of this chapter we shall stick to the title 'question marks'.

The four categories can now be described in greater detail.

'Stars' are relatively new products and are often in the growth phase of the product life cycle. They are enjoying high shares of the markets in which they operate. Obviously they represent precious opportunities for their companies and need to be looked after with attention and skill. They are today's breadwinners. At the same time one must recognise that they may require heavy investment in order to ensure that the high share so far attained in a growing market is maintained.

'Cash cows' are the products that have achieved high market shares but in markets that have ceased to grow. They are often the successful 'stars' of yesteryear. Most probably they have reached the maturity phase and by and large they require limited investment and financial support. On the other hand the 'cash cows' are very useful generators of cash, hence the title.

'Question marks' refers to products under the disadvantage of low market share yet operating in growth markets. They may be former 'stars' whose position has been eroded or products that simply have failed to maintain their share of the market in order to preserve their 'star' status. They offer useful potential for exploitation but require the addition of funds as well as marketing talent before they can enter or re-enter the desired quadrant, namely become a 'star'.

'Dogs' labour under a dual disadvantage: not only do they have a low

market share but they also suffer from the fact that they operate in low growth markets. Prospects are on the whole poor and a strong case for divestment exists. On the other hand, if properly managed, and with a suitable level of austerity, they may be able to generate a positive cash flow whilst they are kept in the firm.

The tool is simple and extremely helpful, especially in complex multiproduct and multimarket environments. It enables the planner to slot the myriad of products, activities and subsidiaries into four distinct pigeon holes, each of which has different managerial, marketing and financial prospects. Such a categorisation can be dovetailed into every aspect of the planning process. Thus manpower planning can benefit from this kind of analysis in so far as one can match individual talents to the specific needs of every unit. The person who is best suited to run a 'cow' is not necessarily the most competent individual to run a 'question mark'. The former must be a manager who can run a tight ship in the most cost-effective manner. The latter must be a highly creative and experienced marketer with strong diagnostic and analytical skills!

Similarly, the planner can use this approach for calculating and evaluating cash flow levels of products falling into each of the quadrants. The aim must be to divert cash from areas that enjoy a short term flow to

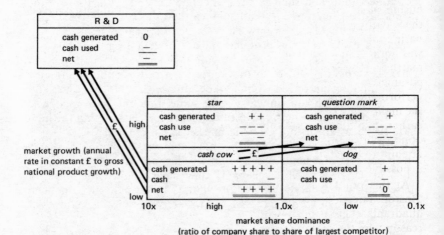

Figure 12.2 Cash flow management. The number of plus signs indicates the level of cash flow; the number of minus signs indicates the level of cash need and/or use. There is a major cash flow from 'cash cows' into R & D in order to improve the product mix and there is a secondary cash flow diverted into 'question marks' to maintain or revive some of these products. (Adapted from G. S. Day, 'Diagnosing the product portfolio', *Journal of Marketing,* April 1977.)

those that can yield longer term prospects of success. Figure 12.2 illustrates an imaginative approach to the cash flow management of products in the portfolio. It is based on the assumption that 'cash cows' are the vital sources of short term cash flow whereas 'stars' are cash hungry. 'Question marks' generate little or no cash, but their cash needs are high, especially if a higher market share is aspired towards. The planner can attempt to calculate and quantify the cash that can be diverted from one quadrant to another. Cash picked up from the 'cash cows' can go into research and development in order to improve the product mix and also to endeavour to ameliorate the market share of the 'question marks'. The whole idea is based on the need to identify the sources of cash on the one hand and the best recipients of that cash on the other. After all, this is the essence of good planning, and the 'business portfolio' approach helps to reflect upon the appropriate options open to the strategist.

The Application of the 'Portfolio' Concept to Marketing Decisions

The 'product portfolio' concept has triggered the imagination of businessmen, consultants and academics alike. In its simplicity it paved the way for a host of modifications, extensions and developments. The basic concept sought to match two dimensions on a matrix. In fact there was nothing new about analysing complex problems through the use of matrices. However, the elegance of the 'Boston effect' was in the way two parameters were chosen: one internal to the firm, namely its own performance, and one external, namely the marketplace itself. This is the main value of the whole concept to the planning process. As stated earlier, planning means the matching of one's own resources to the opportunities offered by the marketplace. In other words one must attempt to dovetail internal resources and capabilities to perceived and if possible quantified openings in the market.

At this point it is important to emphasise that whilst the original 'Boston effect' approach sought to divide the portfolio into four quadrants, there is nothing sacrosanct about that division. There is no reason why the matrix cannot be divided into nine or sixteen or even more 'pigeon holes'. Moreover, whilst the original concept attempted to match market share with market growth rate there is no reason for not attempting to match other disparate dimensions.

A number of examples will help to demonstrate the large number of areas in which a modified version of the 'business portfolio' approach can be applied. The only limit to the number of permutations open to the marketer is probably the fertility of his own creative mind.

CASE 1: INTERNATIONAL MARKETING AND THE 'BUSINESS PORTFOLIO'

A firm wishes to market a new and sophisticated electric shaver on an international scale. It realises that it would be too ambitious a task to attempt to sell the product in all countries. It therefore seeks to identify the most promising countries in which to develop its international presence.

As a first phase an arbitrary decision is taken to restrict the firm's marketing objectives to countries that enjoy a *per capita* income' in excess of $2000. It is recognised that the product, being a luxury item, is more likely to attain a penetration in countries that enjoy a certain standard of living. Thus one can narrow the field of concentration into a more manageable catchment portion of the world.

Now comes the big problem: having identified a few score countries that fall into the desired 'typology' one must accept that some or many of them are not necessarily the most suitable opportunities for the marketing company in question. 'Country A' may rank very high on the *per capita* income' league and also have a high population. Yet the same country may rank as a poor opportunity for our specific marketer owing to an inherent weakness in the firm's structure or capabilities vis-à-vis that country. The firm's image there may be an insurmountable barrier to market penetration or the firm may lack the experience to manage the intricate, local distribution structure. On the other hand, 'country B', which appears to be a less attractive market, may prove a lot more compatible with the organisation's skills and strengths. The ideal target market is of course the one which offers the highest objective and quantitative opportunity coupled with the highest compatibility with the marketing company's specific strengths and capabilities.

A modified version of the 'Business Portfolio' concept can be a most valuable aid to a structured screening effort. All one has to do is design a matrix with two dimensions:

(a) *The countries explored*   We can divide countries by their level of commercial attractiveness into three groups: 'high', 'medium' and 'low'. Each of these terms can be supported by measurable criteria encompassing such items as population size, economic development, stability, level of industrialisation, consumer habits, local competition, etc. All these are facts which can be quantified.

(b) *The firm's compatibility with each country*   This is an internal assessment of the firm's own inventory of strengths and weaknesses vis-à-vis each country in the short-list assembled during the earlier phase. Once again 'high', 'medium' and 'low' can describe the firm's perceived compatibility in relation to each country.

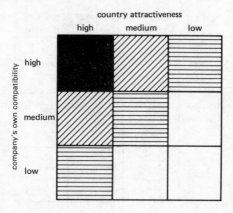

Figure 12.3 Choice of country. Black area indicates primary opportunity; diagonally hatched areas indicate secondary opportunities; horizontally hatched areas indicate tertiary opportunities; blank areas indicate countries to be avoided.

A 'box' with nine 'pigeon holes', as described in Figure 12.3, has thus been established. The marketer can now pursue the discipline of analysing the data available to him and slot every country into its appropriate box by comparing the opportunity identified to the firm's own ability to penetrate that country. At the end of the exercise he should have a pretty shrewd idea as to which are the 'primary', 'secondary' and 'tertiary' opportunity countries to go for. It is a far cry from the Boston approach. Nonetheless, some recognition of parentage can be perceived.

CASE 2: 'BUSINESS PORTFOLIO' IN CORPORATE PLANNING

An ingenious evolution of the 'Boston effect' can be detected in the so-called 'directional policy matrix' used in the Shell organisation. The purpose of this matrix is to identify the most interesting areas in which the firm should invest additional resources and those areas which ought to be considered for a policy of divestment.

Two parameters are selected for study:

(a) The commercial and marketing attractiveness of the various industrial sectors in which the firm is operating. These are of course commercial facts capable of measurement.
(b) The firm's own competitive capability.

The former, (a), is divided into three sectors: *attractive, average* and *unattractive*. The latter, (b), is divided into *strong, average* and *weak*.

prospects for sector profitability

		unattractive	average	attractive
company's competitive capabilities	weak	disinvest	phased withdrawal/ custodial	double or quit
	average	phased withdrawal	custodial/ growth	avis
	strong	cash generator	growth/ leader	leader

Figure 12.4   Directional policy matrix.

The combination of the two axes gives the planners nine areas for analysis and strategic consideration. Succinct titles were given to each of the 'pigeon holes', as shown in Figure 12.4. 'Leader' is self-explanatory; 'Avis' stands for a sector in which the firm appears to be 'second, but is trying harder', etc. Once the management accepts the terminology and understands the full implications the tool gradually becomes extremely meaningful within the planning process. The manager of a 'cash generator' should understand the financial, marketing, and managerial implications as much as the manager of a 'cash cow' in a Boston-orientated firm does.

This particular case helps to illustrate how flexible the tool can be. Instead of four boxes we have nine. The direction of the axes is reversed from the conventional Boston approach and the titles totally changed albeit equally quaint. 'Leader' means 'star'; 'disinvest' means 'dog'; and so on. Why not?

CASE 3: A SALES AID FOR A TRANSPORT COMPANY

A large road haulage company has come to realise that in the context of its operations there are some cargoes which are more cost-beneficial than others. For many years the company has been offering an 'undifferentiated' product in the sense that it consented to carry all cargoes irrespective of their nature. A new marketing manager took the view that it should be possible to run a much more profitable and effective operation by concentrating the firm's marketing and selling activities upon a range of cargoes capable of utilising the firm's capacity, as far as it was possible, to the optimum. Thus the underlying objective was to determine what would constitute an optimum 'cargo mix'.

Moreover, the marketing manager felt that the outcome of such an analysis could form the basis of an excellent sales aid. If salesmen could be provided with a 'hit parade' list of cargoes in a descending scale of 'desirability' it would enable them to decide how much sales effort was justified vis-à-vis each prospect. Cargoes at the top of the 'hit parade' would be worth fighting for; those at the bottom should be avoided like the plague. That is an ideal 'sales aid'.

At the same time the marketing manager realised that a cargo which was generally attractive to the transport industry was not necessarily the most suitable for his own firm's capacity due to vehicle configuration, route structuring and depot location.

A simple screening device was compiled with the view of matching (a) cargoes and their commercial attractiveness, and (b) the firm's own infrastructural characteristics and needs.

Figure 12.5 illustrates the results of the study and the numerical quantification ascribed to each cargo analysed. Salesmen knew that cargoes marked with a '9' (3×3) were the 'star' cargoes and that those marked with a '1' (1×1) were the 'dogs'.

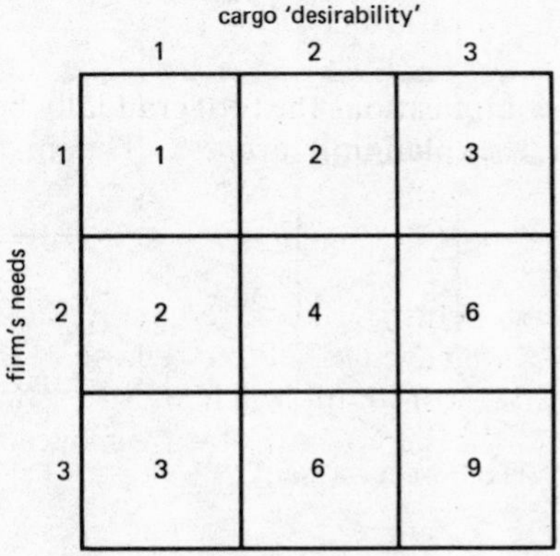

cargo 'desirability'

	1	2	3
1	1	2	3
2	2	4	6
3	3	6	9

(firm's needs — vertical axis label)

Figure 12.5 Cargo analysis. Under the heading of cargo 'desirability': 1 = low; 2 = medium; 3 = high. Under the heading of firm's needs; 1 = low; 2 = medium; 3 = high. As regards the cargoes themselves: 9 = perfect; 6 = very good; 4 = average; 3 = make weight only; 2 = last resort; 1 = avoid at all costs.

CASE 4: BRANCH SELECTION FOR A BANK

A bank with many thousands of retail outlets wishes to design screening criteria for (a) selecting new branches, and (b) identifying branches for amalgamation, running down and/or closure.

The success of a branch normally depends on the combination of two factors: (a) the size and characteristics of the catchment market and (b) the bank's own ability to provide a service compatible with the needs of the target market thus defined. The former includes such elements as the size of the market, its socio-economic and demographic nature, and the level of business and commercial activity in the area. The last-mentioned item encompasses the expertise and personal resources available to the branch, the bank's image, and of course the bank's own objectives and aspirations. The ideal location is the one that offers a sizeable market and which corresponds highly to the bank's aspirations and capabilities. Both are capable of quantification and screening.

Figure 12.6 shows the kind of matrix that emerged after considerable external study as well as internal self-flagellation.

The main aim was to identify the 'high-flyers'. The tool was very successful in helping to achieve this objective.

THE MARKETPLACE

		high	medium	low
bank's aspirations and capabilities	high	'high—flyers'	possibles	?
	medium	possibles	?	'dead loss'
	low	?	'dead loss'	'dead loss'

Figure 12.6   Branch selection for a bank.

CASE 5: 'CREATIVITY' AND THE 'PORTFOLIO' CONCEPT

This may sound like the ultimate abuse of the 'business portfolio' concept! Yet it is a good example of how simple the whole device is in spite of its fancy titles and sophisticated origins.

In my own activity as an organiser of creative sessions for clients with the objective of developing new products and/or new ways to market products in difficult environments I resort to traditional techniques such as 'brainstorming', 'synectics' and 'morphological analysis'. The essence of these techniques is that one seeks to generate a large quantity of ideas. In the early stages of the creative process one looks for quantity of ideas rather than quality. One of the fundamental conditions of a successful creative session is that judgement is suspended and that every idea, however bizarre, is recorded on the list of ideas to be screened at the next step.

The next stage of the process is the very laborious task of screening all the ideas assembled with the view of identifying those which deserve further in-depth study. This phase of work can be very tedious and I have encountered many participants on such sessions giving up the whole exercise in despair. The trouble is that the more prolific the group the more ideas emerge and the larger the number of ideas the more difficult it becomes to screen them in a systematic and intelligent way.

The 'business portfolio' approach provided us with the kind of tool we desperately needed. In screening ideas we recognised that the attractiveness of an idea was not enough. The idea, however original and exciting, must be compatible with the firm's own resources, constraints and objectives. An idea can be excellent, but if it offends the firm's image and perceived standing in the market it has to be rejected. Similarly a good idea may have to be rejected if it is incompatible with a code of practice laid down by the firm's professional affiliation. Thus we have two dimensions to be matched: (a) the idea itself, its originality and attractiveness; (b) the firm's own objectives and its ability to cope with the idea in question – let us call it 'compatibility'.

Obviously the former must be judged on its commercial merits independently of the firm's internal constraints; the latter must be appraised on the basis of internal assessment of what is right and what is wrong for the company itself. This is a very useful exercise that can be conducted by a committee. Ideally it should be a different group from the one that generated the list of ideas in the first place. Nonetheless, the

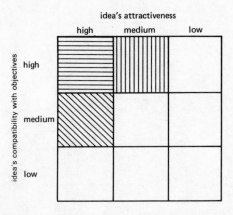

Figure 12.7 Creativity and the business portfolio concept. Horizontally hatched area indicates an excellent idea compatible with stated objectives and needs; vertically hatched area indicates a fairly good idea compatible with stated objectives and needs; diagonally hatched area indicates a fair idea only partially compatible with stated objectives and needs.

group must consist of managers who are capable of giving every idea the benefit of the doubt before deciding to reject it!

Figure 12.7 illustrates the kind of matrix that we use on such occasions.

PART IV

Marketing in Service Industries

13
Transport Needs Marketing

'Marketing is a useful concept for firms manufacturing consumer or industrial goods. It is inappropriate to enterprises operating a service such as transport or distribution.'

This is the kind of statement which is often echoed in the corridors of companies whose main business is to provide a logistics service. The idea that the marketing concept applies only to those firms that have a physical product to offer is indeed slow to die.

While everybody acknowledges that a firm producing detergents needs to apply the marketing concept with all its rigours, one tends to feel that a company running a fleet of lorries carrying produce can do so without applying any marketing principles. Somehow there must be a flaw in the thinking that leads to such an idea. In fact, it may be a partial explanation for the high rate of failure that one encounters among firms operating in transport and distribution – the inability to achieve a fair return on the capital involved rather than absolute profitability. In the field of transport it is inevitable that one must talk in terms of returns in so far as this is such a capital-intensive industry. Furthermore, as we shall see later, if one acknowledges that the concept of product life applies also to the 'service life cycle' in the field of transport and distribution, it is essential that one plans one's service in such a way that the capital invested in a new service is recovered during the life of such a service. If one wishes to plan in terms of profitability, it is the aggregate profit over the life of the product that matters and not just profitability over individual years. The marketing implications of such a notion are quite far-reaching. The marketing function is normally entrusted with the task of planning products or services capable of earning sufficient funds within the firm's overall objectives. In most cases this would mean that by the time the service has to be dropped or modified, the full investment therein must be fully recovered and on top of it an adequate return must be shown. If this is the task of marketing, it is difficult to argue with the need to have a sound marketing function.

The purpose of this chapter is to emphasise the importance of a sound marketing approach to organisations in the business of 'generating the utility of time, the utility of place and the utility of convenience' for its customers. The creation of these utilities is what transport and distribution services are all about.

One of the weaknesses of marketing is the difficulty in defining the meaning of the word in such a way that no doubts, confusion or ambiguities can arise from the definition itself. A large number of definitions have emerged since the so-called marketing concept first saw daylight in the mid-1950s. Most of the definitions that have been propounded over the years tend to confuse rather than elucidate the real meaning of the term.

The most practical definition suggests that marketing is *the process whereby the firm, in whichever sphere of activity it happens to operate, seeks to identify, quantify and anticipate the needs of its markets (present and potential) and take the necessary steps for satisfying such needs.* Whilst undertaking this task, one must remember that the whole purpose of the effort is to help the firm to meet its corporate objectives. These may be expressed in financial terms or in some other less quantifiable criteria.

A Checklist

At this point, most businessmen would retort that this is precisely what they normally do. They would claim that there is nothing new in this philosophy and belabouring the point is an utter waste of time. The following checklist might convince the doubters that the idea expressed, albeit simple in the extreme, is worth pursuing:

- Are you able to state with some accuracy what your market share is in each segment in which you operate?
  Yes/No
- Do you know why your customers use your service in preference to competitive products?
  Yes/No
- Are you able to assess how many more years your product or service is likely to last?
  Yes/No
- Do you know what level of satisfaction exists among your customers?
  Yes/No
- Do you know the price elasticity of your service?
  Yes/No
- Are you sure that your sales force is adequate?
  Yes/No
- Do your salesmen cover the best opportunity areas?
  Yes/No
- Do you know how many potential users of your service are aware of your existence and the type of service you offer?
  Yes/No
- Do you promote your service by objectives?
  Yes/No

- If yes, are you able to say how effective your promotional effort has been?
  Yes/No
- Do you experiment with new ideas which might help you to improve the service and level of satisfaction of your market?
  Yes/No
- Do you control your marketing effort in such a way as to learn what to do or not to do in the future?
  Yes/No

A manager in the field of transport and distribution who is able to answer all these questions with 'Yes' is probably in possession of most of the marketing inputs that a firm requires and need not continue to read this chapter unless he feels that it would be useful to be reminded of his personal virtuosity!

The Marketing Mix

The 'marketing mix' is a concept that is well understood among marketing personnel of any company operating in consumer goods. It is less well understood among managers of industrial products firms. Managers of transport and distribution organisations often ignore its existence.

The marketing mix is based on the notion that consumer satisfaction, being the underlying purpose of the function, can be achieved through the integration of a number of variables. It is the judicious and well balanced mixing of these variables which in the ultimate would achieve

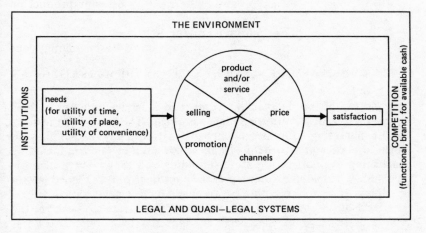

Figure 13.1 The marketing mix within the marketing environment.

maximum consumer satisfaction. The mix differs from industry to industry, from company to company, and quite often during the life of the product. Furthermore, the marketing mix must take full cognisance of the major environmental dimensions that prevail in the marketplace. This latter point adds a dynamic flavour to the marketing mix in so far as it has to be changed from time to time in response to new factors in the marketing scene.

Figure 13.1 describes the marketing mix variables in relation to the external and uncontrollable marketing environment. For the purpose of this paper the mix is being portrayed in the context of the transport and distribution industry. Thus, instead of talking in terms of product, price, distribution, promotion and selling, which are the variables applicable to the marketing of consumer goods, the diagram refers to the product and/or service, price, channels, promotion and selling. The difference is probably more semantic in nature than substantive, but nonetheless helps to make the concept acceptable to an industry that can seldom identify the product in such a term.

The significance of Figure 13.1 is that a well planned marketing effort is based on the development of a marketing mix which will be satisfactory to the customer in all its variables. Thus, if the level of service is fully acceptable but the price is wrong, the mix will not achieve consumer satisfaction. Similarly a mix which is perfect in every respect except in its promotional effort cannot be classified as a satisfactory mix. Mixing the perfect mix is the art of marketing, and the manager who has developed that skill is worth his weight in gold.

In the next few sections every ingredient of the mix will be explored in turn, with a view to highlighting a number of issues of importance which a successful marketing effort in the transport and distribution sector envisages.

The Product and/or Service

THE PRODUCT AND/OR SERVICE AS SEEN BY THE MARKETING MAN

The notion of 'product' in the context of a service industry such as transport and distribution presents a problem. The product is the heart of the marketing effort in any enterprise. It normally takes a physical form, a cluster of well defined and visible utilities of form including packaging, supportive literature, branding and so on. The product is touchable, visible and kickable. If the consumer is not satisfied he can complain and, it is to be hoped, receive a replacement. Satisfaction is derived from a spectrum of features, most of which are physical, and the whole assemblage of 'satisfiers' is supported by a number of less physical attributes such as reliability, convenience, etc. Even these attributes have physical undertones in so far as failure manifests itself in the product not performing as it should. Thus a television set would meet the customer's expectations by being of a certain size, having a pleasing design, possessing control buttons that are easy to manipulate; all these are physical characteristics. At the same time the consumer would prefer a product known for its reliability and durability – these are less physical, but nonetheless failure of any of these would soon manifest itself in a physical inconvenience to the consumer.

The 'product' in the case of transport and distribution activities normally has no shape and no utility of form. The shape and colour of a distribution vehicle in which goods are being transported from the Midlands to Scotland is of little or no relevance to the customer; neither is the speed at which the vehicle travels; nor the quality of petrol or fuel that propels the engine. What is of importance is the timing of departure and estimated time of arrival coupled with a fair certainty that the goods will arrive at their destination in one piece. The product in such circumstances is certainly not the vehicle itself.

Similarly, when a holidaymaker talks about crossing the Channel with his car he normally knows that he has a number of options: crossing by ferry, hovercraft or air ferry. In marketing terms the vehicle upon which the car is ferried across the channel is quite immaterial. All three options perform the same task. All three produce the same cluster of utilities: *utility of place*, viz. getting the car and its passengers safely across an awkward route interruption; *utility of time*, viz. allowing the car's passengers to get across at speed and at a time of their choice; and *utility of convenience,* viz. crossing the Channel in relative comfort and convenience. The product is therefore basically the same – it is the respective attractiveness of the various utilities which would make one option more acceptable to one consumer as against the other.

This is a vitally important concept to a person operating in transport and distribution. The product is not the technology or the infrastructure used in meeting market needs. The product is what the service purports to achieve in terms of the various utilities – time, place and convenience. By this token a *9 a.m. flight from Heathrow to New York, leaving daily and punctually, offering an efficient and courteous service and in an aircraft belonging to an airline with an excellent safety record* is the product. The fact that the plane is a Boeing 747 belonging to British Airways is as irrelevant as the fact that Schweppes Bitter Lemon is packed in a glass bottle made by United Glass. To the Boeing Corporation, the Boeing 747 is a product; to British Airways the aircraft is a container for ferrying passengers and goods at speed over long distances and in relative comfort at maximum safety and economy.

Every marketer in the transport and distribution sector must therefore define his product objectives with great clarity, and these must be consistent with the marketing goals underlying the firm's activities. This must always be done with an eye to meeting the main task, namely satisfying consumer needs rather than meeting operational and production demands. This statement sounds simple in the extreme. However, in practical terms, it is not always easy to dissociate one's thinking from the infrastructural tradition of the firm. Hence, a railwayman tends to think in terms of trains, a road haulage man in terms of lorries, and a shipping man in terms of ships. If the marketing concept were to penetrate the firm's culture in depth, these managers would automatically think in terms of the markets and segments they service. This is fundamental to a marketing-orientated philosophy; it is easy to propound in a brief chapter – it is difficult to implement in the rugged realities of the transport and distribution world.

The following examples help to emphasise the point:

(a) 'Transporting gas from a gas field to a bulk terminal' is a product.
(b) 'Transporting gas from a terminal to a filling depot' is another product.

The facilities used are probably identical; nonetheless, the products are different.

Similarly, 'distributing fresh produce on a daily basis to supermarkets' is a totally different product from 'delivering produce to primary markets'. Once again, the vehicles used may be the same; the 'products' are totally different.

On this basis an airline will find that it offers a very large range of products within a set of corporate and marketing objectives. Every route and every departure time constitute a clearly defined service or product. Each such product has its own life cycle and performance levels. Indeed, the plane that leaves Heathrow (No. 1 Building) for Orly Airport at 9 a.m. is a different product from the flight that leaves Gatwick at 10 a.m. for Charles de Gaulle Airport. In marketing terms, each of these flights would meet the needs of different target groups and each flight is capable of being measured not only in accordance with the level of satisfaction it generates but also in terms of the resources used. A good marketer always tries to identify the characteristic of the consumers that he seeks to satisfy before he actually designs a product or service. In this instance, the service is expressed in the airline's timetable and concomitant conditions.

In our example the situation is further complicated in so far as the 9 a.m. flight from Heathrow to Orly may have two subsegments: those who travel by First Class and those who prefer the cheaper Economy Class. It needs very little common sense to know that if the First Class is always empty and the Economy Class is always full on this particular flight, somebody has made a marketing mistake at the planning stage.

In summary, the products that one should be talking about in the transport and distribution sector often get overlooked because of the capital intensity of the infrastructure itself. The products are the various levels of service that the firm renders, thus satisfying specific needs through the creation of the utilities of place, time and convenience.

In other words, the range of products or services that a company in the transport and distribution sector offers is far greater than its physical facilities indicate. Indeed, it is a very useful exercise for a firm in this field to break down its existing markets and sub-markets in relation to the kind of service it is capable of rendering. It is a useful way of seeking to identify the really valuable opportunities – the 20% of the products that are capable of yielding the 80% of the revenue or profit.

THE PRODUCT AND/OR SERVICE LIFE CYCLE

The concept of product life cycle is well understood among marketers operating in consumer and industrial goods. It is not always appreciated that the theory applies also to the kind of product or service which is offered by companies in the transport and distribution sector. Thus, the road tanker has completely superseded the delivery of oil products in barrels. This means that one product has died and another product has replaced it. Similarly, the faster flight that the jet aircraft has brought about has superseded the piston aircraft service. Presumably, had the piston aircraft been capable of speeding up its performance to 600–650 miles per hour coupled with improved comfort, we would have been travelling in such planes even today. The technology has helped to improve the product of the airlines and by so doing has shortened the life cycle of the previous product of those airlines.

The product and/or service life cycle concept is described in Figure 13.2. Five stages normally occur over the life of the service:

(a) *Introduction* The service is introduced; level of awareness

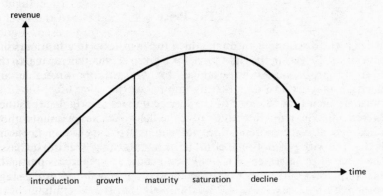

Figure 13.2 The product and/or service life cycle.

of its existence is low; rate of acceptance is nominal. Inevitably profitability is non-existent or low.

(b) *Growth* Service acceptance is rising through the results of the promotional effort; satisfied customers talk about the service in question, thus creating further demand.

(c) *Maturity* Revenue still grows but at a relatively reduced rate; penetration of market approaches optimum level; competition increases and places pressure on margins.

(d) *Saturation* Revenue reaches a peak and it is virtually impossible to go above that level. Pressure on margins becomes severe. Competition is heavy.

(e) *Decline* Revenue diminishes; newer and better services gradually oust the product from the marketplace.

The important aspect of the life cycle concept is the fact that in most cases peak profits are achieved well before the service has attained peak sales. This means that a company that fails to perceive that a product or service has a limited life may discover too late that the breadwinner has ceased to support the firm. This is where sound marketing planning can save the company from unexpected disasters.

Furthermore, it is also important to remember in this connection that the marketing function has the task of shifting the relative levels and emphasis given to the various ingredients of the marketing mix during different stages in the service life cycle. Persevering with the same mix throughout the life of the service is courting trouble. In this respect there is very little difference between the principles that one applies for marketing a motor car and marketing the Inter-City rail service. They both have a life cycle and they will both eventually disappear. Estimating their relative lives is the kind of challenge that the marketing personnel of both companies must face.

The Price

Price is the instrument through which the firm seeks to attain its profit objectives. Selecting the right price for a given service will mean that the ultimate profit might be attained. In contrast, the wrong pricing decision may lead to a marketing failure. At the same time, the price must be such that the user of the service derives the right satisfaction therefrom. The trouble with price is the fact that it is quantitative and unequivocal; once chosen it does not lend itself to easy manipulation, as is the case with promotional effort or personal selling. If a firm increases the number of salesmen, it is unlikely to cause any repercussions in the marketplace. On the other hand, a change in price, up or down, is there to be seen by everybody, and it is unlikely that the reaction to such a change will be a passive one.

Determining an appropriate price for one's service in the field of transport and distribution must be based on careful research and analysis. The following major pressures must be considered with some care: (a) competitive practices; (b) elasticity of demand; (c) influence of legal and quasi-legal constraints.

COMPETITION

The idea of competition in transport and distribution activities normally. assumes a wider meaning than in consumer and industrial goods. It encapsulates three possibilities:

(a) *Functional competition* Here one tries to identify the alternative services open to one's customers for attaining a certain functional aim. One must not lose sight of the fact that it is the creation of the utilities of time, place and convenience which is the underlying purpose of the service that one renders. Thus, in comparing the price of various alternatives available to the customer, the marketer must analyse the full cost–benefit relationship that the customer is likely to derive from each of these alternatives. If the product is the transporting of passengers from London to Liverpool, the functional options are (i) air travel; (ii) rail travel; (iii) bus; (iv) car. In each instance, one has to identify the additional costs that surround the use of each service, e.g. travel from the airport to the centre of the city, parking, meals during a long journey, etc. Until all the relevant factors have been identified and compared, the pricing decision is likely to be based on inadequate data.

(b) *Brand competition* Here the choice open to the service user is between two or more identical services. The traveller to New York can choose one of a number of identical products – nonetheless, he may choose the one rather than the other on the basis of non-price considerations. Some passengers prefer one airline to all others for no better reason than the quality of the cuisine they have managed to identify. Essentially this is the kind of brand loyalty that most airlines wish to develop, and it is not very different from what detergent manufacturers strive to achieve. The winner in the brand competition game is the one who manages to offer the most attractive and credible cluster of embellishments to the product known by marketers as USPs ('unique selling points'). Some of these USPs can be tangible, others intangible. In the transport business such items as punctuality, safety record, smiling conductors or drivers can prove to be vital ingredients in the competitive arena.

(c) *The disposable cash competition* Under this heading, the competition is focused on the cash available to the consumer or user for a given activity. Both individuals and firms have limited cash resources and, before choosing a service to the exclusion of others, they seek to gauge the relative priorities and demands on the disposable cash available. This may mean in extreme situations that an efficient manufacturer will opt out of distributing his goods in parts of the country (or the world) which absorb excessive demands on his available cash. This inevitably will mean that the provider of transport services to such geographical locations will see his market reduced. Once again, this is a question of cost–benefit assessment. The marketer in transport and distribution activities cannot dissociate himself from this vital aspect of his customers' needs.

ELASTICITY

Here the marketer must establish the effect that price variations will have on the volume of sales. 'Will a higher fare deter people from using my service?' or 'Will a reduced price enhance the level of demand?' Without research it is difficult to verify the point and, in the absence of such information, the company will have difficulty in taking a decision. If there is no elasticity, there is no point in reducing the price for one's service; all one would achieve is a reduced margin. On the other hand, if demand elasticity does exist, it should be possible to calculate the optimum price within a defined set of objectives. Once again, this is an important marketing decision.

LEGAL AND QUASI-LEGAL CONSTRAINTS

The price of a transport and distribution service is often guided by legal and institutional pressures outside the marketer's control. Rail fares are controlled by governmental policies; air fares are subject to IATA agreements; sea freight rates are subject to shipping conferences. The marketing planner in such situations is trapped in a situation in which the price ingredient of the marketing mix is outside his jurisdiction. He is thus forced into a non-price competition and has to rely on the other ingredients of the mix for achieving desired results.

Distribution Channels

One does not normally associate the question of channels of distribution with transport and distribution services. Nonetheless, it represents an important activity in many situations pertaining to this industry. An airline needs travel agents; shipping companies need loading brokers; road haulage firms often resort to commission agents. The identification of channels, the selection of the most appropriate channels and their motivation is an important part of the marketing effort. One cannot escape from the notion that channels are required for the following reasons:

(a) Specialist channels of distribution can perform the task more effectively and, very often, more economically than the marketing company itself can.
(b) Customers often find the use of middlemen a convenient service. In other words, the need to have channels is imposed upon the company by the habits of the marketplace itself. It is difficult to visualise a satisfactory airline service without the intermediary help of travel agents.

While the choice of channels can be an obvious decision in certain circumstances, there are many cases in which a considerable amount of creativity has to go into the selection of the most useful and acceptable middleman structure. A good marketing man must never take things for granted. We accept the idea that rail tickets can be bought from a vending machine; we recoil somewhat from the idea of buying air tickets from vending machines. Why not? Vending machines are as much a channel of distribution as travel agents and therefore a creative marketer should explore, analyse and consider the validity of far-fetched ideas of this nature.

The important point to remember in this connection is that the choice of channels is determined by a number of factors which are not entirely within the marketer's control:

(a) The ideal channels may not exist.
(b) Existing channels may refuse to handle your service.
(c) The present channel structure is incapable of devoting sufficient time and effort to your service.

This is a difficult area which calls for considerable attention and effort from the marketing organisation of most companies. Furthermore, even where the choice of channels appears straightforward enough, one must ensure that the channels are sufficiently well motivated, financially and otherwise, to devote sufficient time and attention to one's products. Most airlines will admit that travel agents have their personal likes and dislikes of individual air carriers. A good marketing effort demands that a firm ensures that dislikes are obliterated and likes are fostered and capitalised upon.

Promotion

This is another ingredient of the marketing mix which causes managers in transport and distribution firms to raise their eyebrows. This attitude is regrettable because promotion is as essential in service companies as it is in consumer goods. The objectives of the promotional effort may be different, the budgets may be smaller, but the underlying philosophy is similar.

The word 'promotion' normally includes the following:

(a) *Advertising,* i.e. paid messages communicated through media.
(b) *Sales promotion,* i.e. non-media communication such as demonstrations, sales aids, samples and exhibitions.
(c) *Publicity,* i.e. the communication of significant items of news in media without the sponsor paying for such mentions.

All these promotional activities have an important role to play in the pursuance of the marketing objectives of transport and distribution firms. How else can I find out that British Road Services have introduced a new service? How else can I discover that LASH Services are an economical proposition for transporting bauxite to my plant? Alternatively, how am I going to become aware of the fact that the ABC Company is now running an integrated distribution cum merchandising service – in other words, they can replace my own merchandising effort? Without awareness there is no knowledge and without knowledge one cannot expect to sell one's service.

The kinds of promotional objectives that are relevant in the transport and distribution business, and which are capable of quantification, are as follows:

(a) To create *awareness* of the firm's service among potential users. (If the level of existing awareness is known to be $x\%$, the aim may be to increase it to $(x + 10\%)$.

(b) To generate detailed *knowledge* of the firm's product and service including details of cost–benefit relationship, price, and other pertinent information.

(c) To improve the firm's image among existing and potential users so as to improve the customers' *attitude* towards it. The main objective being to prepare the firm's target group towards being more receptive to the new service which will be launched in the near future.

(d) To eliminate perceived misconceptions.

(e) To advise existing and potential customers of special offers or modifications of the service.

(f) To advise the marketplace of new channels.

These are a few examples of the kinds of objectives that underlie promotional strategies. It is essential for the marketing man to define his promotional objectives with great clarity, and wherever possible they must be quantified. Indeed, where no objectives exist, the task of measuring the promotional effort's effectiveness is hopeless.

The choice of media is another important aspect for the marketer to consider. The media must be such that maximum exposure can be attained among members of the firm's target group. In this connection one must remember that most companies operating in the field of transport and distribution possess one of the most valuable media, viz. the firm's own livery. The company's vehicles, ships, planes and/or trains lend themselves to a very creative promotional styling. A well designed and attractive livery can enrich the company's image and promotional goals.

Selling

The role of the salesman in transport and distribution firms varies enormously from company to company and depends on the kinds of service it offers. The size of the sales force is determined by the number of customers that the firm expects to obtain within its marketing objectives. Furthermore, the kinds of channels that have been selected for selling the company's service will have a major influence on the level of personal selling that the firm has to undertake.

In the case of mass markets like passenger traffic, the promotional task of the salesman is normally carried out by counter staff, booking office personnel, etc.

In firms operating cargo-carrying services, the personal selling effort assumes the role of problem-solving advice to customers. In fact, the salesman in such enterprises can be compared to a consultant who helps his clients to plan their logistics activities. He must be very knowledgeable in the relative merits of alternative transport systems; he must be able to compare benefits as against costs; he must be able to help his customers in planning their warehousing systems; he must be familiar with the rules and regulations that apply to transport and distribution activities. All this calls for careful selection of salesmen. They must be trained and motivated.

In Conclusion

Marketing is not the sole prerogative of firms operating in consumer goods. Admittedly, companies in manufactured goods have made better use of the marketing process in their endeavour to ensure that products match more closely the needs and desires of the marketplace. Nonetheless, the process has a very potent role to play in transport and distribution firms. They also have a product, and the success of such a product depends on a thorough and painstaking research as to what the market really needs. Having established the exact needs of the market, the firm can proceed towards the development of a marketing mix which would satisfy the user in every respect. The ability to design a service which is available at the right price, at the right time and at the right place is as applicable to logistics companies as it is to any firm offering physical products.

14
Banks and the Marketing Concept

Among the various service industries, the one most likely to face great challenges in the 1980s is the banking fraternity. This is an industry that has enjoyed a relatively peaceful era with considerable growth and, with a few exceptions, a period of stability. The prediction is that the industry is heading for a period of considerable competition not only from other banks, both UK-based ones and overseas, but also from 'functional' competitors such as building societies, the National Girobank and other financial organisations. They are all becoming more professional, better equipped and more aggressive. Competition for the customer's patronage will increase and obviously some banks will fare better than others. In the competitive game there are always winners and losers.

The winners will be the banks that learn how to incorporate the marketing concept with all its rigours into their organisational environments. This point must be emphasised. Many banks have marketing departments that perform portions of the marketing task. However, very few banks have recognised that marketing is a way of life, an organisational attitude which takes many years to develop. The majority assume that by building a marketing department that can carry out a number of research projects and/or design pretty and colourful new brochures they have fulfilled the need to improve the bank's marketing effort. They might have taken the first step in this direction, but it is a very small step indeed. It is enough to walk into some of the branches scattered along the high street to realise what a poor marketing orientation exists in these banks. All one has to do is talk to friends and acquaintances and ask them about their experiences with their respective banks to be innundated by sob-stories about how they have been treated at one stage or another by some bank official. This is a more important aspect of marketing than spending fortunes on advertising and sales promotion activities. Or at least it is as important. If banks believe in the usefulness of the marketing concept, they must apply all its principles with the same rigour that a manufacturer of fast moving consumer goods normally does. There is little point in selecting bits of the marketing process and introducing those in a diffused manner.

The word 'banking' conjures different meanings to different people. To the man in the street it means a location in the high street where he keeps his money, stands in queues to deposit cheques, draw cash, collect travellers' cheques and so on. Not surprisingly this is what one calls 'retail banking'. As the name implies it represents an institution that deals with the public at large and in many respects the rules of retail marketing apply to the management of a branch. The main problem is that whilst a shop in the high street sells in the main a tangible product, the bank deals with many intangibles, as we shall see later. From the bank's point of view the retail outlet is a place where they can 'borrow' money from the consumer, thus raising the funds which are needed by them in order to 'lend' to others.

It is appropriate to mention here that in the UK the retail banking system is dominated by the 'Big Five' known as the 'clearing banks'. This quaint description emanates from the importance attached to the function of 'clearing' cheques, credits and debits throughout the banking system. The stimulus towards developing this sophisticated arrangement came from the creation of the Post Office National Giro. Not wanting to be left behind the clearing banks established their own Giro system. This is certainly a case where the advent of a competitive threat proved to be a prod to innovation.

The 'Big Five' established the so-called Committee of London Clearing Bankers (CLCB) that owns the Bankers' Clearing House that is responsible in turn for all the 'clearings' in England and Wales. This is the organ that handles the physical paper exchange of cheques and other documents. Another offshoot of CLCB, the Bankers' Automated Clearing Services Ltd (BACS), is the body that uses electronic data processing as the basis for clearing operations. Non-clearing banks have special arrangements with a selected 'clearer', thus being able to pass all transactions through the system. The whole system is sleek and seems to function well.

There are other types of bank. There are many banks that have no contact with the public at large. They do not offer current accounts to the man in the street and do not lend small amounts of money to individuals. They only deal with large amounts and effect substantial loans to major clients like governments, local authorities, large companies and other banks. In order to be able to make such loans they must borrow large amounts from institutional lenders. The margin between the interest they pay and the interest they collect, sometimes minute, represents the bank's gross contribution. This type of bank is stated to be in the 'wholesale banking' business. In marketing terms this kind of activity comes closer in character to the way industrial marketing is transacted. The lessons learnt from enterprises that market industrial goods to industry are congruent in this type of banking.

The word 'banking' also encompasses the activities of the so-called 'merchant banks'. These represent institutions that provide a broad range of services to the industrial, commercial and financial communities. They act as professional advisers in financial matters; help to raise funds; assist in mergers, acquisitions or divestments; provide investment counselling and sometimes participate in business ventures on their own account. The range of activities of merchant bankers varies considerably from bank to bank. Marketing to such organisations has many faces and depends on the individual *modus operandi* of each of them. Nonetheless, in my experience some merchant bankers suffer from the paucity of marketing expertise, especially where they need to assist their clients in screening acquisition candidates. They seem to be most competent in evaluating the financial quality of candidates but are often unable to perform an effective marketing audit in relation to the same companies.

In practice the division between retail, wholesale and merchant banking is not always as clear-cut as is implied. Many banks operate at all three levels. Some of the big banks operate strongly as high street retail bankers whilst at the same time they perform wholesale activities and also merchant banking activities. Each part of the business carries different marketing responsibilities.

For the purpose of this chapter I wish to concentrate on some of the marketing issues pertaining to retail banking. This is the area where the greater challenges will have to be faced and greater marketing effectiveness will be called for in the years to come.

The Marketplace for Retail Banking

Very few industries can claim that virtually every adult citizen in the community is a potential customer. Banks can certainly make such a claim. Nonetheless, if one looks at the achievements of the industry in terms of 'market penetration', the outcome is not that exciting.

The reasons were summarised most succinctly by Mr Brian Pearse, a general manager with Barclays Bank, who recently said, 'If in the 1970s we failed in one area of our business it was to persuade our personal depositors that they were wanted. This we must remedy in the 1980s'. At least one senior banker has recognised that some marketing opportunities were lost.

What is the bank's 'product'? In an earlier chapter ('How to vector

Table 14.1 Bank accounts in Britain 1979.

Type of account	Adults holding accounts (%)
bank current account	55
building society account	45
bank deposit or savings account	35
National Savings Bank (via Post Office)	25
none of these	15

Source: Inter-Bank Research Organisation.

markets', Ch. 3) a strong plea was made to marketers to think in terms of what the product does for the customer and not what the product means to the marketing company itself. How much does a bank know about its customers and what motivates them to bank with one bank to the exclusion of others? What is the bank's 'product' as seen through the eyes of the customer?

The following checklist may help the bank's marketing strategist to reflect upon the needs of the people that the bank is trying to satisfy:

(a) *How much do you know about your customers?* This question should be answered in the following terms:
- Social class and demographics
- Life-style, interests, hobbies and spending habits
- Employment, professional affiliation and general progress in their career
- Attitudes towards savings, security and capital formation generally
- Newspapers and reading habits.

If one cannot answer most of these questions one obviously would not know what to communicate to one's clients nor how to communicate with them. Moreover, in the absence of a better understanding of one's clientele one is unable to determine the typology of one's perfect customer.

(b) *Are you satisfied that your customers are happy with the level of service they obtain from your bank?* This question should be answered in the following areas:
- The location of the bank
- The time it takes to receive attention and/or service
- The general demeanour of counter staff or management of the branch
- The ability of clerical staff to deal with difficult problems
- The level of knowledge of clerical staff in response to queries.

(c) *The bank's clerical staff represent the branch's sales force – are you satisfied that they try to sell the bank's services whenever appropriate in an effective way?* On this latter point I was once present in a branch belonging to one of the large 'clearing banks' when an old lady walked in and asked the clerk for advice on how to invest small amounts for a little grandson. The clerk directed her to the building society across the road! Who was at fault here the clerk himself who manifested such lack of interest in the welfare of his own bank or the management who had failed to communicate to him his role as a sales ambassador for the bank at all times?

(d) *Do you know the market share that a branch has achieved in its geographical catchment area?* Appropriate information here would include the following:
- The share of socio-economic segments

- The share of commercial and business opportunities in the area
- The branch's position vis-à-vis competitors in the vicinity.

Without such knowledge the bank is unable to identify the specific strengths and weaknesses of the branch in its marketing environment. All one can hope to do in the future is to continue to operate in the same way but more efficiently. This may simply mean that the bank would be 'doing the wrong things better'.

(e) *Do you know what new services your customers may require in the future?* Good marketing means *inter alia* the anticipation of customers' needs and seeking to develop products or services to satisfy them. Bad marketing means responding to such needs only when competitors have stolen a march and paved the way in that direction or when customers have started to agitate at the lack of action on the part of the marketing organisation.

The former strategy is known as anticipatory marketing, the latter is reactive. Many banks tend to pursue a more reactive approach than an anticipatory one. Obviously a bank that is able, through careful research and competent forecasting, to anticipate the needs of say three to five years from now may well prove to be among the winners.

(f) *Do you know what the customer is prepared to pay for the service you provide him with?* Everything has its proper value in our society. The final arbiter as to what is the correct price for a product or service is the customer. A customer may be prepared to pay a premium for certain intangible utilities which he considers valuable. Wise is the person whose perception of what a product is worth coincides with the value ascribed to it by the customer! In most cases one needs to refer to the marketplace for validation of one's price hypotheses.

We read a lot nowadays about the new pricing policies of the clearing banks. Running a branch is becoming a costly business and banks must find a way of recouping some of the increasing costs. However, the fact that there is divergence among the charges policy of the major banks indicates that confusion prevails as to what is the right price for the service rendered. In the circumstances the more marketing-orientated banker must be able to answer the following questions:

- Have you determined through some research the most appropriate and least irritating charge system to be applied? Some banks may regret the fact that they formulated a policy without reference to the consumer, especially if customers may decide to use the new charges as an incentive for considering changing their bank.
- Do you know what elasticity exists in the various segments you serve?

- Have you considered the impact that the new charges may have on customer loyalty? Traditionally banks have benefited from customers' loyalty. It would be a great pity if some of this loyalty were to be lost through a clumsy introduction of bank charges without adequate preparation and a supportive communication programme.

(g) *How effective is your communication system?* The clearing banks are competing with each other as never before to attain a greater penetration of the market. It is no secret that with 45% of the UK adult population still without bank accounts this country lags behind many of the industrialised nations. Somewhere along the line the banks have failed in their communication strategy and must endeavour to identify the weakness which has allowed this situation to prevail. The following questions need to be answered:

- What is the attitude of both 'users' and 'non-users' towards the banking fraternity? This is a study that ought to be undertaken by the industry as a whole at fairly regular intervals. A strong case for 'primary demand' development seems to exist here; i.e. primary demand for banking services as against 'selective demand' for a specific bank.
- Are banks trusted by the public?
- Is your own bank enjoying a favourable image? The fact that banks can declare inflated profits during a period of inflation and recession hardly helps to endear them to the public. Moreover, the fact that even a Conservative government finds it necessary to impose a windfall tax on banks is hardly a fillip to a bank's communication aims.
- What is the image of the branch's management? Are they considered as helpful? Friendly? Cheerful? Empathetic? Competent? Reliable? Discreet? Modern? Or the opposite? In this connection I came across a branch manager who instructed his counter staff to address every client by his or her name whenever possible: 'Yes, Mr Smith'. 'Here is your £50 Mrs Brown', etc. What a superb attempt at improving personal communication with clients! On reflection one must admit that it is not that difficult to implement such a simple strategy. After all most customers present themselves with suitable 'visiting cards' in the form of cheques, paying-in books and credit cards.

Strategies for Better Marketing in the 1980s

I must emphasise at the very outset that I have no intention of telling bankers how to run their affairs. It is a complex industry which requires a considerable amount of technical knowledge. It is one of the oldest service industries and has many traditions based on a wealth of experience and professional standards. Moreover, it is an industry that has been very dynamic in adapting itself to new technologies and investing in them.

The one weak area which seems to apply to most banks in the UK is the marketing function. Although most banks have a rudimentary marketing department, more effective with some than with others, hardly a single bank has a fully fledged, well integrated marketing system that can be compared in its effectiveness to the marketing function that one encounters among the more sophisticated manufacturing organisations. How many banks have a marketing director on their main board?

This weakness stems from a few obvious reasons:

(a) Success often stifles the need to explore and incorporate new concepts into an organisation.
(b) The industry, by the nature of its recruitment policies and specialised nature of its knowledge requirements, suffers from considerable in-breeding. Very few banks would consider recruiting senior people from outside the industry. This unfortunately means that most banks would be reluctant to enrich their marketing function with marketers from other industries.
(c) A prejudice seems to exist in the banking world against 'marketing' as exercised by manufacturing companies. An educational programme is required to change this attitude if the industry is going to derive the full benefit of an effective marketing function.

Nevertheless, a few banks have recognised this weakness and have made a valiant effort towards developing a marketing arm to their organisation. The thoughts expressed here are aimed at strengthening the resolve of these banks towards developing a truly marketing-orientated approach to running a bank in the 1980s.

The main areas for attention are given under the six following subheadings.

THE NEED FOR EDUCATION THROUGHOUT THE ORGANISATION

It is always useful to remember that the word 'marketing' encapsulates two separate concepts. The first (marketing with a small 'm') is an operational set of activities such as researching markets, planning, developing products or services, advertising, selling, selecting and managing channels of distribution. These are all clearly defined 'doing' tasks. The second meaning (Marketing with a capital 'M') is a more philosophical notion. It represents an attitude towards the marketplace and the customers. Such an attitude should percolate throughout the organisation. Every member of the organisation is invited to think about 'our precious customer and his needs' at all times. It is a corporate ethos almost like a religion. Members of the organisation from the chief executive to the switchboard operators are expected to develop an attitude of a deep-rooted empathy towards the firm's clientele. In every contact that the firm undertakes with its customers the aim must be to deal with them in the manner that one would expect to be dealt with oneself in similar circumstances. Under the first heading the firm seeks to incorporate a range of methods, tools and techniques into its managerial processes. Under the second heading the firm endeavours to develop an *attitude*, a way of life. Some firms have managed to develop perfect competence in the former area but failed in relation to the latter. Others have stimulated the right attitude but have been slow in developing the operational side. Indeed some companies run their affairs in a most marketing-orientated way without even using the word 'marketing' in the firm! The firm that manages to combine the two concepts into its corporate life is obviously the potential winner of the 1980s!

My message to the banking industry is that developing a marketing function with a small 'm' is not enough. On the contrary the attitudinal side of marketing is probably the more important and should come first. It is the greater of the two challenges. Marks & Spencer seldom talk about marketing. Yet few companies are more marketing-orientated and responsive to customer needs!

Changing attitudes is one of the greatest challenges of management development. It calls for a patient, persistent and persuasive programme of indoctrination – and at all levels. A good place to start the long-term aim of changing the bank's attitude is probably at the 'induction training' of new recruits. New trainees are usually keen and impressionable and the first few lessons immediately after joining are the ones best remembered. How many banks tell their new trainees the day they join that 'the customer is king and don't ever forget it!'

How many banks give a similar message to their telephonists? It is quite obvious to me from some of the letters written by branch managers that have been shown to me over the years that they have not been exposed to such an essential brainwashing process.

The fundamental strategy is clear: the first step for a bank wanting to improve its marketing performance is to design a development programme endeavouring to make every member of the bank's team more customer-orientated. In seeking to achieve this objective one can make use of the bank's house magazine, special bulletins, notice boards, special booklets, records and any other available medium. It is a vital project that can be described as *'marketing Marketing'*.

HARNESSING IDEAS FROM OTHER INDUSTRIES

'This idea is not for us. It may be suitable for marketing cereals'.
'We are bankers, not detergent manufacturers!'
'Brand management?! Surely it is not relevant to our type of business!'
These are some of the responses that I encounter from bankers. A deep rooted resistance exists among them towards ideas and/or strategies that emanate from non-banking organisations. Once again this is an attitudinal problem which a progressive and forward-looking bank must attempt to eradicate. There is little doubt that some industries have had more experience in the field of marketing and an excellent track record in developing imaginative and successful marketing strategies. Why not learn from them? The cross-fertilisation of ideas from other businesses is bound to be a source of important stimulation and innovation. Bankers must learn to resist the temptation of rejecting ideas just because they originate from a non-banking environment. In this connection it is refreshing to see that the various credit-card operations have adopted creative ideas that stem from the experience of successful companies in the direct marketing field.

May I suggest that it might be a good strategy for banks to recruit into their organisation some marketing talent from non-banking companies. In pursuing such a recruitment policy they must ensure that the people selected are capable of helping to develop the 'gospel-spreading' task described in the previous section. Furthermore, such individuals must possess a tolerant and empathetic personality. One cannot afford to sell the marketing concept to an organisation which is slightly resistant to it by means of an aggressive bulldozing method.

MARKETING INTEGRATION

In Chapter 2 the problem of marketing integration was discussed in some depth. Service industries have on the whole been slow to integrate marketing into the mainstream of decision-making and control systems of the firm. Banks are probably among service organisations that have been least successful in integrating marketing activities into the strategic thinking of the enterprise. 'Marketing', where it does exist, tends to be a peripheral function to the bank's managerial structure or is confined to what are in effect components of the marketing process, e.g. advertising, marketing research, corporate identity.

Once the educational task described earlier is at an advanced stage, the bank's senior management ought to apply themselves to the need to integrate the whole marketing process into the bank's planning and control systems. Probably one day in the not too distant future every bank will have a marketing supremo at main board level. His job will be to undertake the various integrative tasks that his function envisages, i.e. (a) to integrate marketing planning with the overall planning process of the bank; (b) to integrate the various marketing activities that are being conducted round the bank; (c) to integrate the various components of the marketing mix in respect of specific 'products' or services.

For more details on this subject it is recommended that the reader refers back to Chapter 2.

IMPROVING MARKETING INTELLIGENCE

Most banks suffer from a serious paucity of marketing data about their clientele. This applies to corporate customers and private clients alike.

Where the customer is a company or some other commercial or institutional organisation they tend to solicit and analyse information of a financial nature in the form of balance sheets or annual reports. However, the bank seldom enquires about clients' marketing problems or market standing. The general attitude is that as long as the money side is healthy all is well with the world. Companies have been known to generate profits and cash flow in spite of the fact that most of their products have reached dangerous stages in the life cycle. The company is simply milking its 'cash cows'. If bankers are willing to accept that marketing in the 1980s has to be conducted in the spirit of 'joining' one's clients, they must learn to understand more about the marketing environments of such clients. The 'joining' concept, described more fully in Chapter 10, implies that the main aim of an effective marketing effort is literally to become a spiritual partner with one's customers. The banker's aim must be to become so involved in his clients' welfare, plans and aspirations that in marketing terms he has 'joined' them as a permanent counsellor and sounding board. In order to achieve such a posture one must understand the customer's marketing environment and not just his cash flow performance. Very few industries offer a better opportunity to develop this kind of relationship than banking does. Strangely enough the old-fashioned branch managers of half a century ago probably performed a better marketing job than their present-day counterparts. This was mainly due to the fact that far fewer people had bank accounts and the manager could devote more time to each client. Secondly, the mechanisation and automation processes have depersonalised the relationships between clients and bank personnel. It is much more difficult to relate to a number than to a human being.

As far as corporate clients are concerned it is strongly recommended that managers attempt to develop dossiers about each company's marketing activities. The aim should be to learn about their customers and not just to snoop. The dossier should include such information as the following:

(a) The firm's products and their relative unique features.

(b) The standing of the firm in the marketplace vis-à-vis its main competitors.
(c) ·The firm's pricing policy. Are they leaders or followers? Are they aware of the price elasticity of their various products? If they are not, the banker is justified in encouraging them to research this vital point.
(d) General trends in the marketing environment of that client.
(e) The quality of the communication system and/or sales force.

Undoubtedly a knowledgeable banker is a formidable ally for any corporate client to have and a superb 'unique selling point' for the banker to offer.

In this connection it is useful for a banker to analyse his corporate and professional clientele with the view of identifying specific segments in which the bank appears to have made a strong penetration. Sometimes a bank attains such a position without realising that it has done so – and often without being able to explain why it happened. I recently came across a branch that appeared to have 'cornered' the solicitors in the area. Obviously this is a useful 'input' for future planning purposes.

Collecting and analysing data about the private account holder is more difficult because the average bank has so many of them. Nevertheless, no branch can plan its marketing strategy for the future without a better understanding of whom its clients are and what proportion of the catchment market it represents. In theory every branch manager wishes to open as many new accounts during the year as possible. Small accounts are also welcome – 'Tall oaks from little acorns grow!' However, a manager can take a passive posture and wait for people to step into the bank and enquire about how to open an account or adopt a more forthright attitude and seek new clients out. On the other hand, he cannot parade up and down the street with a sandwich board extolling the bank's virtues. His venture into the marketplace must be subtle, professional and based on a perfect understanding of the best target to aim his effort at. If he finds that a large number of his clients are golfers, let him become a golfer or take some steps to support the local golf club. If he discovers that many of his clients are doctors from the local hospital, let him develop some social contact with members of the hospital's environment. He must do everything within his power to fight the anonimity that modern bureaucracy is imposing upon us.

The main point to remember is that a lot of the information about clients is available in the bank's records or can be easily collected without impinging on a person's time or privacy. After all, bankers do keep records of an account holder's financial reliability and punctuality. Surely it would not take much effort to add some data about the person's non-financial habits and interests. To take a simple example: if a bank were to discover from its new-style records that they have a large

number of music lovers in their area, it might be a good idea to develop a
new 'product' in the form of a special loan for the purchase of a musical
instrument! An integrated communication programme to music lovers
and music shops coupled with advertising in concert programmes may
be a useful strategy for satisfying existing clientele and attracting other
music lovers to the bank. Unfortunately, in reality most bankers wait for
the client himself to knock on their door and ask for a loan to buy a
piano!

MAKING AN INTANGIBLE SERVICE MORE CONCRETE

When two or more firms compete with an identical product, one of the
marketing tasks is to augment the product through the incorporation of
unique selling points (USPs). The aim of such USPs is to differentiate
the marketer's product from competitive offerings. A USP can take any
form, tangible or intangible, but is only of value when the customer
considers it of usefulness to himself. Many firms have fallen into the trap
of spending a considerable amount of money and effort in developing
USPs which the customer felt were of no use to him. Obviously such
attempts at differentiation are an absolute waste of effort.

A physical product like a car, a camera or a detergent can be
augmented through the addition of a mixture of tangible and intangible
features. A stereo unit or rust-proofing added to a new car are tangible
USPs. Membership of an exclusive club of owners of a certain type of
car is intangible. One can easily verify whether the customer appreciates
the feature added to the product or not. The feedback from the
marketplace is swift and decisive.

The situation with banks is much more complicated. Their 'products'
are highly intangible. The customer has little to touch, see or hear.
Superficially most banks look alike and the services they render appear
identical. What kind of USPs can a bank offer in order to distinguish its
service from its competitors? One bank is proud of the fact that its
statements, unlike those of its competitors', show the names of the
payees of the various cheques drawn during the month. If the customer
values such a service it certainly represents a USP, and what is more it is
a tangible one.

The ironical fact is that firms offering tangible products such as
detergents or beer spend large amounts of money seeking to
communicate intangible, abstract, associations. Heineken beer is a
tangible product yet the firm's communication strategy seems to
concentrate on a highly abstract image – 'the beer that reaches the parts
that no other beer can reach!' What can be more intangible in its
connotations?

At the other extreme a service is a very abstract product. To add
intangible elements to an already intangible 'product' can be self-
defeating. The marketer in service organisations normally, and very

often unconsciously, tries to develop *tangible* clues which the customer is capable of associating with the firm's 'products'. The theory is that the customer can surmise from the quality of the tangible clues that the intangible nature of the service is of high quality. Some marketers have adopted this 'circumstantial evidence' approach without fully realising the soundness of such a strategy. One should always attempt to *encode* intangible attributes into a concrete form. Airlines spend considerable resources in designing very elegant and soothing showrooms. This is their attempt at projecting a concrete image of an amalgam of intangible USPs that the airline wishes to convey to its customers. Advertising agencies, especially in the United States, always attempt to design their offices in styles which convey the agencies' 'personalities' and the nature of the services which they seek to specialise in. All these are concrete manifestations of a range of intangibles. However, before a service organisation can undertake this process of 'encoding' intangibles into concrete clues it must ensure that (a) it knows precisely who its target audience is; (b) it has defined the unique selling points which should be incorporated into the service – such USPs must be capable of meeting the needs of the target market.

It is only at this point that the marketer can start, with the help of the behavioural sciences, to develop the concrete evidence which can convey to the customer the value of the intangible USPs that the firm has decided to develop.

Here lies one of the major marketing challenges for modern banks. The concrete clues that they can communicate to the customers can take many forms: the physical environment of the branches, the furnishing, all the accoutrement of the bank's corporate identity and image, the stationery, cheque books, the general decoration of the walls, even the way members of the staff dress. If you want a 'go-go' bank the way the cashiers dress would provide a concrete clue to the personality-image the bank seeks to develop!

However, one point must never be forgotten: the marketing objectives, the nature of the service and the target audience must be crystal clear before the bank can undertake the process of translating a range of intangible attributes into concrete communication evidence.

SALESMANSHIP AT ALL LEVELS

Finally, a bank must remember that selling is not an ugly word. Every member of our society has to 'sell' something at one stage or another. Manufacturers have to sell; professional people have to sell their services; politicians have to sell their ideas and solutions. Similarly, banks have to sell their services. I do not suggest for a minute that branch managers must go out and knock on every single door in the neighbourhood offering their wares. On the other hand, the passive attitude of the past is not good enough in capitalising upon the enormous investment which a prime high street site represents. The branch manager and his staff must be vigilant at all times for 'selling' opportunities.

A person wants a loan to buy a car; why not offer him an insurance policy for the sum borrowed in order to protect his family against contingencies? A person buys travellers' cheques; why not offer him a holiday insurance policy at the same time? Another person pays into his current account the proceeds of an insurance policy that has matured; why not sell to him the idea of a deposit account or a new unit-linked cash-builder? In this area banks are so timid that on many occasions their inaction can be construed as verging on the unethical.

I recently came across an elderly couple who kept a large sum of money in an ordinary current account. They were too old to understand the erosion effect of inflation upon their funds and too complacent about the need to earn maximum interest on their nest egg. Surely it is the duty of a customer-orientated banker to alert them to the options open to them and not just to allow them to hold the funds in a non-interest-bearing current account! I tackled the branch manager on behalf of my elderly friends and accused him of taking advantage of old people. He felt that it was not his duty to advise them what to do with the money, although he acknowledged that he was aware of the stupidity of keeping funds in a current account! He felt that it would be indiscreet of him to interfere with the wishes of his clients in this respect. I felt that it was a serious dereliction of marketing duty.

In Conclusion

In summary, whilst banks consider themselves as very different from the rest of the commercial and industrial world, the marketing concept applies to them with perfect relevance. They are lucky inasmuch as they have all the experience of consumer and industrial marketing to draw upon. They can extract valuable lessons and creativity from the myriad of successful cases recorded in marketing textbooks and anthologies. The main barrier among bankers towards progress in this area is their own self-imposed resistance to accepting the full discipline of a fully fledged and well integrated marketing function. The bank that will open its heart fully to the marketing concept with all its underlying principles will definitely be the star performer of the 1980s.

15
Insurance, Too, Needs Marketing

Of all the service industries in our society the one that markets the most intangible of intangibles is the insurance industry. A person insures his own life and is unlikely ever to enjoy the fruits of his prudence. If he survives the term of the policy, he gets nothing (unless of course it was an endowment policy). If he dies during the term of the cover, he will certainly derive very little posthumous joy from his investment. Nonetheless, many people do take out such policies and must have emotional and behavioural reasons for committing themselves to such an expenditure.

Similarly, a person insures his house and its contents and pays premiums year after year. Until he has had an opportunity to make a claim the policy is a very intangible promise to compensate the householder against a range of losses or damage. In truth the policyholder would prefer not to have to make a claim ever in his lifetime. In fact the insurance company too would be happy if he could go through life without a claim. Thus both parties to the transaction are happiest when no claims are made. Once again the customer obviously has a certain need satisfied by having such a policy, albeit in the majority of cases it represents no more than a promise to pay if certain events take place.

The industry is vast and the number of companies operating therein is large. No industry could reach such a level of size and sophistication had it not been capable of meeting the needs, overt and covert, of its customers. Obviously the insurance industry has managed to do so until now and undoubtedly hopes to continue to do so in the future. Nonetheless, a quick interfirm comparison of performance in the industry soon highlights the fact that some insurance companies are able to manifest far better levels of result than others.

Admittedly insurance is an industry which ascribes different criteria of success than those prevalent in manufacturing companies. Moreover, many of the criteria applied to measuring the performance of insurance firms are at times in conflict with each other and defy true comparability. A company can appear to have generated a satisfactory profit and yet be highly unsuccessful inasmuch as its sales of new policies are sagging or the current sales are to high risk clients. All this will come home to roost in the future. In the short term the firm looks all right. In other words, the nature of the business – and especially the life insurance side – imposes upon management a conflicting choice between short term and long term profitability. In spite of this kind of difficulty one is able to identify at the one end insurance companies that present a dynamic and innovative image and conservative and unimaginative companies at the other extreme. If one believes in distribution curves, one would assume that these two extremes are in a small minority and that the bulk of the insurance firms fall into the larger middle quartiles. What typifies the small segment that falls into the dynamic and innovative group of companies? My case is that what distinguishes them from the others is better marketing. Readers from the insurance industry may disagree with some of my conclusions. Nonetheless, if as a result of this chapter they decide to devote more thought and resources to their own firm's marketing effort I will have achieved my aim.

The Customer and his Needs

The industry is based on the satisfaction of three major needs: (a) the need for security; (b) the need for savings and/or capital formation and (c) the need to meet legal or institutional requirements. The first two are emotive in character and call for one form of marketing and communication. The third is mandatory and the customer has little choice in deciding whether to insure or not. However, he has a choice as to whom he will insure with. Obviously in such circumstances the marketing task is totally different.

Let us explore briefly each one of these set of needs and highlight some of the marketing implications.

THE NEED FOR SECURITY

Security is one of the basic needs of human beings. In Chapter 7 the nature of needs was explored and Maslow's theory on the 'hierarchy of needs' summarised. Safety and security needs are second only to physiological needs. Obviously people who are hungry and thirsty have other needs to satisfy first before even thinking about their desire to protect themselves against loss or danger. This is normally well understood by insurance companies. They seldom try to sell policies to people who live at the lowest level of subsistence, nor to young people who have just commenced their first job.

The need for security and safety is deep-rooted in most people. However, the intensity of this need differs among various groups of individuals. It tends to differ among cultures. Some nations are more security conscious than others, and that often depends on the impact that historical events have had on the general sense of security in these nations. Some races suffer from a greater sense of insecurity than others. In fact some professions seem to breed a higher level of security consciousness than others.

Buying insurance policies is one way of satisfying the need to feel more secure. Other forms of insurance, such as private health schemes like BUPA and motor protection like the AA or the RAC, are also methods of alleviating a person's sense of insecurity. In spite of the fairly useful system that exists in the UK for protecting the citizen against many hazards such as health, social problems and unemployment, many consumers spend large sums of money in order to improve their sense of security and comfort in the face of the hazards of the unknown. It is perfectly human to feel such a need and to want to satisfy it. Many people find that the need for security is insatiable and reach a point at which they start feeling a fresh sense of insecurity resulting from their inability to pay the ever-growing premium load.

In the area of 'security and safety' need satisfaction the effective marketer should attempt to develop the typology of the 'most attractive clients' and provide such an 'identikit' as a sales aid to the sales force. A salesman who can 'home in' on a potential customer who falls within the typology criteria is more likely to sell his 'products' than the one who knocks on all doors indiscriminately.

THE NEED FOR SAVINGS AND/OR CAPITAL FORMATION

The need and desire to amass possessions and capital is part of the process of wanting to feel more secure. A person would talk about a 'nest egg' or wanting to save for 'a rainy day'. It all amounts to the same basic need on Maslow's hierarchy of needs. Some individuals are more acquisitive in their character than others, yet a large number of people consider that having a number of endowment policies or other insurance-linked capital building policies are a worthwhile investment to have. Of course the tax system in the UK encourages this kind of insurance-linked parsimony. Within certain limits one obtains tax savings on every pound that one invests in life policies. It is true to say that life insurance linked with endowment facilities is probably the most tax-efficient way of saving capital. It is interesting to note that in countries which do not offer such tax advantages the structure of the industry in relation to life insurance has taken a totally different course and endowment policies have not gained the same level of acceptance as in this country.

The various permutations that exist for putting money aside for retirement pensions fall into this savings and capital formation category. Essentially the motivating force underlying all these transactions is a combination of emotive and rational stimuli. The emotive factor is the desire to feel more secure. The rational factor is the wish to reduce taxes, to save and to build capital. The level of intensity of these motivators differs from individual to individual and the marketing task of the insurance company is to develop suitable approaches to the various behavioural segments they seek to satisfy.

The industry has manifested a considerable amount of creativity in developing a plethora of 'products' to suit most tastes and personality traits. Some of these 'products' emphasise the security angle, others the savings aspect and others offer a judicious combination of both. Under fancy names such as 'level term insurance', 'decreasing term insurance', 'convertible terms insurance', 'renewable term insurance', 'increasing term', 'family income benefit', 'endowment policies', 'unit-linked insurance', etc., are a few of the 'products' that the consumer has to choose from. Among the myriad of offerings he is sure to find the 'product' that will meet his needs. Unfortunately not many customers understand the jargon of the industry. The average person is mystified by some of the terms that the insurance fraternity use and one can assume that many potential sales are lost to the industry as a result of this communication constraint. Moreover, those who purchase their policies through brokers, the middlemen of the industry, soon find out that the brokers are more interested in satisfying their own need to earn money through the commission they get than meeting the needs of the clients. Very few customers realise that before going to brokers they must sort out their own objectives as to whether they want protection or investment and the level of cover they require.

One of the areas in which the industry has failed to perform an effective marketing job is the area of communication with the ordinary citizen. Those companies which have mastered the communication game with the marketplace stand a good chance of becoming the star performers of the industry.

THE NEED TO MEET LEGAL AND/OR INSTITUTIONAL REQUIREMENTS

There are some areas in which insurance cover is prescribed either by the legal system or by some institution with whom the consumer has developed some financial relationship. Car insurance is prescribed by the Road Traffic Act. This specifies the minimum type of insurance that satisfies the law. It covers the driver only for claims made as a result of causing death or injury to someone else in an accident on a public road. Here there is nothing emotional about the nature of the cover. The law demands it and the driver has to comply with it. At this point the more security-conscious person would add bits of cover ranging from a third party, fire and theft to a comprehensive cover. The first cover is mandatory, the latter discretionary. The marketing process relating to each is obviously different.

Similarly, employers have to take a cover protecting all employees working on their premises against accidents that might occur there. This is laid down by the legal system and the only discretion left to the employer is the choice of the insurance company with whom to effect such a cover.

There are many situations in which the consumer is forced to take insurance cover of one sort or another at the insistence of an institutional third party. Hire-purchase firms will normally insist that the buyer of a motor car on hire-purchase takes a comprehensive policy. Building societies and nowadays banks demand that the purchaser of a house with a mortgage takes a household policy. Very often they even insist that such policies are taken with a company of their choice. Some holiday operators demand a holiday and cancellation policy taken through their own agency. In such situations the consumer ceases to be an important member of the 'decision-making unit'. He is a 'user', but of limited influence upon the transaction. The main 'influencer' and/or 'decider' is the institution that demands that a suitable cover is effected. The stimulus for such a compulsory insurance is partly for protecting their funds (building societies wanting to protect their mortgage investment) and partly as a source of extra income from the commission earned.

This is probably an over-simplification of the reasons why people take insurance cover of any sort. However, the aim was to emphasise the fact that the motivating force that stimulates people to spend money on insurance ranges from the very basic need to feel secure to the very rational need to comply with legal and semi-legal requirements.

The insurance industry, on the whole, understands these behavioural elements, but does not always know how to build them into effective communication programmes.

The Marketplace

So far mention has been made of the consumer and his needs. No mentioned has been made of the insurance needs of commercial, industrial and institutional organisations. This represents a very large sector of the insurance industry. Firms need to protect their premises, plants, vehicles and personnel. Pension funds have grown at a considerable rate, partly due to the facility offered to employers to 'contract out' of the new state pension scheme which started in April 1978. For many insurance companies this represented an excellent marketing opportunity and indeed some companies capitalised on this opportunity in a very effective way.

The dilemma that many insurance companies face as far as the marketing function is concerned is the dual nature of the marketplace. The market consists of consumers, householders and ordinary citizens on the one hand – in fact every person who owns a car, a house or any possessions can be a potential buyer for insurance policies. On the other hand the market consists of the tens of thousands of companies, large and small, who employ people and own premises. The former entails consumer marketing; the latter comes very close to manifesting all the characteristics of industrial marketing. A company may decide to specialise in marketing its services to the consumer direct, in which case all the challenges of consumer marketing have to be faced. Or it may decide to adopt the 'industrial' route and concentrate its activities on the corporate sector. All the rules of industrial marketing will need to be applied. Quite a few firms, especially the older ones and the well established ones, seem to tackle the marketplace in both ways. Somewhere along the line they seem to fall between two stools and carry out the marketing task in a sub-optimal fashion. This is particularly true of organisations that rely on brokers, the middlemen, for a substantial portion of the corporate insurance sector but have a direct sales force for the consumer side of their business.

The word 'insurance' covers a vast number of 'products'. Few industries talk in larger sums of money, especially when one refers to the amount of 'insurance in force'. A staggering example is the amount of 'life insurance in force' in the UK, which in 1979 amounted to £125 500 000 000! As a proportion of the UK's gross national product it amounts to around 80%. Of course it is a fairly meaningless ratio, but it places the vastness of the figures in their proper perspective. At the same time the insurance industry is one of the very few industries that has great difficulties in answering a very simple question: 'How much do you spend every year on marketing as a proportion of your premium income?' A straw poll which I conducted a couple of years ago among insurance firms taught me a simple lesson: those who could answer this question and provide chapter and verse on how they spend their marketing money are among the companies that share analysts consider as the high-flyers of the industry. The obvious dilemma arises: are they high-flyers because they seem to perform their marketing task effectively or do they carry out their marketing job well because they are high-flyers? It is difficult to know which is the correct answer to this 'chicken and egg' question. However, in seeking to identify a good company to invest in or to acquire in the insurance business I have a simple criterion: check their marketing effort. If it is effective and creative you are on to a good thing!

For the rest of this chapter I propose to concentrate my comments upon the life sector of the insurance business. It is probably the most dynamic and, in terms of potential market growth, the most exciting sector of the industry.

The 'Marketing Mix' for Life Business

People in the industry are often offended when they are reminded that marketing life policies is not very different from marketing pharmaceuticals or detergents. The knowledge required by individuals operating in the insurance business is vastly different from the one required in other industries. However, the underlying principles and tools of marketing are the same in all three industries. A marketer of pharmaceutical products who is able to acquire the complex knowledge of the insurance world and master its terminology and jargon is well on the way to becoming an effective insurance marketer. Like banks, insurance companies believe that they are a law unto themselves and will very seldom consider recruiting marketing personnel from outside the industry. This is probably a very short-sighted attitude which will constrain those suffering from it from achieving progress in their marketing performance. It deprives such companies from a useful injection of experience and ideas from other industries which have had a valuable track record in performing successful and complex marketing programmes.

As a first step it is recommended that companies that wish to enrich their marketing function take a conscious decision to rid themselves of the self-imposed embargo on talent from outside the industry. On reflection most firms should identify many good reasons for pursuing such a strategy and very few for rejecting it. Clearly, before such new recruits become fully operational they must undergo a period of training in the industry's special areas of knowledge, but I cannot accept that any of the mysteries of the insurance world are so daunting as to perplex an intelligent individual from another industry.

In support of the contention that marketing life policies is no different from marketing other products let us explore the marketing mix of the average life company. If one accepts the marketing mix of a manufacturing company as *product, price, promotion, selling* and *distribution*, it would be interesting to see how far these elements are germane to marketing life assurance policies. A similar analysis can be undertaken in relation to other types of insurance offered by the industry as a whole.

THE PRODUCT

The life business has a plethora of 'products'. In the past these products were designed with a thoroughbred 'production orientation' in the sense that the company sought to ensure that whatever policy the consumer bought the company's risk was mitigated to the very utmost. Actuarial computations, life expectancy tables and risk analysis were the paramount factors upon which products were designed and the type of person that the company would insure determined. The welfare of the firm came first, second and last. The individual who deviated marginally from the firm's norms of minimum risk was rejected. Unfortunately for such an individual a rejection by one firm could place a nasty black mark on his escutcheon inasmuch as being rejected by one company must always be disclosed on every subsequent proposal form. The rejecting company had no empathy or mercy towards the person thus rebuffed. Hardly a consumer-orientated approach! Moreover, the industry took no cognisance of people's real needs. Each company sought to sell its products whether they were suitable for the individual in question or not. The result was that many policies lapsed through disenchantment or through a simple inability to pay the premiums.

Competition, the consumer's best friend, has brought about many changes to the industry. The biggest change is an insidious one: many products have reached the end of their life cycle and their sale has dropped dramatically. New products have emerged in large numbers and because of the pressure of competition have been developed with greater vigilance towards the consumer and his needs. Whilst the industry seldom uses the expression 'unique selling points', many policies have been designed with a clear aim to incorporate special features that would enhance their marketability. Thus, without a clearly stated strategy, the industry has gradually shifted to a more marketing-orientated philosophy. However, even today very few insurance firms undertake systematic research into what the consumer really needs and what he would prefer to buy. 'Marketing orientation' is often based on the marketer's own perception of what the customer needs rather than on a scientific evaluation of what these needs are in a dynamic marketplace. The result is that a large number of new products has been flooding the market and that the consumer is often confused as to which of these products is the most likely one to meet his personal needs, emotional or otherwise.

At the same time it is important to emphasise that the consumer of today is different from his counterpart of a few decades ago. First, he is less loyal to one insurance company. He would change his allegiance at the drop of a hat, especially if he could see a material advantage in changing insurers. Secondly, he is a lot more vigilant about the 'value for money' that he is getting. The consumer of twenty or thirty years ago assumed that the 'product' sold by a blue-chip firm must be good. The consumer today does not accept such an assumption. He will consult the *Which?* report. He will talk to friends with some experience and will attempt to ensure that the policy he buys offers him good value. In this sort of environment it is evident that product innovation must withstand the scrutiny of a much more sophisticated type of consumer aided by institutional watch dogs.

A major environmental element which affects the product acceptability of policies, especially those purchased as an aid to savings or capital formation, is of course inflation. Inflation is probably the single most important factor which will affect product management of the life business for quite a few years. Even if inflation comes down in the next few years, there is little doubt that the consumer has developed an obsession about the impact of inflation on his savings. He is bound to favour a policy which offers some kind of indexation or protection against the erosion of the value of the pound. Hence the success of such products as the 'unit-linked' contracts or the 'property-linked' policies.

The following checklist may be helpful to the insurer who wishes to plan new products on a more marketing-responsive way than hitherto:

(a) Identify the kinds of customers you currently have and attempt to define, within broad principles, their typology.

(b) Consult a representative sample of your clientele with the view of establishing (i) their current level of satisfaction with your products; (ii) their perceived needs for the future; (iii) the extent to which your products are likely to continue to satisfy these needs.

Remember that the best product strategy is the one which is anticipatory in nature – the one that seeks to respond to needs as and when they develop. The imitative strategy whereby one follows the leadership of the more creative members of the industry often places the insurer at some tactical disadvantage.

(c) List the major features that your customers are looking for in the 'ideal' insurance contract.

(d) Analyse the products offered by the competitors that you particularly respect and identify the USPs that they have incorporated in their policies.

(e) Scan the international scene and try to list the innovative products that are being offered in foreign countries.

In this connection it is important to realise that a product that is very successful in one country will not necessarily be equally successful in the UK and vice versa. Environmental, cultural, legal, tax and institutional factors often make a product attractive in one country but less so in others where different conditions prevail. Nonetheless, identifying successful approaches in foreign countries can often provide a useful source of ideas for innovation.

(f) Establish a continuous dialogue with a number of your customers with the view of ensuring that your firm is keeping a 'finger on the pulse' of the marketplace. The discussion group approach can be a useful device in this area. It is relatively cheap to conduct and often provides most valuable input to better product planning.

(g) Ensure that you are fully conversant with the way consumer bodies evaluate the quality of products in the industry. Quite often these bodies measure the quality of products in a different way than the industry itself does.

(h) Evaluate at frequent intervals the quality of your administration and claims service *as seen through the eyes of the customers*.

It is useful to remember that insurance policies encompass a large number of intangible features. One of these intangibles is the promise to pay on maturity, death or some other event a certain sum of money. When such an event occurs the intangible becomes very tangible to the next of kin or to the insured himself. The way claims are handled – the speed, the human touch, the general professionalism of the administrative machine – is an integral part of the 'product'. The only person who can judge at this point whether the 'product' is good is the claimant himself. The effective marketer should monitor the level of satisfaction among recent claimants as part of his product management.

(i) Where your products are sold through brokers, solicit from time to time some feedback as to how they view the standing of your products.

Such studies are often best performed by independent third parties such as market research organisations or consultants. They are more likely to obtain objective responses to questioning.

The insurance marketer who actually undertakes all these tasks should feel confident about his approach to the marketplace. Provided that he maintains an up-to-date evaluation of all this data he is likely to respond to the needs of consumers in a dynamic way, thus giving his own company a cutting edge in the competitive game.

THE PRICE

What is the right price for a life assurance policy?

To an actuary or an underwriter – the production people of the industry – the price is a function of the risk involved. It is possible to quantify the risk as against the revenue of each policy. As long as a notional contribution can be shown they are happy. To the marketer the proper price is the one which the customer is happy to pay. If both prices coincide it is excellent. If a gap exists a dialogue must take place between the two approaches and a consensus must be reached. However, the marketing creed ordains that the acid test is the customer's viewpoint – if he is not satisfied he simply votes with his feet.

On the other hand, those who base their costings on actuarial and underwriting considerations are entitled to insist that the marketing perception as to what the right price is should be based on an objective, thorough and reliable analysis of the facts. Until such validation is obtained the more production-orientated price-fixers are justified in sticking to their guns.

The following 'inputs' should equip the marketer with the appropriate ammunition for determining a clear-cut, marketing-orientated pricing policy:

(a) Are you familiar with the pricing policies of your competitors for comparable products to your company's?

(b) Have you analysed the various 'value for money' studies that exist in your industry, including *Which?* reports?

There is little doubt that such studies offer (i) an understanding of how the consumer is encouraged to think in relation to the cost of the various policies that are being offered; (ii) an interfirm price–benefit analysis; (iii) an objective assessment of the marketer's own products and their perceived 'value for money'. Thus, when a *Which?* report says that policies specially designed for women do not represent the 'best buy' (as one did in June 1979), the marketer who ignores such a message does so at his peril.

(c) Have you attempted to gauge the price elasticity of specific policies? Some products are more price sensitive than others. Not knowing the relative level of elasticity is a major constraint on the ability to take intelligent price decisions.

(d) Have you attempted to estimate the extra money which your customers are willing to pay for the additional USPs that you have incorporated into your products?

THE PROMOTIONAL MIX

The insurance industry is spending relatively small amounts in relation to their premium receipts on the various tools of the promotional mix (advertising, sales promotion and publicity). Many companies spend less than 0.25% of their total premium income and less than 2% of total *first* year premiums. Not surprisingly a good portion of this money is spent in a manner which falls short of the high level of professionalism which one encounters in 'fast moving consumer goods' companies.

Traditionally advertising and the other promotional tools have been less critical in the marketing mix of insurance firms than personal selling. Whilst promotion represented derisory budgets, *selling* has always represented a hefty chunk of the marketing cake. This was due in the main to the sales commission structure of the industry. The bulk of ordinary life policies is still sold on a one-to-one basis. The salesman (whether a full time employee of the company or an independent agent) is the essential intermediary between the customers and the firm, both at the moment of the sale and during the life span of the policy. Sales commission on the first year premium can be as high as 100% and thereafter in the order of 5–10% of the premium renewals. Normally the larger and more prestigious the company the lower the commission paid. However, agents of such firms would expect a lot more promotional back-up to support their selling effort.

The situation is changing and will no doubt continue to do so in the future and for the following reasons:

(a) With increased competitive pressures the consumer is becoming more resistant to salesmanship. Promotional back-up will become essential in order to assist the salesman in his work. Creative sales aids will be called for.

(b) Selling is becoming extremely expensive in terms of cost per call and productivity. Alternatives to salesmanship must be considered.

(c) Direct and mass marketing techniques have proved successful in certain situations.

(d) The rapid changes in product offerings call for a greater effort in creating awareness among customers of a dynamic range of products and benefits.

In the light of these observations it is fair to assume that the modern marketer in the insurance business will need to acquire considerable skill in a field in which he could have afforded in the past to have had fairly superficial expertise.

More specifically, the marketer should consider the following questions:

(a) Have you defined your firm's promotional and communication objectives? If so, in what terms? In this connection the reader is advised to refer to Chapter 11, 'Advertising by objectives'.

(b) Do you know what percentage of your target audience is *aware* of (i) your company's name and main characteristics (in terms of size, standing, image, the products it offers, the quality of its service, etc.) and (ii) the unique features of the firm's products (if any, of course)?

(c) Are your clients capable of decoding the communication aids that your firm publishes (literature, sample policies, price lists)? This is an area that many insurance firms have neglected partly because of the legalistic nature of the products and partly through lack of empathy. The fact is that many clients simply do not understand the meaning of many phrases and terms in the small print. Hardly a marketing-sensitive stance.

(d) Have you identified the obstacles to a successful sale? Readers should refer to Chapter 9, 'Back to first principles on sales aids'. The whole issue is covered there in some depth and provides a useful input to the way sales aids should be approached in the insurance industry as well.

(e) Are you measuring the effectiveness of your various promotional expenditures?

(f) Do you know what the consumer's attitude is towards life assurance companies in general and towards your company in particular?

SELLING

Personal selling is one of the important communication tools of the life assurance business. Insurance salesmen are the life blood of the industry. They are often maligned and treated with irrepressible contempt. Nevertheless, without an effective sales force very few insurance companies would have achieved the position which they have. At the same time the more vigilant firms in the business must realise that the traditional way of selling policies is bound to undergo major changes. Whilst salesmanship is unlikely to disappear, heavier productivity demands will be placed upon it and greater marketing support will be required.

Moreover, few companies in the insurance industry recognise the importance of planning and organising the sales effort as an integral part of a total marketing strategy. The sales force, however effective it may be, tends to operate as an independent arm of the firm, and the realisation that selling is one component of a well integrated marketing mix seems slow to sink in.

The following checklist might help the marketer to reflect upon the major issues:

(a) What is the role of the sales force within the marketing mix of your company? This question calls for specific answers on the kind of objectives which should be ascribed to the selling effort. These can be defined in terms of policies to be sold, premiums, customers to be served, brokers to be visited, calls per day, etc. (see Chapter 10, 'Improving the productivity of the sales force'). These objectives must be consistent with the marketing objectives of the firm and must be integrated with each ingredient of the marketing mix.

(b) What size sales force do we require in order to meet the marketing objectives of the firm?

(c) Are there any practical and economical alternatives to selling with which the firm should experiment?

(d) What kind of sales aids should we provide our salesmen with in order to make their task simpler and more effective?

(e) Are we providing our salesmen with an adequate system of training and development? How much do we spend on training each salesman? How is this amount compared with competitors' spending?

(f) What is our sales force turnover and how is it compared with the norm of the industry as a whole?

(g) Is the productivity of our sales force growing? How is this productivity compared with our competitors?

(h) Is the remuneration 'package' satisfactory and sufficient to maintain the right level of motivation?

(i)   Have we given each salesman a territory which would provide
      him with a suitable opportunity to perform?

(j)   Are we keeping our sales force up to date with new product
      knowledge and developments in the legal and quasi-legal
      environments which may help or hinder a successful sale?

(k)   Have we organised ourselves to collect ideas from salesmen in
      the field and/or to cross-fertilise such creativity?

DISTRIBUTION

The distribution system of the industry is wide-spread and well
established. All the basic rules of selecting, motivating, managing and
controlling channels of distribution apply to the life assurance business
with equal force. In deciding to choose the middlemen route the
insurance firm must bear two major considerations in mind:

(a)   A channel decision affects every ingredient of the marketing
      mix.

(b)   Channel decisions invariably involve the firm in commitments
      of a long term nature.

In other words channels strategy must not be developed in a hurry; the
implications of decisions in this area must be evaluated with care!
The following questions are pertinent in this all-important area:

(a)   If we could start life afresh, what kind of distribution
      system would be compatible with our marketing objectives?
      This may be an academic question inasmuch as the freedom to
      start life afresh seldom presents itself to any company. However,
      it offers the marketer an opportunity of taking a fresh look at
      the firm's present distribution system and of comparing it
      with what he might conclude to be the ideal channel. If the two
      perspectives are congruent, so much the better.

(b)   Have we analysed the various middlemen we have and their
      relative performance? A Pareto analysis might be appropriate
      here.

(c)   What is the middlemen's attitude towards our firm? Brokers
      seldom sell one firm's products. Most brokers have strong views
      about the firms they represent. It is useful to research the
      way they view the firm, its products and its general service.
      Without such information it is difficult to develop better
      communication strategies.

(d)   Is our commission level comparable to the ones offered by our
      competitors.

(e)   Do we monitor the performance of our channels of distribution
      on budgetary control approach?

(f) Do we take steps to create distributor loyalty?
(g) Do we allocate sufficient funds towards training and developing our channels of distribution and their personnel?
(h) Do we maintain an efficient communication system with every distributor?

In Conclusion

It seems evident that insurance, in spite of all the mystique which people in the industry have surrounded themselves with, is as capable of marketing orientation as any other industry. The marketing mix concept applies in its entirety to this service industry despite the intangible nature of its products. At this point the reader from the insurance world can go back to the beginning of this book and read every chapter knowing that the words 'insurance', 'policies', 'life cover', 'premiums', 'brokers', etc., can be inserted with perfect congruence into the same slots that talk about the traditional ingredients of the marketing mix. Insurance deals with people and so do all other industries. As long as one markets to people the rules of marketing apply to all!

PART V

Case Studies

16
Case Studies

Introductory Note

Of the various teaching methods employed in business schools and other management training establishments the case study approach is still one of the most frequently used. It is based on the belief that a student can attain managerial understanding and competence through the study, contemplation and discussion of actual situations. The case study method does not purport to be a device for transmitting knowledge, concepts or principles of current business practice and thought. The prime objective is to provide students, either as individuals or as groups, with an opportunity to develop the skill of diagnosing the important issues that need to be resolved and the questions that must be answered. In real life managers often have to select courses of action without all the facts they would wish to have. Users of the case study method have to do likewise.

The 'Harvard' approach tends to use very detailed cases running at times to scores of pages. They usually contain considerable data about each function of the enterprise: marketing, finance, production and personnel. The effective use of such cases requires considerable time and my experience has taught me that they are more appropriate to long courses than short programmes. Briefer cases form an excellent vehicle for discussing managerial problems in seminars, workshops or other short courses. Reading the material is less time consuming and more time is available for discussion, exchange of views and cross-fertilisation of ideas. With suitable tutoring short cases offer a most effective platform for exploring alternative solutions to managerial problems. This in turn represents an admirable learning opportunity either from one's tutor or from other participants on a course.

The cases incorporated in this book describe a range of fairly typical marketing situations. They do not claim to represent examples of effective or ineffective marketing. They illustrate, in the main, problems which I have had to grapple with in my consultancy career. All the names of the companies described and the personalities involved are fictitious. Any similarity to the names of real companies or people is purely coincidental.

Suggested topics for discussion and exploration are incorporated at the end of each case. By referring back to the text of the appropriate chapter the reader may derive some suggestions as to how the problems described can be approached.

The Cases Studied

MEDI-SYSTEMS INTERNATIONAL INC.

Whilst this case relates to an international marketing research project, it is easy to visualise how similar situations can occur in a domestic environment. The firm is planning to launch a new 'product', namely 'turnkey' hospitals. The aim of the exercise is to identify among all the countries of the world the dozen or so opportunity markets towards which the firm should direct its marketing attention. Only after an initial screening process has taken place can the firm undertake the in-depth collection of marketing data. The case offers an opportunity to discuss the way a researcher can narrow the number of available 'candidates' to a more meaningful and manageable number. The principles developed can apply with equal relevance to the process of narrowing the field of search for acquisition candidates, segments in a domestic market, the most suitable location for retail outlets, etc.

ELDORADO SHIPPING COMPANY LIMITED

This company appears to be performing well in its marketplace. Its market share is in line with the capacity it owns. Nonetheless, the firm is not sure that its performance is optimal in relation to the opportunities. The case offers a useful vehicle for discussing the whole question of marketing productivity and the kind of criteria of success that a firm should ascribe to its marketing activities.

OPTICOL PRODUCTS LIMITED

A major row is brewing in this case between the marketing and the R & D departments. The R & D department has developed a new product which the market does not seem to appreciate. This is not an uncommon problem. The case can be discussed from a number of angles: the problem of integration especially between marketing and R & D; the need to develop better internal communication among functions; production orientation vis-à-vis the marketing concept; the role of marketing research in a production-orientated organisation.

PHARMACIA LIMITED

This case study highlights the problem of communication with reluctant members of a 'decision-making unit', especially in the light of increased costs of sales representation. The whole question of productivity of a firm's selling and promotional efforts can be discussed here. Moreover, the need to explore the behavioural constraints to effective communication could form a useful topic for further discussion.

LENSING & EYEGLASS OPTICIANS

This short case study offers an opportunity to consider creative ideas for solving an awkward challenge: the code of practice of the industry (opticians) supported by the legal system prohibit any kind of promotional activity. How does one communicate with one's clients in such a restrictive environment? The emphasis in this case should be placed on the exploration of creative ideas rather than the discussion of specific methods.

ZIPPO TRANSPORT LIMITED, BLN AIRWAYS, TRANSITO SERVICE LIMITED, AND WALPOLE TOURS LIMITED

All four case studies deal with the question of developing effective and productive sales and/or communication aids. Following the discussion of each one of these cases the principles outlined in Chapter 9 may help to fill in some of the gaps.

Medi-Systems International Inc.

Medi-Systems International Inc. (MSI) is a subsidiary company of one of the largest international pharmaceutical firms. It was first set up by way of a major diversification from the parent company's over-reliance on a small, albeit exceedingly profitable, range of ethical drugs. The philosophy behind the MSI development was the notion that there is a substantial global need for the development, design and building of 'turnkey' hospitals. Brief research has indicated that many countries, especially the emerging OPEC economies, would welcome the opportunity of placing orders for a total hospital system. Such a system would include the total design and building work, equipment, supplies, recruitment, selection and training of personnel, and the actual start-up of the hospital activities.

MSI was organised to run its affairs in an independent fashion from the parent company. Substantial funds were set aside for developing this business. The parent Board's instructions to Dr Herrmann, the Chief Executive of MSI were as follows:

'Your objectives are

1   To develop the "package hospital" concept on an international scale.

2   To attain a break-even point within two years.
3   To attain a 10% return on investment during the next two years.
4   To attain a 20% return on investment in subsequent years.

In selecting the most suitable geographical areas for development attempt to ensure that the countries thus selected are (a) politically stable; (b) large enough to need a number of hospitals over a fairly short period; (c) capable of developing an adequate number of nationals to assume managerial, professional, medical and nursing tasks within a reasonable period.

Within these constraints you have a total freedom to develop the business in the way which you feel will best benefit the Company's stakeholders'.

MARKETING THE CONCEPT

Dr Herrmann was a competent manager with an excellent record in the pharmaceutical industry. He was a qualified doctor and had also gained an MBA degree from a renowned business school.

On taking control of the MSI project he realised that a thorough study of world needs in hospitals was essential. Whilst he knew a lot about hospitals in Europe, the USA and other developed countries, he knew very little about the kinds of hospital that the less developed countries needed. He was in some difficulty in determining the most promising parts of the world to explore. Moreover, a vast number of questions kept cropping up:

(a) 'What kind of "product" should we offer? Large or small hospitals? General or specialist types? Standard or "made to measure"? What facilities and equipment should we incorporate?'
(b) 'How do we determine our pricing strategy?'
(c) 'Is there substantial competition and if so what are the strengths and weaknesses of our competitors?'
(d) 'What are the special commercial and financial features that the ideal "package" should include?'
(e) 'How do we promote our "product"?'
(f) 'Do we need to appoint middlemen?'

Many other questions arose during the discussions. One thing became clear to Dr Herrmann: before accepting the objectives set for him by the Board, he needed to evaluate the whole project from both marketing and financial viewpoints.

APPROACH TO MARKETING CONSULTANTS

Dr Herrmann came to the conclusion that, as a first step, he needed to invite a firm of marketing consultants to undertake market investigations on a global scale. He envisaged that these investigations would entail a two-phase approach.

1　A quick analysis of available data on every country with the view of pinpointing a 'short list' of the best opportunity markets. Criteria for the selection of 'short list' countries should be defined at this stage.
2　An 'in-depth' study of the 'short list' countries in order to submit a positive and practical 'input' for planning purposes. Such 'input' to include details of market environments, needs, institutional structure, legal constraints, competitive offers, etc.

Dr Herrmann's expectation was that at the end of Phase 2 he would know everything that a good businessman needed to know in order to plan an effective marketing effort.

With this objective in mind he approached four firms of consultants with a request for suitable proposals.

YOUR TASKS

1　Discuss the case and its implications with the view of *specifying the kind of information that you feel MSI requires in its endeavour to develop detailed marketing plans.*
2　Suggest a step-by-step *methodology for collecting the appropriate data* both in relation to Phase 1 and Phase 2.

Eldorado Shipping Company Limited

Eldorado Shipping Company Limited (ESCL) is a well established company operating a regular shipping service between the UK and Eldorado, a Caribbean island. The line started its operations about twenty-five years ago as an offshoot of a large aluminium company. Its initial success stemmed from the fact that it was able to carry a full cargo of bauxite from Eldorado to the UK and the only marketing effort which the line had to concentrate upon was return general cargo from the UK to the island. The inward cargo virtually covered the line's total cost of running the business and the revenue from the outward freight represented to a great extent the company's profit.

However, over the years the nature of the business of the parent company changed, ESCL became a fairly independent company in its own right and the bauxite cargo became a less and less significant part of its operations.

In 1979 the line's Managing Director died suddenly and Mr Sticker, the Marketing Director of a well known forwarding firm was recruited by 'head-hunters' to replace him. Mr Sticker insisted upon joining the company that he be given clear terms of reference as to what the Board of Directors who represented the major shareholders expected from him by way of performance. He was anxious to know whether they expected better results all round and if so in what terms.

The Board placed the ball back in Sticker's lap and asked him to carry out an in-depth business appraisal. They felt that such an investigation would show whether the firm was performing well in the marketplace and whether it was capable of general improvement. 'You tell us what you feel the company can achieve in the future and translate that into corporate objectives. Obviously we would welcome better revenue and better profits and a higher market share', they stated during a Board meeting.

With this 'input' in mind Mr Sticker set out to investigate the performance of the line. He soon discovered that the firm's executives knew very little about the marketing environment of the business. They also knew little about the interfirm comparison of performance. In the absence of such data, he felt, it was difficult to determine the level of performance which Eldorado could legitimately aspire to achieve in the future.

The following information was probably the only relevant material available:

(a) *The market* This is as shown in Table 16.1.

Table 16.1   The market for the Eldorado Shipping Company Limited.

	1977	1978
value of imports from Eldorado to the UK (at CIF value)	£14.36 million	£15.85 million
value of exports from the UK to Eldorado (at FOB value)	£15.67 million	£17.08 million
tonnage from Eldorado to the UK	92 260 tonnes	98 400 tonnes
tonnage from the UK	71 250 tonnes	77 625 tonnes
ESCL's share of tonnage carried from Eldorado	67%	68%
ESCL's share of tonnage carried from the UK	59%	59%

(b) *Competition* ESCL had three ships. There were two competitors, each having one ship. All five vessels serving Eldorado were of more or less the same size and capability. Thus the company's managers felt that in terms of productivity and market share ESCL's performance was satisfactory.

(c) *Profits* ESCL was a profitable line. Its profits fluctuated between £300 000 and £400 000 per annum. However, no analysis of the return on investment and/or capital employed had ever been calculated. Sticker felt that the time has come to try to define objectives not only in terms of profits but also in terms of other criteria which are meaningful in relation to the capital and effort invested in the company. Moreover, he believed that the resources employed in the company might be used much more effectively if the nature of the business could be geared more clearly to defined market and segment opportunities.

YOUR TASKS

This is a very brief description of a fairly common situation. The company appears to be performing well but in fact nobody seems to know whether this performance is optimal in relation to the realities of the marketplace. One needs to assemble information which would make a better evaluation of the firm's effectiveness in the marketplace possible.

With this comment in mind try to list the following:

(a) The information which Mr Sticker needs to assemble in order to appraise the company's real standing in the UK–Eldorado market.
(b) The criteria of success which should be ascribed to ESCL's marketing effort. In other words in what terms would you seek to specify the company's marketing objectives?
(c) Having defined the 'criteria of success', suggest the methods you would use to collect the appropriate information which would help you to measure the attainment of the standards of performance implied by the marketing objectives that you feel are meaningful in the circumstances.

Opticol Products Limited

Opticol Products Limited is a firm specialising in the manufacture and marketing of eye-care products. The firm's products are sold internationally. The company was established in 1936 by two brothers, Charles and James Collins, with the main objective of manufacturing lenses both for consumer and industrial applications. The former were supplied via the optical trade; the latter were supplied to manufacturers of optical instruments such as telescopes.

The two brothers were qualified engineers and both developed a passionate interest in the world of optics. However, they were not experienced businessmen and certainly did not understand the way goods should be marketed and distributed in a complex marketplace like the optical trade. The result was that although the firm enjoyed an excellent reputation for high quality products it was suffering from a very serious financial problem and the two brothers were heavily indebted to their bankers. The future looked very gloomy.

The war saved the firm from bankruptcy. Demand for lenses for military applications was tremendous and whilst prices were controlled on the basis of 'cost plus' calculations the firm's growth and profits were excellent throughout the war years. 'Cost plus' pricing meant that the buyers, mostly governmental bodies, paid a price which represented actual cost plus a percentage for profit. That meant that inefficiency was rewarded inasmuch as in paying the 'cost plus' price no cognisance was taken of the level of productivity or quality of the process used. All one had to do was to declare the costs and be prepared to have one's costings audited by independent inspectors. Provided the figures looked correct one obtained a price representing the cost plus the pre-agreed margin for profit. Thus the higher the cost, the higher the margin. Opticol finished the war in a very strong financial state. Nonetheless, the two brothers realised that their honeymoon was over and that they ought to use the newly acquired strength towards developing a sounder future.

POST-WAR DEVELOPMENTS

At that point the two brothers decided that the firm should be split into two separate businesses:

(a) *Opticol Industrial* This division specialised in the manufacture of lenses for industrial applications only.

(b) *Opticol Lenses* This division supplied lenses to the so-called 'prescription houses'. These are the organisations that fit lenses into spectacle frames on behalf of opticians and/or eye clinics. In other words the division had very little contact with the opticians themselves or with the consumers. Lenses were purchased by these 'prescription houses' and their criteria of choice were mainly quality and price. In most instances the price was the most important criterion inasmuch as all suppliers of lenses seemed to have an identical quality.

The first division started well but its strength declined over the year because (a) Japanese incursion into the European markets reduced the demand for lenses and (b) most of the large manufacturers of optical instruments started making their own lenses as part of a vertical integration strategy.

By 1965 Opticol Industrial's problems became very acute and the division was sold as a going concern to a major competitor. This was the end of the chapter as far as the industrial division was concerned.

Opticol Lenses also had its share of difficulties because of the pressure on prices imposed by the 'prescription houses', and also because of the lack of significant 'unique selling points' associated with the products themselves. On the other hand, the firm's executives were fully aware of the fact that by the time the consumer pays for a pair of spectacles the price of the lens increases by around 300% from what Opticol get for it. This convinced the Collins brothers that they should develop a strategy whereby their channels of distribution should be shortened. They felt that they should strive to bypass the 'prescription houses'.

The result was that the firm decided to enter the contact lens business. Contact lenses are supplied to opticians direct. Moreover, in order to steal a march over competitors Opticol decided to ensure at all times that their products would be the most advanced, the most reliable and with a rapid delivery service. The objective was to deliver always, if at all possible, from stock.

In order to ensure that these objectives would be met, a strong team of technicians was assembled and set up as a R & D department. A Mr Leitch was put in charge and his instructions were: 'You must know what developments are taking place all over the world. Our aim is to develop contact lenses which are better and cheaper than anything else available in other countries. We look to you as the provider of new products which will enable us to be the leaders of the industry in the world. If you can do this our future is assured'.

Substantial budgets were placed at the disposal of the R & D department and Mr Leitch assembled an excellent bunch of specialist researchers such as plastic technologists, polymer chemists, machinists and ophthalmologists. The team was all set to innovate.

However, the whole approach to the establishment of the R & D department was fraught with problems in so far as an élitist climate surrounded their role. The R & D people were regarded as the saviours of the firm. The marketing people resented this special role ascribed to them. The financial people felt that too much money was placed at their disposal without attaching criteria of productivity and results. The Collins brothers were adamant that success depended on unique products being developed and therefore it was inevitable that the R & D personnel would be elevated to a special position.

NEW PRODUCTS

The R & D department proved its worth fairly quickly. A whole range of contact lenses was developed and some of them proved to be real winners. The most successful development was a hard lens made out of acrylic by a matched die process. The lens itself was not very special but the quality of the edges was so good that patients could place the lens on the eye without any problems and the level of comfort was much higher that that of any other hard lens. Moreover, the cost of production was so low that the firm could make large margins of profit. Big stocks were produced in a large variety of prescriptions and in 99.5% of the cases delivery could be made within twenty-four hours!

This development was most successful. It helped the firm to establish itself in direct contact with opticians, it helped to develop a good image for Opticol in the market and it justified the investment in the R & D establishment.

From this point onwards the firm went from strength to strength. The financial position improved and the character of the firm changed radically. Opticol became a major force in the growing market for contact lenses. Market share of this lucrative segment of the optical trade was around 27%. A large number of ancillary products such as lens solutions and special boxes for lenses were launched with good results.

The one major threat on the horizon was the realisation that many competitors all over the world were working on new ideas and new materials and the fear that the 'product life cycle' of existing products was short provided a major spur to enhanced R & D activity.

Rumours were rife about the advent of 'poly-hema' polymer as a useful material for soft lenses. Poly-hema is a plastic material which remains soft when in contact with liquidity or humid surfaces. The eye generates sufficient humidity to retain the softness of poly-hema. Poly-hema was invented in Czechoslovakia and an American firm was in the process of buying a licence. The poly-hema can be cast into rods; the rod can be sliced into buttons and these buttons can be machined into lenses. It is a fairly lengthy process and the cost of production is high. However, lenses made out of poly-hema can be very comfortable to wear.

It is important to remember that in many countries one cannot sell lenses or similar products for eye-care without obtaining special approval from the authorities. In the USA one needs to obtain the approval of the Food and Drug Administration, which is very difficult and expensive to get. All the potential poly-hema contenders were in the process of investing large amounts of money towards obtaining a Food and Drug Administration licence.

In 1975 the first poly-hema lens approved by the Food and Drug Administration arrived. It triggered the imagination of the optical trade as well as the public and great inroads were made into the hard lens market. At the polymer end long and tedious litigation developed between the patent-holder and his various licencees. Nonetheless, a large number of firms started buying 'buttons' and machining lenses. Many sophisticated alternative processes were also developed such as centrifugal casting and injection moulding. The net result was that the market got flooded by soft contact lenses.

OPTICOL STRATEGY – THE X-LENS

Opticol felt that it was missing out on the soft lens development. Mr Leitch decided that what he ought to do was to develop a lens which was soft but had additional properties. He went to work with his team on a project which they called the X-lens. It was a very secret project; not even the marketing people knew the details of the programme that was being pursued.

The objectives of the project were as follows:

(a) To produce a soft lens comparable in properties to the poly-hema development in the USA but based on alternative polymers.
(b) The method of production must be very cheap.
(c) The lens must be permeable to gases and water.
(d) The lens must be very thin.
(e) The lens must be capable of being worn for long periods.

At the end of a year's development work sample lenses were produced and introduced to the marketing and selling personnel. All the objectives were achieved with the exception of cheapness. The development costs were so high that the amortisation of such costs over the prescribed period of three years (the Finance Director's policy, approved by the Board) added at least £2 per lens to the costs. The total cost per lens was £5, i.e. £10 per pair. The cost per pair of hard lenses was £2.

The marketing people were not very excited by the results. They felt that whilst permeability to gases and liquids was a technological breakthrough, the consumer would not see any benefit in such an attribute. The optician would have great difficulty in explaining the merit of such a property.

The fact that the lenses could be worn for long periods, including during the night, could be very interesting but, they felt, that demand for such a lens would be slow to develop.

Opticians were visited by R & D personnel and were assured that they thought the development was superb. Nonetheless, they were reluctant to say whether they would place orders for such a lens or not. Their argument was that until a customer asks for a lens by name they could not push it – especially where the price is so high. Unfortunately there are severe restrictions on advertising lenses to the public in the UK. In other words the level of awareness of the new lens would remain low for a long time.

THE DILEMMA

The situation looked very worrying to Mr Leitch. Here he was sitting on one of the greatest breakthroughs in optical technology and the signs were that the lens would not be a success. He was convinced that it was the fault of the marketing people who were taking their revenge for the secrecy with which the whole project was shrouded.

The marketing people were emphatic that whilst the lens looked good it incorporated properties that neither the opticians nor the consumers appreciated. Mr Leitch felt that good marketers should be able to change customers' attitudes and should be capable of making the customer want what was obviously good for him.

This argument went on and on and meanwhile the project was at a standstill.

In 1977 a major competitor launched a 'permanent lens' at a price which was comparable with the ordinary poly-hema soft lens. By all accounts it proved to be a great success. The Opticol permanent, gas-permeable lens never saw daylight.

YOUR TASK

Discuss the implications. In particular, consider the ways in which the kind of problem described could be avoided in the future.

Pharmacia Limited

Pharmacia Limited is a company manufacturing and selling ethical drugs. Ethical drugs can only be obtained on doctors' prescriptions. In other words, the general practitioner who sees the patient is the ultimate 'decider' who determines whether Pharmacia products will be dispensed.

In order to promote the products the company employs a field force of medical representatives. They are all extremely well trained in clinical and product knowledge.

The company's Marketing Director has diagnosed a few serious threats:

(a) The cost per representative call has increased from £8 to £14 over a two-year period. This is partly due to inflationary cost escalation and partly due to the fact that the number of calls per day has decreased.

(b) Many doctors appear to be reluctant to see salesmen and insist upon literature, samples and promotional material being left with the receptionists. Others limit the length of a visit to a few minutes only. This makes the quality of the communication very ineffective.

The pharmaceutical industry's code of practice has imposed severe limits on advertising expenditure.

YOUR TASK

Define the kind of research that the firm ought to undertake with the view of improving the effectiveness of the communication process.

Lensing & Eyeglass Opticians

Lensing & Eyeglass is a firm of opticians offering a comprehensive service in the eye-care business. They own 60 outlets in the UK.

Because of a very rigid code of practice of the industry coupled with legislative constraints they are not allowed to advertise or otherwise to promote the existence of their retail outlets. This in fact means that the only promotional tools available to them are as follows:

(a) The design of the shop windows. In this area they have come to recognise that one must strike a balance between the need to look professional and clinical and the need to attract the attention of the passers-by.
(b) 'Word-of-mouth' by satisfied clients.
(c) Recommendations by doctors.
(d) Annual reminders to existing patients that the time has come for a new test.

The firm never attempted to measure its market share either nationally or on a regional basis. However, they have recently discovered a disturbing trend: the number of 'cases' (namely the number of people who visit the practices to have their eyes tested and if necessary to have new glasses or contact lenses dispensed) per annum is static. This means that growth is under threat. The other disturbing fact is that the 'takings per case' (the average expenditure per patient) is growing at a lower rate than inflation.

The firm's marketing director feels that urgent steps should be taken to achieve three important and interrelated objectives: (a) to increase the number of 'cases' per annum; (b) to increase the 'takings per case' by at least 10%; (c) to find a way of increasing the level of awareness of the firm and its practices among non-users without infringing the law and/or the industry's code of practice.

YOUR TASK

Consider creative ideas for assisting the firm to achieve these challenging objectives.

Zippo Transport Limited

Zippo Transport Limited is a road haulage firm specialising in the transportation of medium to heavy cargoes (25–75 tons). It is estimated that in that segment of the market there are around twenty competitors. On the other hand, at the top end of the market, viz. carriers of cargoes over 75 tons, the number of competitors goes down to four or five companies only.

Zippo's Marketing Manager is anxious to identify the firm's 'unique selling points' in order to incorporate them in the company's literature and also to assist the salesmen in making more persuasive presentations to clients. He recognises that as long as the company cannot claim 'uniqueness' it is bound to be trapped in a highly competitive game with a resultant pressure on prices.

As a first step the Marketing Manager discussed the subject with his colleagues and then with a large number of customers. The main aim of these discussions was to identify what unique selling points (USPs) the firm's customers perceived in Zippo's service. The company's management was not very confident that Zippo had any USPs worth talking about.

After some deliberations the Marketing Manager came to the conclusion that Zippo was able to list the following characteristics: reliability, punctuality, excellent company image, friendly drivers and office staff, security of cargoes in transit, speedy handling of complaints. All these items seemed useful, but only regular customers were aware of the difference that existed between Zippo's service and other companies' service.

In other words, even where Zippo did in fact excel in its service it was of little practical value inasmuch as customers were not aware of such a level of excellence.

The Marketing Manager realised that the time had come to identify with some clarity the USPs that customers welcomed, to proceed towards developing them and of course to equip the sales force with the appropriate aids that would facilitate communication with clients and potential clients.

The Marketing Manager invited a number of marketing communication consultants to assist in solving the problem.

YOUR TASKS

You should assume the role of one of these firms of marketing communication consultants and simulate the kind of proposal that they feel would have been appropriate in the circumstances.

In particular try to cover the following points:

(a) List the possible USPs which Zippo could profitably incorporate in their communication aids. Do not be afraid of recommending new and creative ideas.
(b) Recommend a creative approach to the development of communication aids incorporating the suggested USPs listed above.

Remember that the whole approach must be considered within an economical budget. The emphasis is on creativity and not on extravagance.

BLN Airways

BLN Airways is an airline specialising in air cargo only. It operates along no specific routes. It offers its services to any shipper in any country and to any destination. The only constraints are those imposed by institutional and legal bodies which limit the landing rights of the airline in various airports.

The company capitalised in the past on a number of opportunities which occurred as a result of political events. Thus it carried vast quantities of cargo during the Berlin blockade. It also carried considerable freight to and from Vietnam when the US forces were active in that country.

More recently the company developed a strategy whereby it would carry any cargo on a semi-'tramping' basis. In other words it was willing to stop anywhere provided the cargo was interesting and future prospects were good.

Mr Newall, the company's marketing director, stated the firm's USPs in the following terms:

(a) 'No other airline is prepared to run such a buccaneering service. We are flexible – we are prepared to go from and to anywhere, any time and at frequent intervals provided the money is good.'

(b) 'We can offer an advisory service as to packing, documentation, transportation to departure point and from arrival point. Moreover, we are in the position of producing a comparative analysis of alternative modes of logistics.'

(c) 'Our personnel are trained to be helpful at all times. Complaints about the slightest lack of courtesy are being dealt with swiftly and ruthlessly. I expect everybody in the firm to treat our clients with a broad smile.'

(d) 'Being a fairly small firm we should be able to give an immaculate and personal service. However, we do not compete on price. Our customers can expect the kind of service that no large airline can offer but we do not claim that we are always the cheapest operator.'

Unfortunately only existing customers recognise the quality of the firm.

A marketing plan has been prepared. This new plan envisages an increase in the number of the airline's *users* by no less than 200%. The firm's management realises that this entails a formidable selling effort coupled with a highly creative communication programme.

YOUR TASKS

Start from the assumption that the firm's USPs as defined by Mr Newall are valid and sustainable. Your group should consider the problem and recommend the following:

(a) The kinds of communication aids that the salesmen should be equipped with in their endeavour to meet the ambitious objectives set (viz. 200% increase in the number of users).

(b) Methods for measuring the effectiveness of these aids.

Transito Service Limited

Transito Service Limited is a transport company specialising in the physical distribution of 'difficult' cargoes. The firm's founder, Mr Duguid, always felt that the best formula for escaping from the rigours of competition was to do things that nobody else was prepared to do. The result of this philosophy was that the company became a specialist organisation in the transport of cargoes which called for highly sophisticated equipment with a heavy capital investment.

At the same time the specialist nature of the business meant that the firm was able to command relatively high prices for its various 'products'. Thus the company was able to offer a comprehensive service in the carrying of semi-fabricated chemicals in a viscous state which needed rigid temperature control and minimum vibration on the road. Another service which the company offered was the transport of explosives. Both services were very limited in their markets but prices were high and margins excellent.

Mr Duguid instructed his marketing department to identify other 'products' which might fulfil the segmentation philosophy that characterised the company in the past. He insisted that any segment thus selected should be researched, measured and also be substantial enough within the firm's objectives and resources. With these instructions in mind the marketing personnel felt that an interesting opportunity might be to develop a creative distribution service for fragile cargoes such as glass and china. They believed that with the company's knowledge and experience of 'difficult' cargoes such a service would be highly compatible with the rest of the business.

The market was researched in some depth and the conclusion reached that the glass, china and tableware industries had a definite need for an efficient and economic service for delivering goods from factory to customer's door.

A marketing plan was set in motion to include a total system aimed at meeting the industry's needs as highlighted during the research project. The system that emerged incorporated a number of useful features: (a) special stackable trays to do away with the very expensive chests and casks traditionally used; (b) cages designed to accommodate the above trays in transit – these being collapsible when not in use; (c) depots to handle smaller consignments; (d) a computer system to handle complicated physical distribution problems pertaining to a multi-delivery project; (e) a guarantee system against breakages and/or losses in transit; (f) an advisory service capable of assisting clients with logistics problems; (g) a commercial service to include, wherever necessary, invoicing, factoring, debt collecting, refunds and similar services. The aim was to provide a comprehensive system capable of ridding customers of the total distribution task.

The new service was test-marketed and proved of great interest to a number of customers. The firm decided to launch it nationally with the hope of extending it to the whole of Europe within a year.

Although cost per mile was higher than the more conventional method of carrying such goods, the total cost after allowing for the cost of packaging, breakages, complaints, rejects, etc., was around 30% cheaper. Moreover, the intangible benefits such as general customer satisfaction and overall improved efficiency made the service even more attractive.

It was agreed by the firm's marketing personnel that salesmen should be equipped with a sales aid which truly reflected the USPs of the service and altogether could facilitate communication with potential buyers. A highly creative 'communication and sales aid' was sought and the firm was prepared to invest the necessary amount in the right material.

YOUR TASKS

Attempt to place yourself in the position of an adviser to the company's marketing personnel. With this idea in mind discuss the problem in your group and prepare a brief presentation as to how you would approach the problem of designing effective 'sales and communication aids'. In particular endeavour to (a) define the communication objectives that the 'aids' required will need to meet; (b) suggest ideas that might fulfil these objectives – obviously such ideas must be capable of economic and effective implementation. The emphasis must be on creativity as well as on commercial viability.

Walpole Tours Limited

Walpole Tours Limited is a tour operator with a difference. It organises 'packages' for people who want to partake in cultural and intellectual activities during their holidays. Thus the holiday catalogue of the company includes painting holidays, art appreciation 'packages' such as a 'tour of the Leonardo country' and 'visits to Mozart land'. A tour of the various 'musical instruments centres' was particularly popular.

The firm is small but very successful. Its tours are heavily subscribed and most customers return very happy with the physical arrangements as well as the cultural content of the 'package'. Nonetheless, there is a fly in the ointment: the company is spending too much money on communication. If one adds up the cost of promotional activities (advertising, sales promotion and publicity) as well as the cost of personal selling to the travel agents, one reaches a total figure of £24 per passenger. In the three previous years the respective figures were £12, £15 and £19 in chronological order. These figures do not include the actual commission paid to the agents.

Mr Stifflip, the Marketing Director, is concerned by this alarming trend. He has invited a marketing communications consultant to assist the company with this problem. The consultant has come to the conclusion that the firm's communication strategies are extravagant and not cost effective inasmuch as the firm is dealing with a limited segment and because there is so little knowledge about where this segment is located and who belongs to it a lot of redundant exposure takes place. Thus an advertisement in the national press is tantamount to the use of a 'sledgehammer' to crack a nut'. 'Walpole Tours caters for a specific segment and it needs to acquire more knowledge about the members of this target group. If we knew more about them we could perhaps communicate with them in their homes . . . ' is the consultant's main message. 'Spending £24 per passenger – £72 per family if there are three of them – is a ridiculous sum to spend on each sale!' he keeps stressing.

The firm realises that before re-defining its approach to communication it needs to determine a typology of its clientele.

YOUR TASKS

(a) Endeavour to design a research programme with the view of learning more about the firm's customers. Specify the parameters that need to be identified and measured if an effective communication strategy can be developed.

(b) Consider possible communication methods that could be used in a situation where the marketplace is narrow and the number of possible users relatively low. The main aim is to find a method which is more economical than the present one.

Bibliography

This book covers a very wide range of topics. There is no one single book which attempts to cover the entire field in one volume. The reader who wishes to explore any of the topics discussed here in greater depth is invited to refer to the appropriate books or articles listed hereunder:

Part I: The Marketing Concept – A Strategic Perspective for the 1980s

Abell, D.F., *Defining the business: the starting point of strategic planning.* Englewood Cliffs, N.J.: Prentice Hall Inc. (1980)

Arndt, J., How broad should the marketing concept be? *Journal of Marketing,* January 1978.

Bartels, R., *The history of marketing thought,* 2nd edn. Columbus, Ohio: Grid (1976).

Berridge, T., *Product innovation and development.* London: Business Books (1977).

Buckley, A., A blueprint for acquisition strategy. *Accountancy,* September 1979.

Drucker, P.F., *Managing in turbulent times.* New York: Harper & Row (1980).

Fitzroy, P.T., *Analytical methods for marketing management.* Maidenhead: McGraw-Hill (1976).

Hughes, G.D., *Marketing management: a planning approach.* Reading, Mass.: Addison Wesley (1978).

Kitching, J., Acquisition in Europe. *Business International,* 1973.

Kitching, J., Why acquisitions are abortive. *Management Today,* 1974.

Kotler, P., *Marketing management, analysis, planning and control,* 4th edn. Englewood Cliffs, N.J.: Prentice-Hall.

Kotler, P., W. Gregor and W. Rogers, The marketing audit comes of age. *Sloan Management Review,* Winter 1977.

Krausher, P.M., *New products and diversification,* 2nd edn. London: Business Books (1977).

McCarthy, E.J., *Basic marketing: a managerial approach,* 6th edn. Homewood, Ill.: Richard D. Irwin (1978).

Majaro, S., *International marketing – a strategic approach to world markets.* London: George Allen & Unwin (1977).

Meeks, G., *Disappointing marriage: a study of the gains from merger.* Cambridge: Cambridge University Press (1977).

Rines, M. (Ed.), *Marketing handbook,* 2nd edn. London: Gower Publishing (1981).

Salter, M.S., and W.A. Weinhold, *Diversification through acquisition: strategies for creating economic value.* New York: Free Press (1979).

Salter, M.S., and W.A. Weinhold, Choosing compatible acquisitions. *Harvard Business Review,* January/February 1981.

Part II: Marketing Within its Management Development Context

Abell, D.F., and J.S. Hammond, *Strategic marketing planning.* Englewood Cliffs, N.J.: Prentice-Hall (1979).

Argyle, M., *Bodily communication.* London: Methuen (1975).

Berne, E., *Games people play.* London: Penguin Books (1967).

Briston, J.H., and T.J. Neill, *Packaging management.* London: Gower Press (1972).

Chisnall, P.M., *Marketing: a behavioural analysis.* Maidenhead: McGraw-Hill (1975).

Engel, J.F., D.T. Kollat and R.D. Blackwell, *Consumer behaviour,* 3rd edn. New York: Holt, Rinehart and Winston (1978).

Festinger, L., *A theory of cognitive dissonance.* Stanford, Calif.: Stanford University Press (1957).

Harris, T.A., *I'm OK – you're OK.* New York: *Avon Books* (1973).

Midgley, D.F., *Innovation and new product marketing.* London: Crown Helm (1977).

Plummer, J.T., The concept and application of life style segmentation. *Journal of Marketing,* January 1974.

Prince, G.M., *The practice of creativity.* New York: Harper & Row, (1970).

Rogers, E.M., *Diffusion of innovation.* New York: The Free Press (1962).

Part III: Tools of Marketing – A Creative Approach

Aaker, D.A., and J.G. Myers, *Advertising management – practical perspectives.* Englewood Cliffs, N.J.: Prentice-Hall (1975).

Anderson, B.R., *Professional selling.* Englewood Cliffs, N.J.: Prentice-Hall (1977).

Andrews, B., *Creative product development.* London: Longman (1975).

Broadbent, S., *Spending advertising money,* 3rd edn. London: Business Books (1979).

Corkindale, D., and S. Kennedy, *Managing advertising effectively.* Bradford: MCB Books (1975).

Day, G.S. Diagnosing the product portfolio. *Journal of Marketing,* April 1977.

Doyle, S.X., and B.P. Shapiro, What counts most is motivating your sales force. *Harvard Business Review,* May/June 1980.

Enis, B.M., GE, PIMS, BCG and the PLC. *Business,* May–June 1980.

Greenberg, H.M., and J. Greenburg, Job matching for better sales performance. *Harvard Business Review,* September/October 1980.

Lambin, J.J., *Advertising, competition and market conduct in oligopoly over time.* Amsterdam: North-Holland (1976).

Levitt, T., Marketing success through differentiation – of anything. *Harvard Business Review,* January/February 1980.

Lidstone, J., *Recruitng and selecting successful salesmen.* London: Business Books (1976).

Lovell, M., and J. Potter, *Assessing the effectiveness of advertising.* London: Business Books (1975).

McNiven, M.A., Plan for more productive advertising. *Harvard Business Review,* March/April 1980.

Nicholl, D.S., *Advertising: its purpose, principles and practice,* 2nd edn. London: Macdonald & Evans (1978).

'Performance appraisal series'. *Harvard Business Review* 1972.

Robinson, S.J.Q., R.E. Hitchens and D.P. Wade, The directional policy matrix – tool for strategic planning. *Long Range Planning,* June 1978.

Skinner, R.N., *Launching new products in competitive markets.* London: Associated Business Programmes (1973).

Part IV: Marketing in Service Industries

Adolfse, J., and F. Vervoordeldonk, Strategic planning and policy making in banks. *Long Range Planning* **12** (3), June 1979.

Dutter, P., Life company marketing strategy: key to profit growth. *Best's Review,* February 1978.

Ford, W.F., Innovation and evolution in the banking industry, 1976–1985. *Business Economics,* January 1977.

Gummesson, E., The marketing of professional services – an organisational dilemma. *European Journal of Marketing* **13** (5), 1979.

Ham, M.J., The profit impact of market strategy in the insurance industry. *Best's Review,* December 1978.

Harmer-Brown, F., Do the banks make good use of advertising? *The Bankers' Magazine* **222** (1607), February 1978.

Kotler, P., *Marketing for nonprofit organisations.* Englewood Cliffs, N.J.: Prentice-Hall (1975).

Mason, J.B., and M.L. Mayer, Bank management and strategic planning for the 1980s. *Long Range Planning,* 1979.

McIver, C., and G. Naylor, *Marketing financial services.* London: The Institute of Bankers (1980).

Moran, D.E., Improving branch office performance. *Management Focus,* May/June 1979.

Robertson, D.H. and D.N. Billenger, Identifying bank market segments. *Journal of Bank Research* **7** (4), 1977.

Shankleman, E., The Clearing Banks' slow struggle to be corporate marketers. *Industrial Marketing Digest* **4** (2), 1979.

Shostack, G.L., Breaking free from product marketing. *Journal of Marketing,* April 1977.

Shostack, G.L., Banks sell services – not things. *The Bankers' Magazine,* Winter 1977.

Sonen, L.A., Locating bank branches. *Industrial Marketing* **3,** July 1974.

Turner, W.D., A better measure for retail banking performance. *The McKinsey Quarterly,* Spring 1979.

Wilson, A., *Professional services and the marketplace.* Stockholm: Marknadstekniskt Centrum (MTC) (1975).

Index